The
DAVID MYTH
in Western
Literature

The DAVID
MYTH

in Western Literature

edited by

*Raymond-Jean Frontain
and Jan Wojcik*

Purdue University Press
West Lafayette, Indiana
1980

Library of Congress Catalog Card Number 78-69904

International Standard Book Number 0-911198-55-5

Printed in the United States of America

To

Harold Watts
and Margaret Frontain

two who dance with David

Contents

Preface

*F*ew biblical stories are richer than that of David, and few have been as inadequately explored. Only Christ's public ministry and crucifixion, Adam's creation and fall, Job's suffering and reward, and Samson's folk heroics have inspired an equal or larger number of additional literary works, and all of them have been explored in depth, either in relation to individual works or in full-length studies of the traditions themselves. Comparatively little has been done on David.

The reason for this is implied throughout the following essays: of all these biblical heroes, the character of David is perhaps the richest in paradox and so the most difficult to grasp. Samson, for example, is the foolish strongman who, in some traditions, finds enlightenment in suffering; his experience is limited to this central one; his significance is single. David's life, on the other hand, is crowded with more experiences than all the patriarchs' together, and in that mass of experience are so many contradictions that no easy statement can be made about him. Readers the first 2,000 years were so confused and even frightened by the multivariousness of this hero, and by the implications of his experience, that they consistently tried to reduce him to a single meaning; with the Song of Songs, the books of Samuel are among the most consistently allegorized works in the Old Testament. But as the opening essay in this volume shows, such a reading cannot predominate: David is the biblical man for all seasons.

Organizing a special session on the David myth for the 1976 annual meeting of the Modern Language Association, the editors were struck by the wealth of David criticism that is written today and by the confused state of David studies. Individual scholars, generally unaware of others, were writing to explore a particular tradition. This volume is an attempt to give some organization to David scholarship; it is preliminary to the more exact and encompassing statement on the significance of David's presence in Western culture that can be made only after these statements are digested by the scholarly community and the many directions they suggest are more fully explored.

The essays are organized chronologically, generically, and thematically. For example, they suggest a response to David in Reformation England, in colonial Puritan America, and in modern-day Israel. They offer generous slices of the language that has been used to talk about David in lyric and epic poetry, in drama and fiction, and in sermons and other religious writing, thus making the book a sort of "David reader" or a history of cultural styles used in response to him. And each essay reveals another facet of the enormously complex personality of the biblical character: David the penitent, David the adulterer, David the epic and folk hero, David the military leader, David the poet.

One of the most interesting facets of this volume is that the richness of David's character is reflected in the variety of literary forms that are used to talk about him. The scope of interest in David over the last 2,000 years gives the word "literature" in the title a broad reference; it includes freely imaginative works, such as Cowley's epic and Drayton's heroic poetry; Smart's, Roethke's, and Amichai's lyrics; and Faulkner's novel *Absalom, Absalom!* And there are sermons and devotional writings as well—literature by the rabbis and church fathers, by Reformation polemicists and Puritan preachers, where David's image dances more solemnly, even stridently, to the moral music of those days. By "literature" is meant any imaginative interpretive writing that gives David's story a new setting.

This volume does not pretend to completeness. It would be impossible to cover all aspects of David in all literary cultures. There are no essays on David in Jewish and Yiddish folklore, for example, or in Spanish Golden Age drama, and the order of essays leaves some gaps in chronology and changes focus with surprising dexterity on occasion. We rely on the introduction, which traces the transformation of David primarily within English and American literature and within the religious traditions these literatures rely upon, to supply continuity, directing the reader in the footnotes to those areas already satisfactorily explored and so not duplicated in this effort. We limit ourselves primarily, though not exclusively, to English and American literature because this is the work the majority of readers will be most familiar with, and some determining focus had to be imposed on a study of so large a body of material.

Contributors quote from whatever translation of the Bible best suits their purpose, and the editors have standardized their references to Bible titles according to the traditional division of I and II Samuel and I and II Kings, rather than I, II, III, and IV Kings.

The editors thank Cherylynn Knott for assisting with the typing and Dr. Jacob Adler for putting the material resources of the Purdue Department of English, which he heads, at their disposal. Their gratitude is great to Verna Emery, of the Purdue University Press, who saw their manuscript through to completed book form, and to Jim McCammack, who is responsible for the book's physical design.

Introduction:

Transformations of the Myth of David

Certain stories are called classic when they remain unsurpassed for providing patterns to think or imagine one's way through a particular human concern. The story gets the pieces on the board for generation after generation of players, or, as Horace measured it, for at least a century: "*Est vetus atque probus, centum qui perfecit annos*" (*Hor. Ep.,* II.i.39). And the greater the story, the larger number of concerns that can be imagined through it. The David story is classic in this sense.

Its paraphernalia provide formulae for talking about the ironies in the life of a prodigiously talented man, the relation between personal virtue and tragedy, and the pulls of secularization against piety when a religious culture tries to become a more practical one. It has allowed poets to talk about poetry, religious teachers to sermonize on religiousness, and military leaders to advocate military preparedness. The David of Samuel and Kings is a warrior, a lover, a poet, a killer, and a restorer. His character is a paradox: at one point he dances spontaneously before the ark; on other occasions he plots with cunning the changing course of Saul's disposition toward him. He is the Lord's anointed and the supposed author of the holy Psalms, as well as a murderer and adulturer. He forgives Saul admirably and Absalom excessively. There is a large alphabet here for centuries of authors, following the biblical narrators, to draw upon, as well as wide space for individual interpretations. In fact, writers of I and II Samuel were already retelling it, taking up material about David they found in archives and folk literature to shape his story to their own hopes some 500 years after the events they describe: that a future son would be born of David's family who would rule a glorious kingdom forever, thus reversing the sad fortunes David's more immediate sons had brought the kingdom to. One thing the literary history of the David story shows is that stories can "stretch."

Commenting upon the plethora of David plays in the late nineteenth and early twentieth centuries, Murray Roston notes that "the stories of David's life were, by their freedom from the supernatural and by their striking realism, ideally suited to the needs of the twentieth-century dramatist and they were exploited accordingly."[1] But it is not simply the post-Darwinian age that has been attracted by the absence of miracles or other unnatural happenings in the books of Samuel; it is almost as if, in beginning his story with a people's clamor for a secular as opposed to a religious leader, the author was respecting the desire of generations of readers for a more humanly realistic story than was known before, for a work that is almost entirely man-centered. This is the story of living, breathing, passionate, fallible men, the mistakes they make, and the consequences of those mistakes; the author keeps divine intrusion into their world to a minimum. Much more than the other books of the Old Testament, I and II Samuel study man's relation to the divine and to each other, rather than divinity's relation to men, and are characterized by a psychological realism unparalleled in either testament.

Yet one of the most striking things about the tradition of retelling or reinterpreting the David story is that appreciation of its realism can arise after almost two millennia of typification and allegory. The story has resilience. (Jan Wojcik's study shows how, almost systematically, the earliest readers of David's story averted their eyes from its naked realism to see only moral exempla.) For the pre-Renaissance world—from the time of the earliest religious interpretations through the European Middle Ages—David's significance was as a type, one of the richest and most fully exploited. For the Jews, he satisfied the type of the Old Testament hero: an improbable choice for a ruler by human standards, yet selected by the inscrutable Yahweh and raised over more likely candidates as Jacob was raised over Esau, Joseph over all his brothers, and Israel over all other nations. He is twinned with Saul as Abel, Jacob, and Joseph are twinned with near relations in their stories to dramatize the dichotomy between what the Christian Saint Augustine centuries later calls the "city of God" and the city of men. His career reflects the development of the Israelites themselves: enjoyment of God's favor is interrupted by a fall from grace through sin; repentance and sincere contrition effect a reconciliation with the Lord. (Charles A. Huttar explores the significance of the penitential David in both a Jewish and a Christian context.) He was important to the Jews, both historically as their greatest king and spiritually as the author of the Psalms, and as a model for the man of God.

For Christian audiences David is a type of Christ, the assumption being that Jesus of Nazareth was the Messiah who, it was prophesied, would sit on David's throne and reestablish his lost kingdom. Meditating on this prophecy, for example, Milton's Christ thinks of

> the Shepherd lad,
> Whose offspring on the Throne of *Judah* sat
> So many Ages, and shall yet regain
> That seat, and reign in *Israel* without end.
>
> [*Paradise Regained*, II.439–42]

Like David, Christ was a shepherd—but of souls, not actual sheep. David's triumphs against adversity, especially in his defeat of the giant Goliath, were seen to foreshadow Christ's victories against Satan. In medieval drama David appears in the *Ordo Prophetarum* or *Prophetae* with such other prominent non-Christian figures as Jacob, Moses, Isaiah, Jeremiah, Daniel, John the Baptist, and the Erythrean Sibyl as a witness to the divinity of Christ. As Elmer Blistein comments, "The Psalms of David are important in the liturgy of the Roman Church; David the King is not. When David does appear in the liturgical drama, he appears as a Prophet rather than as a King; he speaks as a Psalmist rather than as a warrior."[2] His only mark of distinction is the slingshot he carries in his hand. In act 3 of the French *Mystère d' Adam* he is made to speak in what the playwright imagines to be his individual character, but again his appearance has no particular significance except in the procession of other prophets and he is not singled out in any way. Like most other figures in medieval drama, he is considered as an allegorical figure or a type rather than as a character who deserves dramatization in his own right. This lack of concrete particularity reflects a mimetic that is no longer our own.

With the Renaissance, David's story becomes a major thematic source for an almost uncountable number of writers with varied religious and secular concerns.[3] He was, first of all, the lover and eventually the husband of Bathsheba, whose unchecked animal appetites had tragic consequences for him, his family, and the community he governed. George Peele's *The Love of King David and Fair Bethsabe, With the Tragedie of Absalon*, Antoine de Montchrestien's *David ou l'adultère*, N. Chrestien des Croix's *Amnon et Thamar*, Hans Sachs' *Comedia: Der Dauid mit Batseba im Ehbruch* and *Tragedia: Thamar die Tochter König Dauid mit irem Bruder Amnon vnd Absalom*, Tirso de Molina's *La venganza de Tamar*, and Calderón's *Los cabellos de Absalón* are but a few of the plays on this subject written in the golden age of European drama. David's love/lust for

Bathsheba was also a popular subject in Renaissance erotic Ovidian poetry,[4] for like the Song of Songs it provided poets with both a religious justification and a biblical model for writing highly sensuous verse. In fact, such emphasis was placed on the sensual component of his nature that by the late seventeenth century David was no longer a tragic figure whose appetites caused his fall, but the subject of burlesque! In the famous opening lines of *Absalom and Achitophel*, John Dryden satirizes the libertine tendencies of Charles II when he emphasizes David's pagan enjoyment of the flesh:

> In pious times, e'r Priest-craft did begin,
> Before Polygamy was made a sin;
> When man, on many, multiply'd his kind,
> E'r one to one was, cursedly, confind:
> When Nature prompted, and no law deny'd
> Promiscuous use of Concubine and Bride;
> Then, *Israel*'s Monarch, after Heaven's own heart,
> His vigorous warmth did, variously, impart
> To Wives and Slaves: And, wide as his Command,
> Scatter'd his Maker's Image through the Land.[5]

Christopher Smart's "A Song to David" was, in part, an effort to refocus critical attention on David as a sacred hero and religious poet when, in the mid-eighteenth century, it was suggested by serious men that his sinfulness demanded his expulsion from Sacred Writ.[6]

Related to this insistence on David's earthly appetites was another tendency to thematize his this-worldliness as his heroic qualities — manifested most clearly in his wrestling with wild beasts and in his defeat of Goliath — became an important subject for the Renaissance brief epic. Barbara Lewalski points out that as early as A.D. 430 advocates of a Christian literature were denouncing pagan heroic subjects and poetic manners while pointing to David's feats of physical prowess as a subject worthy of a poet's efforts, and "in the period 1550–1650 the great majority of Old Testament poems were brief epics about a single hero: the warrior heroes David and Judith were most popular."[7] In such poems as Michael Drayton's *David and Goliah*, Robert Aylett's *David's Troubles Remembered*, Abraham Cowley's *Davideis*, and Jacques de Coras' *David, ou la Vertue Couronée*, David's prowess is seen as the physical incarnation of moral energy which evokes a sense of wonder in the reader; he may, then, be seen as a sort of religious "Herculean hero," a superior mortal whose *virtu* and *élan* put him outside the common moral order. (Anthony Allingham discusses Drayton's transformation of the biblical David into a baroque epic hero.) He even becomes a touchstone for other epic heroes to be compared to, John Milton casting his blind, unarmed Samson as a young David, confident of the Lord's protection, challenging the Philistine giant Harapha/Goliath.[8] The continuous representation in the sculpture of this period of David as a beautiful naked youth just before or after his slaying Goliath—most notably by Donatello, Verocchio, and Michelangelo[9]—is but further indication of his importance as a symbol of the Renaissance ideal of man confronting adversity in this world, as opposed to the medieval ideal of his isolating himself from malevolent forces and patiently awaiting delivery into the next world.[10]

Finally, David's relationship with Jonathan was vaunted by such writers as the Christian humanists in their handbooks on education and princely behavior, and by Spenser in "The Legend of Friendship" (*Faerie Queene*, IV.x.26-28) as an ideal of male friendship—the only Christian example to be included with such classical ones as Damon and Pythias, Hercules and Hylas, Achilles and Patrocales, and Pylades and Orestes. (Ted-Larry Pebworth analyzes Cowley's synthesis of the classical concept of friendship and the Neoplatonic conception of love in the David and Jonathan passages of the *Davideis*.)

David and Bathsheba, David and Goliath, David and Jonathan—this regular coupling of his name with that of a lover or an enemy marks an important departure from previous presentations of him where he appears only in relation to Yahweh or to Christ. However, to imply that with the Renaissance David was entirely secularized, is misleading. He was an important model for renewal in the Reformation, the very age responsible for his secularization (Edward A. Gosselin defines two opposing views of the Reformation David), and he never really loses his religious significance even when it is overshadowed by other considerations. After Christ, for example, he is the most important figure in the literature of colonial Puritan America, appearing in a countless number of sermons, poems, and devotions. (Marie L. Ahearn analyzes one use of David in seventeenth-century sermons to impart religious significance to a secular activity.) Even today he still has more significance in many minds as the supposed author of the Psalms than as the seducer of Bathsheba. It is the extraordinary depth and suggestiveness of the David figure which allows him to mean such different things to so many different readers, and to bear the weight of so many different interpretations. As certain modern writers have observed, he is a symbol of the complexity and ambiguity of human experience itself.

Reformation and seventeenth-century England demonstrate the political significance of the David myth. Early Protestant reformers alluded to David's refusal to slay Saul, and to Absalom's tragic death after rising up against his father, to support Henry VIII's split with Rome; John Bale's thinly disguised argument for the allegiance of the English bishops to Henry rather than to the pope in *Kyng Johan* is supported throughout by references to David, Saul, and Absalom.[11] Court writers, and even James himself, often depicted the first Stuart monarch as either the divinely anointed David or his wise and wealthy son, Solomon. Confronting the frivolous and Frenchified court of Charles I, Puritan dissenters found in the mad and unjust reign of Saul and in his replacement by David, a man of the people, a precedent for dealing with a morally corrupt man who was head of both the body politic and the community of the church. In the pamphlet wars that ensued across the middle portion of the century, Royalists and Puritans alike claimed David in support of their cause, interpreting to their own purposes the significance of David's refusal to slay the Lord's anointed when given an opportunity for revenge, and the meaning of his cry in Psalm 51, "Against thee only have I sinned!"[12]

In the imaginative literature of the period, Thomas Fuller addresses his trilogy of poems—*David's Heinous Sin, Hearty Repentance, Heavy Punishment*—to Charles, casting himself in the role of Nathan at the end of the final poem and warning the king of the problems he will face if he does not repent of his sins and reform; the story of David's sin and repentance—like Nathan's parable of the unjust landlord—is Fuller's prophetic warning. A tangential development of this theme occurred earlier in the revenge tragedies which turn on the question of whether the virtuous and sinned-against man has the right to kill his corrupt and sinful oppressor. (Gene Edward Veith analyzes the relation of the biblical David to the best-known revenge hero in English drama, Shakespeare's Hamlet.) And in the aftermath of the bloody civil wars, new uses were found for the political David: Andrew Marvell sought to justify Cromwell by describing him as a Davidic king, while John Dryden—in what is certainly the most famous retelling of the David story in English, *Absalom and Achitophel*—found in the events of II Samuel 15–18 what George deF. Lord calls a remarkable vehicle for his "preoccupation with a cosmogonic myth of restoration, recovery, or renewal after exile, defeat, or destruction. . . , [for] the restoration of royal authority after a period of rebellious disorder." As Lord suggests, the David story "may well have been *the* central political myth of seventeenth-century England."[13]

With Europe's rediscovery of Longinus in the early and mid-eighteenth century, the sublime quickly grew to be an important literary principle and David was translated once more, this time as a poet. With Solomon and Moses, he was, of course, long the Christian ideal of the poet. In his first pastoral eclogue, for example, Petrarch depicts himself as wandering about, following the music of two sweet-singing shepherds (Homer and Virgil), but finds their music is surpassed by that which comes from a cave beside the river Jordan (David's).[14] Thomas Lodge's reply to Puritan Stephen Gosse's attacks on poetry is typical of the thinking of his age:

> Among the precise Jewes you shall find poetes . . . Beroaldus can witness with me that David was a poet, and that his vayne was in imitating (as S. Ierom witnesseth) Horace, Flaccus, and Pindarus; sometimes his verse runneth in an Iambus foote, anone he hath recourse to a Saphic vaine, and *aliquando seimpede ingreditue*.[15]

Attempts were even made to discover the secret of David's prosody, Renaissance Hebraists being especially active in "quantitative interpretation of biblical prosody"—a sign, says Israel Baroway, that Scripture was regarded no longer as a mere repository of divine law but was also "a sheer revelation of divine Beauty—Beauty, whose mystery must be fathomed."[16]

It is only in the nineteenth century, however, that David is valued not as psalmist or religious poet, but as the harpist whose playing cured Saul of his black melancholy and madness; his significance increases as those notions of poetry usually associated with the Romantic movement come to dominate Western culture. In Sir Thomas Wyatt's *Seven Penetential Psalms*, David cured himself of a spiritual postcoital depression as he repented his sin with Bathsheba; his music was a form of prayer. There was no suggestion in the poems that his cure resulted from his identity as poet or that poetry itself was a healing force. By the middle of the Victorian period, however, Robert Browning was able to claim in "Saul" that David's superior spiritual state results from the deeper perceptions allowed him as a poet and that his song is a wine that is capable of revitalizing Saul's doubting faith.[17] The poet has become, as Matthew Arnold claimed he would, the new priest of society, taking from traditional religious leaders care for the individual's spiritual well-being. (Thomas F. Dillingham uses Christopher Smart to illustrate the model that David the psalmist gave Christian poets to follow; M. L. Lewandowska examines how the popular belief that David is the author of the Psalms has affected one modern poet's work.)

The modern age has found the David story as broad and various as the Renaissance did; its uses of the myth are likewise multiple. The

David story serves, first of all, as a vehicle to analyze post-Darwinian man's spiritual malaise.

> What shall I do? Go through the Tyrol, Switzerland, Deutschland,
> Seeking, an inverse Saul, a kingdom, to find only asses?

asks the speaker in Arthur Hugh Clough's *Amours de Voyage* (IV. 31–32), whose condition is much the same as that of Browning's *angst*-ridden Saul or the contemporary speaker in the first of Yehuda Amichai's Saul and David poems: spiritual paralysis and malaise. (Noam Flinker treats Amichai's use of the Saul and David story to chart the spiritual geography of modern man.) A large number of twentieth-century writers on David have interpreted Saul's madness and black despair as a loss of faith in the rightness of the world that only David, in his pastoral joy and innocence, can still feel. This treatment of the theme is related to a serious psychological interest in the myth; such writers as D. H. Lawrence in *David; A Play*, André Gide in *Saul*, and David Pinski in *King David and His Wives* attempted to dramatize, with varying degrees of success, the psychological motivations of Saul and David in their contrasting states of religiousness and their differing modes of sexual response. In the "Godliness" chapters of *Winesburg, Ohio*, Sherwood Anderson makes a gripping indictment of the materialistic "manifest destiny" of an American fundamentalist Christianity that has lost its pastoral delight. The generational conflicts of Jesse, Louise, and David function as perverse and grotesquely ironic modern equivalents of the Old Testament Abraham-Isaac and David-Goliath types; in his depiction of Louise's need to be spiritually and physically fulfilled, Anderson gives a poignant reworking of the David story's religion-sex motif.

With interest in the psychological came exploration of the sexually perverse, and suggestions of a homosexual relationship between David and Jonathan, as well as a frustrated homoerotic attachment for David by Saul, that for centuries were treated with great delicacy or ignored entirely, were finally explored. Herman Melville's *Billy Budd*, André Gide's *Saul*, and Michael Mason's story of that same title make allusion to or dramatize Saul's possessive desire for the beautiful young shepherd who joins his court; Melville and Mason see Saul's pursuit of David, with his armies across deserts and plains, as an attempt either to repress his homosexual longing by killing its inspiration or to revenge himself on a beloved who spurns him. D. H. Lawrence repeatedly used the David and Jonathan relationship as a model for the "blood-brothership" he thirsted for in his own life,[18] while James Baldwin uses the biblical story as a foil to a relationship *manqué* in *Giovanni's Room*.[19] In "The Giant on

Giant Killing," Pulitzer Prize–winning poet Richard Howard suggests that David's conquest of Goliath was not so much martial as amorous.

> No need for a stone! My eyes
> were my only enemy, my only weapon too,
> and fell upon David like a sword,

explains the defeated giant in a soliloquy delivered from the grave, as he gives a particularly sensuous description of the young boy's body.

From Howard's suggestion that there is more than usually is seen in the relationship between David and Goliath, as given by Donatello in his famous statue (the poem is subtitled "Homage to the bronze *David* of Donatello, 1430"), one infers a final major use of the myth: as a suggestion of the relativity of all human perception. Readers of the original story in Samuel have for centuries been forced to try to reconcile certain obviously contradictory statements. For example, did Saul first meet David only after he had killed Goliath, as is implied in I Samuel 17:55–56, or had he known him previously as the harpist who was sent to cure him of his evil spirit? And why does he seem unaware of Samuel's anointing the boy? Surely news like that would have spread quickly through all Israel, despite whatever precautions Samuel might have taken.

The seams of the various folk traditions, joined to form the chronicle of Samuel, show quite clearly in the narrative. Related to this are those paradoxes in David's character, mentioned at the opening of this essay, which might easily be interpreted as contradictions, thus suggesting either hypocrisy on his part or clumsy time-serving by the author or editor. In *The King David Report*, East German novelist Stefan Heym suggests the latter, that I and II Samuel form an "authorized" biography designed to whitewash David's lasciviousness, greed, and cruelty by heroizing him once he was dead. The novel, like a number of popular novels which likewise have sought to demythologize this greatest of biblical kings, chronicles the human drama involved in reinterpreting the character of a man it suits one's political purposes to elevate, thus commenting on the processes of writing history and a culture's final recognition of its great religious figures.

William Faulkner, on the other hand, found in the David story an archetypal statement of the complexity and depth of human experience and of the eventual inability of the individual to judge the "facts" that are given him. In *Absalom, Absalom!* Quentin Compson receives the Sutpen–Henry–Charles Bon story from four different perspectives before he is able to grasp clearly the essence of the Sutpen family experience. The David story is symbolic of the frustrating inadequacy of man's faculties of perception in a delusive and often treacherous world, as, ironically, attempts to read it can prove.

A narrative story like David's has a protean identity. It consists of a sequence of action and a set of relationships between narrator and character, and of characters to setting. To the extent that its stuff and sense is so structured, it floats free of the style or the language that is used to express it. The proportions are also elastic. One could tell the David story again, following the plot and characterization closely, except for one item—say Bathsheba deliberately sets out to seduce David in the new version—and drastically alter the tone. One could take the configuration of three names—David, Bathsheba, Uriah—and tell a story of royal arrogance in a wholly different setting that would preserve the hypocrisy and horror of the original. (Faulkner, as Stephen Ross demonstrates, did much more with less, taking parts from the David story about the relationship of fathers and sons in the building of empires, elaborating upon them, and tracing out some sense in the history of the American South prior to the Civil War.)[20] Conceivably, one could graph the possible variations of a story almost exhaustively, but it wouldn't be necessary: anyone with a flair for the way literature works follows the course of the deviation to catch its sense.

The studies that follow show that the retellings go beyond respectful variation. The David narrative is classic literature in the sense Frank Kermode gives to the term. Each new version seems to get something of the original wrong, or, in other words, to catch its meanings in an unexpected light. "The only works we value enough to call classic are those which, as they demonstrate by surviving, are complex and indeterminate enough to allow us our necessary pluralities."[21]

A classic story such as David's is open, sufficiently we could say, to have no certain meaning and no ending. Each interpretation or revision of it expands the sense while joining a very old conversation. We could compare its language to a pliable dough of certain ingredients which one can tear a piece from to knead, mold, and season at will. Something fresh (or sour) can come of it over and over again—long after the reveries of the happy feast David held for his warriors when they regained the ark, and of the horrible feast Absalom held for Amnon, are silent. And each remaking shows as much about the baker as the bread.

One:

Discriminations against David's Tragedy in Ancient Jewish and Christian Literature

Jan Wojcik

The Ambiguous Narrative Perspective
in the Biblical Story of David

*T*he first scene in the Books of the Kingdom, as the Septuagint translators called the four sequential, closely related books which are
now known as I and II Samuel and I and II Kings, establishes the
ambiguous narrative perspective on the whole history to follow.[1] Hannah, one of the two wives of Elkanah, is said to be without child at an
advanced age; her husband, who loves her, must honor her less because
his other wife has produced. The other wife ridicules Hannah; stricken,
she goes to the temple to pray.

   To this point she is obviously made to resemble other barren women
before her in the tradition. (Barren Sarai suffered the insults of Hagar;
barren Rachel was jealous of Leah; Rebecca had no immediate rival, but
she too was barren until Isaac appealed to the Lord on her behalf and she
conceived. Samson's mother is also barren, until an angel announces that
she will bear a son, and she conceives and gives birth.)[2] But in this
narrative, instead of the expected voice of an angel or God, assuring
Hannah that all will be well, we hear Eli, a priest, who is off to the side,
staring as her lips silently mouth her prayer, and who suddenly admonishes her in a loud voice: "Enough of this drunken behavior. Go
away till the wine has worn off" (I Samuel 1:14-15).[3]

   For a moment, he stares at this venerable, typical scene from an
uninformed, realistic perspective. Eli doesn't know that she is praying or
what she is praying about. She isn't a type for him, as she has been made
for the reader. From his ground-level view, he somewhat wearily sees
her as another of the drunkards who probably frequent the place.[4]

   The narrator thus presents the same event from two points of view
simultaneously. Readers see from a high place, privy to the real motivation for Hannah's energetic prayer, from which they are able to look
back to other typical scenes (or forward, as Christian readers can, to the
troubles of barren Elizabeth and the momentary bewilderment of the
Virgin Mary). At the same time, they see her as ridiculous through Eli's
eyes.

Eli is mistaken for only a moment. Hannah assures him she is not drunk; she is praying hard. Immediately, with no narrative explanation, Eli believes her—the silence of the narrative indicates that her sincerity must be obvious—and sends her on her way with the wish that her prayer be answered. Shortly afterward, God "remembers" her prayer when she returns home; she has intercourse with Elkanah and conceives a son. Thus her story has a typical happy ending after all, despite the fact that Eli is never corrected in his misapprehension of her status within the narrative. He never asks what her prayer is, or discovers whether it is fulfilled.

The scene at once begins the "history" that the four Books of the Kingdom review. Hannah's son Samuel will anoint the kings Saul and David, who begin the development of the tribe of Israel into a rich and feared kingdom and whose complex inner struggles for continuing in power eventually bring it down. (The last king in their succession, Jehoiachin, king of Judah, ends his life as a pensioner of the conquering king of Babylon; the political power of ancient Israel is destroyed forever.) The scene also begins the ambiguous perspective on the events of that history. The kings Saul, David, and Solomon as well as the pretenders Absalom and Adonijah continually stare into the murky events unfolding before them, and calculate or miscalculate, but in either case they set in motion tragically shortsighted actions that finally are more irremediable than Eli's mistake. At the same time the narrative overview, shared with the reader, continually keeps the familiar, providential plan of God in view. Nathan the prophet shares this view as well. On the brink of David's decline, occasioned by his murderous adultery with Bathsheba, he looks ahead through the eyes of God to a time when a type of David, "one of his own chidren[,] will succeed to his throne . . . [which] . . . shall stand for all time in my sight" (II Samuel 7:14ff.). In another age, barren of hope, a great leader will again be raised up.[5] There's a typical happy ending in store for the large narrative as well.

Yahweh himself foretells that the secular turn the Israelites want their history to take will lead them into trouble. He complains to the elderly Samuel that the king the Israelites ask for will distract them from worshiping God and from seeing all things from a divine perspective. Instead of the special theocracy he has overseen to this point, the people now want sound economics, a strong military establishment, and a secure environment. Yahweh grants their request after telling Samuel of its consequences. The king, concerned exclusively with worldly affairs, will force citizens to become warriors, attendants at court, concubines, peasants, and lackeys. They refuse to listen. "No . . . we will have a king over us, to lead us out to war and fight our battles" (I Samuel 8:15ff.).

Yahweh is of course equipped to see things accurately. He seems to anticipate the most infamous scene that follows: the greatest king, David, has an army in the field while he seduces the wife of one of his warriors. Throughout the history which follows, kings are so absorbed with battles, even against themselves and other tribes of Israel, that they become, unlike their predecessor judges, unable to "see" the moral state of affairs. What prophetic seers such as Samuel, Nathan, and Elijah see they see too late to avert tragic consequences.

Biblical interpreters of Kings and the David story, from the earliest times to the present, have in general shared Yahweh's moral perspective. The Kings' narrative is intended to show his superior view of the history as the proper one; when the realistic narrative ends in the failure of the worldly life of Israel, it clears the ground for reviving a more intimate and enduring relationship between Yahweh and his people, as Nathan's messianic prophecy predicts. As Eli's momentary myopia is corrected, so will Israel's momentary fascination with secular power. In brief, it is thought that the merging of the narrative, prophetic, and providential perspectives on the story is its meaning.[6]

But from another view it is not altogether clear, in several key episodes, precisely what the narrative attitude is toward the fascinating accounts of kingly nearsightedness. Or to put it another way, precisely how much does the inclusion of this realistic, tragic material temper the Deuteronomists' belief that Providence controls human history absolutely?

For example, the narration views the episodes with Jonathan (I Samuel 18-21) along the lines of sight the story's characters use to perceive events; there is no prophetic perspective here, and events are casually related. Saul, it is said, keeps David at his court after the fight with Goliath, not because he admired his prowess—in fact, he was jealous of him somewhat— but because "he saw Jonathan had given his heart to David and had grown to love him as himself." The text says explicitly that it is because of Jonathan's favor that David advances to a command in the army. Throughout the narrative, only Saul's affection for Jonathan remains strong enough to lull Saul's increasing jealousy over David's achievements, until the balance tips when he hears how much the people have grown to love David too. He hears the women singing: "Saul made havoc among thousands; but David among tens of thousands." Then it is David whose eyes become sharper than Jonathan's. Jonathan at first can't believe David's assertion that Saul's jealousy has grown murderous. He tests David's theory with David's scenario and then helps him flee into exile just in the nick of time, still trying to temper his father's wrath whenever he can. David acknowledges the profound bond between them when he laments at the news of Jonathan's death:

> I grieve for you, Jonathan my brother,
>   dear and delightful you were to me;
> Your love for me was wonderful,
>   surpassing the love of women.   [II Samuel 1:26]

He recognizes that Jonathan's affection for him has unraveled a chain of natural, realistic causes that have brought David to the kingship. Before meeting Jonathan, David had been anointed by Samuel at God's command (I Samuel 16), but it is only after his bravery and cunning have secured Jonathan's help at crucial points that David gets the opportunity to begin his career of command. From the narrative perspective on these episodes it appears that divine selection *and* natural circumstances coincided to advance David's career. Divine will and the realistic turn of events agree. And the balance can be even more finely tuned.

The edge of the narrative irony is keenest in the episodes with Bathsheba, at the turning point in the story. Until now David's career and the fortunes of Israel have been rising. He has endured Saul's attacks against him. His restrained self-defense and his mercy toward Saul's heirs have won him the affection of both the northern and southern kingdoms, now united again. His cunning military strategy and governance have made the united kingdom richer and stronger than it has ever been. He has a large nation and a large, loving family about him. But now his fortunes decline. His relationship with God is shaken for the first time. Soon afterward, his son Amnon imitates his father's impetuous lust and rapes his half-sister Tamar. Her full brother Absalom, in line for the throne, kills Amnon in revenge. A rebellion against David breeds while he is in exile, and the father puts it down only at the price of killing his beloved son. His cry at the end of II Samuel, "Absalom, Absalom, my son!" marks the end of his earthly happiness.[7] In I Kings he is an old dry man, warmed by a young woman he can't love, while his surviving sons plot to succeed him. Solomon (whom he fathered with Bathsheba) wins the internecine struggle and rules in opulence after his father's death; but finally he turns away from Yahweh completely and the kingdom, void of its religious identity, loses its unity and national purpose, eventually to fall piecemeal to outside invaders.

In these episodes the attitude of the Deuteronomists about the precise cause of David's decline is so subtle it all but disappears in the ironic balance they strike between viewing David's sin tragically, as the cause of a chain of natural events, and theologically, as the cause of divinely sanctioned punishment, that brings his fortunes down. A detailed analysis of the narrative perspective can serve as a touchstone for assessing the ancient interpretations of the David story.

The Narrative Perspective
on the Bathsheba Episode

The scene begins (II Samuel 11:2ff.) with David walking about on the roof of the palace, from where he "sees" a woman bathing. He sees nothing but her beauty—no moral prohibitions against taking her, nor her conjugal relationship to one of his own soldiers who is fighting one of his wars. Afterward, Bathsheba sends word that she is pregnant and David immediately sends for Uriah, her husband. The narrative gives no details about his facial expression or his reaction or what he is scheming. The ellipsis respects the integrity of the character's mind and indicates where the narrator cannot or wishes not to look. David's motives are perhaps too horrible to view or too opaque to comprehend.[8]

The narrative presents David's reaction to bad news elliptically twice more. Uriah arrives and is sent home presumably so he can have intercourse with his wife. He refuses, however, because the Israelite soldier is under oath to refrain from intercourse while the army is in the field. The narrative reports, "David heard that Uriah had not gone home, and said to him . . ."— stripping away all but the most essential action to focus on David's maniacal fixation with his immediate problem. Nothing else exists for him (and the narration) but its resolution. This time David gets Uriah drunk in an attempt to make him forget his oath. When the ploy fails, he immediately writes a letter for Uriah to take back to his commander, Joab, ordering the latter to arrange Uriah's death in battle. The haste with which David arrives at the new strategy indicates that now, for him, removing the stigma of his adultery is purely a tactical problem. He plots murder as dispassionately as he tempts Uriah to go to his marriage bed. The story's even narrative hand stresses the terrible evenness of David's fixation.

Uriah's innocent blindness counterpoints David's myopia; Uriah is unaware of the plots against him, unbendingly following his soldier's code of duty—even delivering his own death sentence. But another character in the story recognizes, better than David, his characteristic tendency to fix his mind this way. When Nathan comes to admonish David for his crime, he tells David a parable about a rich man, with many sheep, who steals the beloved lamb of a poor man who has only one. David becomes so absorbed in the story that he misses the obvious parallel. He has what could almost be called an ideal reader's reaction, crying out in anger at the villain's deed: "As the Lord lives, the man who did this deserves to die. He shall pay for the lamb four times over because he has done this and shown no pity." Nathan then says to David, "You are the man."[9] He knows, as Joab knows, that David must be approached indirectly. His intense singularity of perception must be allowed to release itself before David can hear what a calmer eye can see.[10]

It appears that David and Nathan, and the Deuteronomist editors, see the consequences of the sin to be the result of a "vertical" causality. David's sin offends God, who from on high punishes him for it. David asserts before his confession that the offender deserves divine punishment. Nathan, before David's confession, reveals God's intention to "raise up evil against you out of your own house, and I will take your wives before your eyes and give them unto your neighbor, and he shall lie with your wives in the sight of this sun." After the confession, Nathan tells David: "The Lord also hath put away thy sin; thou shalt not die"—an idiomatic Hebrew expression meaning that God accepted David's confession and repentance. But he goes on to say that the child of Bathsheba will die. The following stories in the narrative, in which the child dies (II Samuel 12:18ff.) and Absalom takes possession of his father's concubines (II Samuel 16:21ff.), explicitly concur with the omniscient, prophetic belief that the operating moral economy here is vertical: consequences are a matter between the sinner and God. For every sin there is a debt that must be paid, after which the debt is forgiven.

But the narrative implicitly notes as well the less containable, "horizontal" causes that spread into this scene from previous scenes, and from it into the rest of the story. David's character has had him fixing his energies and gazing on particular tasks all through his story. He could spot Goliath's weakness and Saul's jealousy; he could devise the precise tactics that would ensure his survival in the wilderness. He has been, in addition, passionate and spontaneous throughout. He danced naked before the ark, exchanged tokens of friendship with Jonathan, faked madness when it would save him from the Philistines, and sang emotionally of his love for Jonathan. His fixations in this scene are but excessive extensions of his well-established talent for acutely focusing on a single detail.

And there are implicit indications that his fixation has natural consequences that inexorably undo his triumphs, that this intensity can be tragic hubris. After the war that killed Uriah and delivered Bathsheba to David, it is reported:

> *And it came to pass* that David's son Absalom had a beautiful sister named Tamar, and Amnon, another of David's sons, fell in love with her. Amnon was so distressed that he fell sick with love for his half-sister; for he thought it was an impossible thing to approach her since she was a virgin. [II Samuel 13:1-2]

Amnon follows his father's example in his lusting, not so precisely in his taking a woman who is forbidden him, but in his irremediable maniacal fixation. When Tamar tells him later that all he has to do to be given her is to ask David for her — the law would permit it — he refuses to listen. He wants her now. He rapes her, and then, spent of passion and drunk with disgust, he sends her out. Her laments inspire Absalom's murderous revenge which leads to his alienation from the court, the rebellion which grows out of it, and David's tragic cry of recognition: he is the father of his own deepest suffering. The conventional transitional phrase at the beginning of the passage (emphasized), used frequently throughout the narrative, is the most transparent device by which the narrative could link the events of David's adultery and Amnon's fornication. Literally, it means only that after one thing, another thing happened. It is left completely open to the reader to infer how strongly the causal nexus should be taken, whether David's suffering is divinely prescribed or naturally inevitable. The narrative perspective comes down emphatically on neither.

Ancient Exegetical Interpretations of the David Story

The survey which follows asks a question of the oldest interpretations of the story: What was to be made of the tragic in David's story by readers not interested in it? The approach is unusual for scholarship. It might appear unfair to ask a question that would never have arisen within the ancient exegetical tradition and to ignore its other achievements, at least equally important for its time and place. But the interest here is less in rabbinics or patristics as such and more in how one style of literary understanding, in this case the oldest, tugged at a corner of the David story. The ancient readers are like all those who have followed them in one respect: they take up only part of the story — a part that engaged their intellectual and imaginative need to understand how sacred history developed, and what that history demands of them. David's story was part of their own. It was important for them to know what aspects of his life to imitate or eschew. The way they read his story reveals as much about their minds as about the story's meaning. Other minds would see different things.

What is of particular interest here is what these readers see out of the corner of their eye, so to speak, now and then just catching a glimpse of the shadows David's tragic side casts on his story. Interpretations occasionally lapse into contradiction about whether David should be taken as a moral model; there appear to be significant, perhaps uneasy, oversights. We could say the ancient tradition of interpretation is like any other in its "dis-ease" with a literary text. Sacred literature, like any other, implies much more than can be said about it; even more than what *should* be said about it. The dis-ease of interpretation is the symptom of its authenticity. It shows, if only subliminally, that interpretation knows its limits. The text will survive any reading—even this one.

Obvious evidence of interpretive humility is that, within even these orthodox traditions, exegetes varied—subtly, even perhaps uncon-sciously. They would quote each other's opinions about a text copiously and approvingly, giving the impression that the tradition was unanimous and inevitable. But they would also add insights that grew out of their reading. Sometimes new readings virtually contradicted the old, though always silently, respectfully. The variant readings were the way the earliest readers conceded the text its freedom to talk to any and every age in its own way.

The many ancient exegetical images of David provide some back-ground for explaining the vitality of the David story in Western litera-ture. His importance in Jewish and Christian theology kept his story alive; the variety of the many interpretations draws attention to their final inability to type David sufficiently, and invites continuing media-tions. The enduring narrative continually presents writers and readers with a fascinating character of great imagination, cunning, affection, and lusts. His story conveys to the Western imagination religious images of the profound belief that thoroughly tragic lives can be redeemed.

Jesus' story follows from David's in this regard; in fact, he is called the son of David. David's story and Jesus' story follow their characters to their embrace of a profound failure—from a realistic perspective. David's cunning passion and Jesus' calculated passivity are the strengths that undo them. But after periodic glances to a higher, prophetic per-spective throughout the realistic story, each narrative looks beyond tragedy to its providential consummation. The Gospels revive the

Deuteronomists' view that God controls history as a *tour de force* against its natural rhythms.

The books of Chronicles, written approximately a century after the Deuteronomists wrote Kings (fourth century B.C.E.), retell David's history, again at a time when hopes for the restoration of Israelite political might were remote. They fashion David as a more striking moral model for a future king who will perfectly revitalize Israelite religious ideals — ideals that can flourish whatever worldly climate fate decrees.[11] There is no place in the new rendition for mention of Absalom and his rebellion. The episodes in Kings about David's affection for Jonathan and his affair with Bathsheba are unbecoming and irrelevant and therefore are deleted. Similarly, when David becomes angry with Michal, his wife and Saul's daughter, for her indignation when he dances naked before the ark, he curses not her reserve, as he does in Kings, but her father's family, which his family replaces. He is presented as offering no defense of his exuberant behavior, perhaps because the Chronicles' writers share Michal's view that it was unbecoming.

Unburdened of his worldly preoccupations, David becomes clairvoyant. Instead of the disedifying spectacle in Kings, where a withered old David lay curled up impotent in bed with a beautiful young virgin to keep him warm, while his sons Solomon and Adonijah plot viciously for his throne (until David rises from his bed to bless Solomon at Bathsheba's instigation), Chronicles has David, in a stentorian voice, call his officers, priests, and Levites to his chamber. They hear a formal announcement that Solomon is to take the crown and build a temple. David, in his speech, uses the words Nathan uses in his prophecy, thus showing he shares both the prophet's and Providence's view of the future, undistracted by vanity or bodily frailty:

> "Solomon, my son," he said, "I had intended to build a house in honor of the name of the Lord my God, but the Lord forbade me and said, 'You have shed much blood in my sight and waged great wars; for this reason you shall not build a house in my honor of my name. But you shall have a son who shall be a man of peace; I will give him peace from all his enemies on every side; his name shall be Solomon . . .' Now Solomon, my son, the Lord be with you." [I Chronicles 22:6ff.][12]

This passage shows that very early in the tradition of interpreting the Kings narrative, David is credited with having the prophetic insight that only Samuel, Nathan, and the narrative have in Kings. He becomes the very opposite of a nearsighted, tragedy-prone king. This, as can be seen below, is part of his image in the Haggadah, the Christian Scriptures, and the patristic tradition, as David becomes both progenitor and herald of a future son to succeed Solomon even more gloriously.

One passage that is preserved virtually intact from the Kings account is Nathan's messianic prophecy (cf. II Samuel 7 with I Chronicles 17). But now the entire narrative context makes it much more central to the intention of the book. The Chronicles writers strip the action to the central action in Kings, of David bringing the ark to Jerusalem and laying the plans for the temple at Jerusalem to serve as the seat for his glorious successors. Everything points to a regeneration of the nation's moral and religious identity. Cleaving to orthodoxy again, as the exemplary David did, would result in a religious renaissance that would make the previous loss of material power and wealth irrelevant.

In Chronicles the narrative point of view throughout is as lofty and remote as Nathan's impatience with any kingly errancy. Comparing the two renditions of the Kings history, one sees anew how willingly distracted by the realistic dimension the Deuteronomists allowed themselves in part to be.

David in the Jewish Antiquities of Josephus

Flavius Josephus (37/38–100 c.e.) is the only other ancient writer who rendered the Kings story in its entirety.[13] In his preface he says he wishes to inform his Roman, non-Jewish readers of the nature, fortunes, and "grandure" of the Jews.[14] Then, to make them appear grander, when he paraphrases an amalgam of Kings and Chronicles he deletes elements in the story that would probably seem fantastic, childish, or unrefined to cultivated Stoics. For example, he suppresses one of the episodes about Saul's madness (which corresponds to I Samuel 18:10ff.) and explains another (a repetition of the episode at I Samuel 19:9ff.) quite rationally. In Samuel, an "evil spirit" is said to descend upon Saul as he listens to David play the harp, causing him suddenly to throw a spear at him. Josephus first mentions that Saul's jealousy for David had been aggravated by his recent success against the Philistines. The "evil spirit" that he then describes as haunting Saul could be taken as simple narrative hyperbole for insane jealousy. In his account, Saul is troubled; he calls David to play for him; then, as David plays, Saul hurls the spear. Josephus thus suggests that Saul, motivated by jealousy, plots the whole affair systematically. Josephus removes whatever he can of any hint of demonic possession (Josephus, VI, 213ff.).

Other changes attest a similar refinement. The 100 Philistine fore-skins David must present to Saul as a dowry for Michal become 600 Philistine heads (cf. I Samuel 18: 25; Josephus, VI, 198). Josephus omits the passage at I Samuel 18:1-4 which speaks of Jonathan's loving David as much as his own soul and stripping off his clothing to present to David; in its place he adds parenthetically (after describing Jonathan's amazement at his father's outburst against David) that Jonathan "revered him for his virtue" (Josephus, VI, 206). In place of David's elegiac hymn in II Samuel 1:26,

> I grieve for you, Jonathan my brother,
>   dear and delightful you were to me;
> Your love for me was wonderful,
>   surpassing the love of women.

Josephus puts a plodding summary:

> His grief was made heavier by the thought of Saul's son Jonathan who had been his most faithful friend and had been responsible for saving his life. [Josephus, VII, 5]

In II Samuel 6:14, David strips off most of his clothes and dances with abandon before the ark. Michal, his wife, admonishes him for making a fool of himself in front of the servant girls. David responds that he'll dance again. The narrator, seemingly sharing David's disdain for her reserve, adds parenthetically that Michal became sterile from that moment. In Josephus, Michal comes to David primarily to bless him, adding only a mild reproach for his unseemly behavior.

Josephus' sense of decorum is related to his view of history. He states in his preface that his most important intention is to show that men who conform to the will of God, and do not venture to transgress laws that have been excellently laid down, prosper in all things beyond belief, and for their reward are given felicity by God, whereas, in proportion as they depart from the strict observance of these laws, they can never be sufficiently rebuked for their contempt (Josephus, iii). He believes in what Kierkegaard would call the moral imperative: an economy in which God metes out suffering or happiness in proportion to human sin or obedience. He follows exclusively the higher view of the Deuteron-omists that saw history as a raveling out of a divine plan, while his paraphrase deftly excises the Deuteronomists' recurrent suspicion that human actions have some natural consequences of their own. When David meets Goliath in Josephus, he is "accompanied by an ally invisible to the foe, and this was God" (Josephus, VI, 189). When David has his affair with Bathsheba, the invisible narrative presence broods over the story much more obviously in Josephus than in Samuel, to make certain that the readers know how to interpret what follows:

> Now David, although he was by nature a righteous and God-fearing man, and one who strictly observed the laws of his fathers, nevertheless fell into a grave error. [Josephus, VII, 130]

This moralizing perspective concurs directly with God's; where Samuel says "And the Lord sent Nathan to David" (II Samuel 11:1), Josephus says more explicitly: "God, however did not look upon this marriage with favor, but was angry with David, and appearing to the prophet Nathan in a dream, he found fault with the King" (Josephus, VII, 142). And so, when David acknowledges his sin to Nathan, the parenthetical remark which follows could be either's voice: "for he was, as all agreed, a God-fearing man and never sinned in his life, except in the matter of Uriah's wife."

Josephus' most revealing stamp on the story is the subtle manipulation of the chain of causality he arranges to follow this episode. His Nathan predicts only two consequences: the son whom Bathsheba would bear him would die soon after birth, and one of his sons would plot against him and violate his wives. While the second, more specific prediction (Samuel says "a neighbor" will violate them) seems to suggest some natural connection between the sin and the rebellion, Josephus does not mention Nathan's third prediction (in Samuel) that continuing warfare would result from the sin—a consequence that is less obviously controlled from above than a single rebellion. And Samuel's Nathan prophesies the child's death only after David's confession; by prophesying it before in Josephus, Nathan appears to make it a ploy to coerce the confession.

After David's admission of guilt in Josephus, a curious shift of persona suddenly has God speaking directly through the narrative voice:

> Whereupon God took pity on him and was reconciled to him. And He promised to preserve both his life and his kingdom, for *He said, now that he repented of his deeds He was no longer displeased with him.* [Josephus, VII, 153 emphasis added]

Josephus' God already considers the matter closed.

Josephus finds himself compelled to include the following episode, which contradicts, it seems, God's previous avowal of complete satisfaction—"The Deity caused a grave illness to fall on the child" (Josephus, VII, 154)—probably because he approves of David's stoic manner of bearing his grief. And to preserve the integrity of his story he must include the predicted episodes of Absalom's rebellion. But he makes one more decisive effort to sever the chain of natural causes. He introduces the Amnon episode with a much less transparent transition than the Deuteronomists': "But when the King returned to Jerusalem, a great misfortune overtook his household arising from the *following cause*" (*toiautaes*, literally "this"). The emphatic demonstrative points forward to the self-contained consequences of the Amnon story, and turns away from considering the possibility that David might have had some responsibility for the way his son acts. Now one of David's sons runs up debts of his own that the son, unrepenting, will pay for with his life, after David's ledger, it is made to appear, has been cleared through his repentance.

David in the Exegetical Haggadah: Midrash and Talmud

Twelve years after the return from exile Ezra called together the elders of the Israelite nation and they read the Torah or law together "and they gave the sense and caused the reading to be understood" (Nehemiah, 8:8). The rabbis who followed them carried on their tradition for 1,000 years. Their amplifications of Scripture were preserved and repeated, often with embellishments or corrections or new insights, in so sympathetic a manner that they became a kind of folk wisdom, gathering insights and volume as the traditional material was reverentially passed on.

"Midrash" is the name given to the anthologies of ancient sermons, sayings, and exegeses edited and arranged throughout the Middle Ages to form a running commentary on specific books of the Bible. No effort was made to sort the material chronologically; it is nearly impossible to determine with even approximate certainty when a particular anthology was compiled; and the works are undefined in subject matter—for all the editorial effort to link a commentary to the particular line of a text initially under discussion. Often, one line of Scripture immediately suggested another line to the commentator, which required an interpretation as elaborate as the first line. So it is not surprising to find in such a discursive manner of thinking that biblical characters gradually lose their strict definitions. They tend to become eternally present in the rabbis' minds, their adventures excised from context, their peculiar idiosyncrasies distilled into types. The rabbis adopted what one considered to be the style of God as it is written in the Midrash on Esther:

> From the beginning of the world the Holy One, blessed be he, appointed for each one the lot which was fitting for him. He appointed Adam to be head of all creatures, Cain the first of slayers . . . Noah the first of those saved from calamity . . . Jacob the head of the blameless . . . Joshua the first of the conquerers . . . Saul the foremost of the anointed, David the foremost of singers, Solomon the foremost of builders.[15]

David's image in the Midrash is somewhat more varied than that of a singer, but it is not complex, and certainly not tragic. He is, above all, the great king by whose offspring God looks forward to ruling Israel until the end of time (Genesis Rabba 88:7); he has great strength (Midrash Samuel 20:5 has him killing three bears and four lions single-handedly); he has great poetic gifts (Ecclesiastes Rabba 7:19), even if he was too forgiving as a father (Exodus Rabba 8:1) and overstepped propriety with Bathsheba (Ruth Rabba 8:1).

The commentary in Exodus is interesting for providing an example of the Midrash style and the sharpest criticism David receives in the tradition. Rabbi Shemoth begins by commenting on the line "Now these are the names of the sons of Israel who came into Egypt with Jacob; every man came with his household" (Exodus 1:1), and musing on the proper order to have in a household. He immediately calls to mind a proverb: "He that spares his rod hates his son; but he that loves him chastiseth him often." After this he turns to recalling examples of fathers who did and did not chastise their sons properly. Of David he says:

> Because David did not rebuke or chastise his son Absalom, he fell into evil ways, seeking to slay his father, sleeping with his concubines and becoming the cause of his wandering bare-footed and weeping, and of the slaughter of many thousands and tens of thousands of Israelites, as well as of other sorrows without end . . . .David treated Adonijah in a similar fashion, neither rebuking him nor punishing him, and therefore he became depraved. [Exodus Rabba, 1:1][16]

The interpretation passes over the far more serious first cause of the trouble in David's reign—the adultery—to focus on a mistake in judgment David made in trying to contain the consequences of that first cause. The Midrash intent is not so much to understand particular texts as to understand the things that the texts seem to be about.

There is the same lack of textual focus in Midrash Samuel, which is not an original Midrash but a compilation of all the things said in other Midrash pertaining to Samuel, arranged to follow the text. One section lists the sins various rabbis attribute to David, some of which were mentioned in Scripture, others in folklore, and then explains each accusation as mistaken. The accusation of adultery is softened by mentioning, in the same place, one opinion that David's lust for Bathsheba wasn't all his fault. She provoked it by taking off her dress where she knew he would see her.[17] In the Midrash, David is a name to stimulate thought or associative chains of thought or to stand for an idea. He is not a character to be understood in himself.

David in the Talmud

The Talmud contains exegetical commentaries on the law, and its tradition of writing developed in a manner similar to that of the Midrash. It was edited between 250 and 500 C.E., but its area of inquiry is more specific than the Midrash and its intent more serious: to divine and elaborate the moral principles from ancient texts according to which the rabbis and their contemporaries would mold their lives. As the context of the discussion is moral, the characters tend to become moral examples, positively or negatively.

The Talmud pictures David much as the Midrash does. He is the great king: "Whoever contends against the sovereignty of the house of David deserves to be bitten by a snake" (Sanhedrin 110a; see also Horayot 13a, 11b); he has great strength (Mo'ed Katan, 16b); he is a poet (Berakhot 3b, 10b) and a great scholar (Shabbath 30, Berakhot 49). But his failings come in for more frequent scrutiny and criticism, befitting the inquiry. According to Berakhot, his biggest mistake was taking a census of his people, because he presumed a knowledge that only God should have of how large his family was (Berakhot 62a); Mo'ed Katan criticizes him for rejoicing at Saul's downfall—something Samuel explicitly says he did not do (Mo'ed Katan 16b); and Sotar for calling the Torah songs—again, a criticism with no foundation in Samuel (Sotar 35a).

The two most significant discussions of David's story, from our perspective, occur in Talmud Sanhedrin and Talmud Shabbath. Each forgives David's affair with Bathsheba by shifting the details of the story in Samuel onto very different moral foundations from those in the narrative. Rabbi Samuel ben Nahmani in Shabbath says that David could not have sinned in this epsiode because it is said in I Samuel 18:14 that "David behaved himself wisely in all his ways, and the Lord was with him."[18] He reads this statement as an absolute assertion that could not be refuted by anything else that is said about David in Samuel. Nathan's seemingly contradictory statement in II Samuel 12:9, "Why have you despised the word of the Lord, to do that which is evil in his sight?" needs only to be understood properly. Nahmani reads the historical present tense of the verb "to do" (Hebrew *la-ah-sot*) as a deliberate avoidance of the past tense "he did" (Hebrew *ah-sah*), which would have indicated that David actually did the deed. He explains that David didn't actually lie with Uriah's wife, because Uriah, by not going home to her, acknowledged that during wartime soldiers were "divorced" from their wives. To exonerate David, Rabbi Nahmani ignores the explicit intent of Nathan's admonition and the narrative's intent to show Uriah as a dishonored honorable man.

Rabbi Johanan and Rabbi Raba go further in Talmud Sanhedrin to make of the Bathsheba episode a positive moral example. In commenting on the lines "And he walked upon the roof of the King's house: and from the roof he saw a woman washing herself; and the woman was very beautiful to look at" (II Samuel 11:2), Rabbi Johanan speculates that Bathsheba was cleaning her hair behind a screen when Satan appeared to David in the shape of a bird. David shot an arrow at him, which missed and broke the screen, thus inadvertently revealing the naked Bathsheba. So it wasn't either's fault, initially. Before he interprets the rest of the episode, where David sends for her and lies with her, the rabbi posits another verse from Psalm 17: "You have proved my heart; you have visited me in the night; you have tried me, and shall find nothing; I am determined that my mouth shall not transgress." He puts these words into David's mouth so that David himself seems to comment on this episode directly. With these lines David says that he regrets what he has done, because, by a play on words by the rabbi, "I am determined" is interpreted to mean a "bridle," so that what David really says is "Would that my mouth had been bridled so that I would not have to admit now that 'you have proved me.'"

Rabbi Raba, picking up on Rabbi-Johanan, cites another Psalm line: "Against you, you only, have I sinned, and done this evil in your sight: that you might be justified when you speak and when you judge." He puts these words into David's mouth right after the adultery with Bathsheba, and interprets them with a paraphrase. He hears David say to God: "You know full well that if I wished to suppress my lust, I could have done so. But I thought, let them not say 'that the servant can triumph over the master.'" Rabbi Raba interprets this to mean that David deliberately sinned in order to allow God to assert his superiority over David.[19] David wanted to let himself serve as an example to all human beings that no one, no matter how perfect, can expect to live without sin. (The same idea is discussed in Talmud Abodah Zaralt, where God joins David in his theater so that he might later use David as an exemplary repentant sinner [Abodah Zaralt 4b-5a].) Raba also states that God destined Bathsheba to be David's bride; so he took only what was rightfully his (107a).

These interpretations detach David from his place in this story to make him an icon with which to speculate on the religious or moral truth that happens to be at hand. In the same way that the Deuteronomists appropriate history to express their view, the Haggadah makes its own literature out of its literary sources.[20] But what is curious is how David, thus detached, can come to mean or do anything, even the opposite of what appears in Samuel. Rabbi Rabah, as the Chronicles writer, makes David a prophet, even imitating Nathan's fabulist's style in making up a dramatic fiction to teach a moral lesson to the audience. In this same spirit, the ancient Christian interpretive tradition also makes David a prophet, especially when it hears him singing the Psalms. He looks from his place in history forward a thousand years to recognize Jesus as his promised heir.

David in the Christian Scriptures

A passage in each Gospel makes a curiously oblique reference to David as a forerunner or father of the Messiah, and the passage in the Synoptic Gospels is almost identical (Matthew 22:41-45, Mark 12:35-37, Luke 20:41-44). Jesus is arguing with the Sadducees about Mosaic law and teachings when he suddenly changes the subject and asks: "'In what sense do people say the Messiah is the son of David? David himself, you know, says in the Psalms 'The Lord said to my Lord, sit at my right hand until I make your foes a footstool for your feet.' David, therefore, calls him 'Lord.' In what sense, then, is he his son?'" In all three accounts the question is left hanging. Jesus says nothing further on the matter, only raising the suggestion that whoever the Messiah is, he is greater than David: David calls him Lord.

A claim that Jesus is the one greater than David can be read back into the scene after reading Jesus' subsequent response in the synoptics to the Council's question—Are you the Messiah?—"The words are yours" (Matthew 26:59ff.), "I am" (Mark 14:62), "If I do tell you so, you will not believe me" (Luke 22:67), and in his response to Pilate's question—Are you the king of the Jews?—"I am, as you say" (Matthew 27:11, Mark 13:2, Luke 23:3).

John makes his oblique reference differently. He quotes a snatch of an argument while Jesus is preaching:

> Then some of the crowd who had heard these words said: "This is really the Prophet!" Others said: "This is the Messiah!" But some remarked: "Surely, the Messiah is not coming from Galilee, is he? Does not the Scripture say that the Messiah is to come from the line of David and from the village of Bethlehem, where David lived?" [John 7:40-43][21]

The only response that the text makes directly to this argument occurs when Jesus, this time well before his trial, is asked a similar question by "the Jews": "How long will you keep us in suspense? If you are the Messiah, tell us outright." Jesus answers their challenge: "I told you but you refuse to believe" (John 10:22-30) (that Jesus is born in Bethlehem is not mentioned in John).

There are many more references to the Messiah in John than in the Synoptic Gospels, but in each case there is the same obliqueness. Jesus and the Gospel writers very obviously appear reluctant to equate him with David's line. This is probably because they have a different idea of who the Messiah is—different from the popular conception of a David Revivus. The Messiah is not a secular king or military leader, "come to restore the fortunes of Israel," as his disciples hope at one point, but more a suffering servant and a son of God, or God himself. But claiming this would be tantamount to blasphemy—something not to be risked until the opportune time.

Later, however, Peter speaks more boldly. His sermon in Acts makes David at once both prototype of Jesus and prophet:

> Let me tell you plainly, my friends, that the patriarch David died and was buried, and his tomb is here to this day. It is clear therefore that he spoke as a prophet, who knew that God had sworn to him that one of his own direct descendants should sit on his throne; and when he said [in Psalms] he was not abandoned to death, and his flesh never suffered corruption, he spoke with foreknowledge of the resurrection of the Messiah. [Acts 2:29-32]

Paul's brief admonition in II Timothy 2:8, "Remember Jesus Christ, risen from the dead, born of David's line," and the genealogies linking David's family with Jesus' (Matthew 1, Luke 3) tacitly assume what Peter says explicitly, that Nathan's gaze into the future had Jesus in view. Only after the denouement of his story can his followers make the claim openly: Jesus was the one to come to fulfill the promise to David in a way, perhaps, Nathan would never have suspected.

The Christian scriptural view of David is relatively simple; he has significance only insofar as he shares both as prototype and prophet in the Old Testament foreshadowing of Jesus.

David in the Patristic Tradition

The dogmatic rhetoric in the title of chapter 8, book 17 of Augustine's *City of God* indicates how commonplace Peter's typical identification of David and Jesus had become by the fourth century: *"De promissionibus ad David in filio eius, que nullatenus in Solomone, sed plenissme inveiunter in Christo"* — "About the promises to David about his son, which in no way can be taken to apply to Solomon, but can be most fully found to apply to Christ."[22] This is David's typical identity for the Christian fathers, writing from the earliest days of the church to about the eleventh century. At a prophetic level of perception, his essential qualities become absorbed in Jesus—the figure Christian theologians see while sighting along Nathan's gaze into the aftertimes.[23]

In addition, for Augustine and other fathers, as for Peter, David shares this perception of himself as if he were a prophet of his own family fortunes. The same transferral of Nathan's role occurs, we recall, in Chronicles and the Talmud. In his commentary on the Psalms, composed, preached, and written down between 392 and 418, Augustine notes the heading of Psalm 7: "A Psalm for David himself, which he sung to the Lord because of the words of Chusi, son of Jermini." He relates the heading to the story in II Samuel 13ff., in order to explain it:

> The story which occasioned this prophecy can be gathered from the second book of Kings. David's son Absalom was waging war against his father. Chusi, a friend of David's, went over to Absalom's headquarters to find out and report to David what plans Achitophel was concocting for Absalom. . . .

> However, in this Psalm we need not consider the literal story with which the prophet has covered its hidden meaning, but since we have been converted to Christ, let us draw the veil aside. First let us search out the significance of the names. It is said that Chusi signifies "silence," Jemini "the propitious," and Achitophel "brother's ruin"— names which bring once more before our eyes Judas the traitor, of whom Absalom is a type, whose name signifies "peace of his father." David, in fact, was always ready to make peace with him, even though he, deceiver that he was, cherished war in his heart.[24]

Here David appears to be both immersed in the story as one of its characters and (at the point in the narrative where he is said to be singing this psalm) standing outside the story as a seer, "covering up the hidden meaning" with easily decipherable names. He becomes both character and interpreter in his own story, utterly aware of everything he's about.

At another place, Augustine explains the one moment in the narrative where David, clearly, is not aware of everything as merely the necessary cause of the greater clear-sighted moral awareness which follows. David can only be a model repentant sinner if he sins:

> Now David reigned in the earthly Jerusalem, being a son of the heavenly Jerusalem, greatly extolled by the divine testimony because his sins were overcome by such great piety, through a most salutary humility of repentance, so that he assuredly belongs among those of whom he himself said, "Blessed are they whose iniquities are pardoned and whose sins are covered" [Psalm 32]. [*The City of God*, 20]

These images of David as prototype, prophet, and repentant sinner were part of the patristic discursive thesaurus, coming to mind when the topic turned to the prefigurations of Jesus or the problems of sensual excess. Jerome, Augustine's contemporary, looks, as he always does, more closely at the text than Augustine. But like him, Jerome often reads for moral truths:

> David was chosen as a man after God's heart, and his lips had often sung of the future coming of Christ the Holy One. But as he walked upon his housetop he was fascinated by Bathsheba's nakedness and added murder to adultery. Notice for a moment that even in one's own house the eyes are never safe from danger. . . . And that no one may trust in kinship by blood, remember that Amnon was fired by an illicit passion for his sister. It wearies me to tell you many virgins fall daily, what notables Mother Church loses from her bosom.[25]

For Augustine and Jerome the many episodes in David's story have no necessary continuity. Its most important moments by far are Nathan's prophecy and David's repentance, but other moments such as the fight with Goliath or David's exuberant dance before the ark or the rebellion of Absalom, would be similarly detached from context and held up to refract light on the topic at hand. Without a sense of the continuity of the story, its tragic dimension couldn't be seen at all.[26]

But when certain other writers looked more closely at the text of Samuel they stumbled on a contradiction latent in the casual patristic images of David; the clear-eyed prophet and the adulterous murderer become difficult to reconcile in one character, especially if a commentator takes Nathan's energetic condemnation of David's myopia seriously. Eucherius and Isidore have this difficulty, and through their influence it is passed down. Almost every commentator after them quotes their readings of the Bathsheba episodes verbatim.[27]

The commentary on the books of Kings of Saint Eucherius, written in A.D. 434, begins its discussion "On the Adultery of David" by paraphrasing the Bathsheba episode. This serves to introduce a translation of David into a type of the promised Messiah, Bathsheba into a type of the law of the carnal letter that binds the people until "liberated by her association with the son," and Uriah into a type of the Jewish people whose knowledge of the law the Messiah attempts to raise to new heights:

> When David takes Uriah's wife from him and joins her to himself—because he is a "strong armed man" as his name is interpreted to mean, our redemptor appears in the flesh, and begins to speak the law spiritually, which had previously been held according to the letter. He draws out what is the essential part of the Jewish people and joins it to himself. [1092][28]

But in the most original section of his commentary Eucherius suddenly has to change his tack if he is going to be true to Nathan's intent in the story, subsequently, to admonish David for his liaison. Now Eucherius reads the whole tale as an exemplum of repentance. He calls David's sin "detestable" and points out that God does not permit it to pass without punishment. Then, almost immediately, he begins to deflect the accusation. For Eucherius, David's punishment seems to be only the humiliation of admitting his guilt, although he generalizes that God "either punishes men directly or indirectly through the agency of other men or events"—an idea that could admit some synthesis of divine punishment and natural consequences. He doesn't develop this idea, however. He goes on to say that David hears the phrase "The Lord has forgiven your sin" only after he fully confesses it, thus making the whole story's purpose merely an illustration of the axiom *velox confessio velocior medicina* (A quick confession brings even quicker relief).

Significantly, Eucherius cannot use a single method to interpret this scene. The symbolic content he imposes on the scene and its inherent realism are too much at odds. He needs to shift from allegorizing the literal meaning to accepting it, then to rationalizing it, in order to accommodate the story to his moral beliefs. His convictions outshine his awareness of his inconsistency.[29]

Isidore of Seville's interpretation chokes on the same hard bone a century or so later. His allegorizing is at first more lofty and farther ranging than Eucherius'. Under the heading "On the Sin of David with Bathsheba," he interprets David's name to mean both "mighty of hand" and "desirable"; Bathsheba's name means both a "brimming well" and the "seventh well." Then in a dazzling piece of word and text association, he says:

> Now in the Song of Songs the bride who is the Church is called a well of living water. And the number seven is associated with the Holy Spirit because the spirit descended from heaven on Pentecost on the seventh day of the week. . . . Therefore in the giving of this gift of seven, the Church was established as a brimming well, because there flows into it an eternal stream, and whosoever drinks of it shall not be thirsty for all eternity. [John IV][30]

Uriah's name signifies the Devil. His first name is to be interpreted "my light is of God," but the second, Hethenus— the Hittite—as "cut off." Together, the names mean that he was first a great light bearer, then an angel fallen from grace—Lucifer.

But the text at hand distracts Isidore from his allegory, just as it did Eucherius. He compares Uriah's allegorical sin with David's literal sin in the scene, and then writes a strangely harsh and menacing sentence:

> Ergo, iste quidem David graviter sceleratque peccavit; quod scelus ejus etiam per prophetam Deus arguit increpando, et ipse abluit poenitendo—Just so that despicable David gravely and wickedly sinned, a sin which God accused him of through a prophet's proclamation and cleansed him of through penance. [411, 5]

But then, having cleared the air, as it were, with what had to be said, Isidore slips back into the more comfortable mode of allegorizing, his own "cleansing." His paraphrase of the story is: "The most desirable of all men, when he was walking in the solarium, fell in love with the Church, washing the grime of the ages off her body. He took her from her house of clay into a house of spiritual contemplation. Afterwards he killed the devil that had been plaguing her, thus liberating her from an endless marriage." He concludes with an unabashed, typical association of David with Jesus: "Let us love this David, so beloved, who has liberated us from the Devil through his mercy" (411, 8).

Eucherius and Isidore reveal more than they seem to be aware of. Their close readings discover, if unwittingly, something approximate to the ambiguous perspective on the David story that the Deuteronomists let arrange its events. They don't come close to recognizing David's tragic character, but they recognize the one undigestible revelation of that character. The momentary breakdown of their method of "inverting the sense" (see note 29) approximates, somewhat obliquely at least, the ironic indecision of the final editors about where the ultimate meaning lay in David's realistically tragic but prophetically redeemed tale.

Hope in the coming Messiah predisposed the rabbinical exegetes, as faith in Jesus as Messiah predisposed the early Christian exegetes, to follow Nathan's gaze as the true perspective on the story. The awkward lapses of their Midrash or allergories or figuration over the literal events of the story show at least that they didn't always miss seeing what didn't fit their perceived hope or faith. Finally, however, the disjuncture of the literal and symbolic readings also shows that for more than a millennium after the Deuteronomists arranged the complex tragi-divine comedy of Kings, an interpretation discovering their finely balanced ironic perspective on the glories of the David story could not, perhaps for reasons of great hopefulness, be written.

Two

Frail Grass and Firm Tree: David as a Model of Repentance in the Middle Ages and Early Renaissance

Charles A. Huttar

Non was strengere than Sampson ne non holier than David ne non wisere than Salamon, and yit thei fellen bi wommen." The quotation is from a French homiletic guide (via a fourteenth-century Middle English translation),[1] but the sentiment could as easily have been taken from any of a score of other sources. Examples were the mainstay of the medieval sermon, and no preacher who respected his craft would cite one example when three were available. But the name of David also occurs frequently in another list of examples, for the encouragement of all who, having fallen, are tempted to the still worse sin of despair. If such great offenders as David, Peter, and Mary Magdalene could be restored through penitence, there is surely hope for all.

The chosen examples may vary. The account in the *Golden Legend*, though somewhat more elaborated, is typical enough. There are three kinds of sins: pride, lechery, and avarice. Saul of Tarsus exemplifies the first: he "persecuted the chirche over prowdly." David was guilty of the second, "For he maade advoulterye, and for thadvoulterye he slewe urias his trewe knyght." Avarice was the sin of Matthew, the tax collector. But all three did penance and obtained not only pardon but "multiplied . . . yeftes of grace." Saul the persecutor was "made a right trewe prechour," David a prophet, and Matthew an apostle and evangelist. "And therfor these forsayd thre ben ofte recited that no man that wold be convertid shold have dispair of pardon."[2] Sometimes Zaccheus is substituted for Matthew, sometimes Manasses is added to the list, and often extra examples are given for lechery, drawing on such postbiblical legends as those of Thaïs and Saint Mary of Egypt. But David is nearly always included.[3] "Considering the position from which David fell, let no one be proud; but since David recovered from his lapse, let no one despair."[4] A twelfth-century abbot, Gottfried of Admont, wrote:

> David, king and prophet, was a frail stalk of grass when he saw Bathsheba, and took her, and killed Uriah by the sword of the children of Ammon, committing at the same time two wicked sins, adultery and homicide. Then was David frail grass. But afterward he was made a firm tree, when Nathan came to him, rebuking him out of the mouth of the Lord, by whose words he was inflamed with so great a fire of penitence that he lay on the ground for seven days, not eating

bread nor drinking water. Look, he who was a frail stalk, to how great a treelike strength has he come through penitence![5]

Gottfried found particularly nice imagery for sentiments that seem to have been on every preacher's tongue. Even a sporadic churchgoer could hardly have escaped the myth of David. If his eye strayed to the stained-glass windows, he might see David in his role as an ancestor of Christ, in the Jesse Tree. If he looked at the statuary, there was David as a prophet, king, or foretype of Christ. But more dramatic than either of these was the story of David's sin and repentance. It was by this that Dante, in his *Paradiso*, chose to characterize David as "the singer who for grief at his sins cried out, 'Have mercy on me'" (32.11-12). From the beginning to the end of the Middle Ages and on into the seventeenth century, if the evidence of English sermons is any indication, the role of David as a model of repentance was most prominent in the portrayal of this hero. In the space here available we can only survey this vast subject, giving particular attention to the variety of ways in which tradition has embellished and interpreted the biblical narrative.

To permit the broadest pastoral application, commentators sometimes defined with considerable subtlety the sins of which David was guilty. Nearly always cited along with adultery is the sin of murder, of which the prophet Nathan accuses David in 2 Samuel 12:9. Treachery is also frequently mentioned, referring to David's sending Uriah with his own death warrant.[6] This part of the story must have had a great impact on the popular mind; it embodies a folklore motif that has appeared independently in different parts of the world,[7] and in German the term *Uriasbrief* had by 1476 become "a household word" for such a letter of treachery.[8] In a somewhat different analysis, David's sin is seen as four-fold: besides committing adultery and homicide, he "cast upon truth both deceit and contempt" and "disdained to confess his sins."[9] And one diligent compiler, Nicolaus de Hanape (c. 1225-91), identified no fewer than eight sins committed by David in this affair: "deceit and subtlety," treason, murder, adultery, "luxuriousnesse and incontinency," "unwise lokes," hypocrisy, and "slouthfulnesse and negligence." On the last, he offers this explanation, based on 2 Samuel 11:1: "When other kings were wont to go a warfare, David taried at whom [home]."[10] Two of the sins in Hanape's list, and the sin of pride as well, appear in the very influential *Postilla* of Nicolaus of Lyra (c. 1265-1329), who seeks to identify not the outward acts but the root sins. He said that David sinned, first, *per luxuriam*, second, *per negligentiam*, and third, *per superbiam*.[11] Presumptuous pride is also what Sebastian Brant has in mind when in his *Narrenschiff* (1494) he lists David among those who "synne trustynge upon the mercy of god."[12]

The sin of pride is also central in a Muslim legend of David's sin and repentance. I will give this story at length, as several of its details will be referred to later. David, overhearing a dispute between two of his subjects as to whether he or Abraham were greater, prayed for an opportunity, comparable to Abraham's sacrifice, to show his love for Allah. Three days later, on ascending the pulpit, David caught sight of a beautiful bird, which so distracted him from worship that "he sung fewer psalms" than usual "and grew soft and playful in the most solemn parts of the worship." He cut the service short and followed the bird, coming by sunset to the margin of a small lake, where the bird disappeared. "In its stead there rose up a female form, whose beauty dazzled him like the clearest midday sun." He asked her name, which was Saja, and, learning that her husband Uriah was away with the army, commanded his general to put him in the most dangerous post in the van. Uriah was slain. "David then wooed his widow, and married her at the expiration of the prescribed time."

The day after the marriage, at Allah's command, Gabriel appeared in human form before David, with Michael, and said, "The man whom thou seest here before thee is the owner of ninety-nine sheep, while I possess an only one; nevertheless he pursues me without ceasing, and demands that I should give up my only sheep to him."

The king replied that this was unreasonable, betraying "an unbelieving heart, and a rude disposition." Gabriel interrupted: "Many a noble and accomplished *believer* permits himself more unjust things than this."

Recognizing the reference to his conduct, David was angry. "He grasped his sword, and would have plunged it into Gabriel," but with a scornful laugh the two angels spread their wings and ascended, with this parting word: "Thou hast pronounced thine own sentence, and called thy act that of a barbarous infidel: Allah will therefore bestow upon thy son a portion of the power which he had originally intended for thee. Thy guilt is so much greater, since thou prayedst that thou mightest be led into temptation without having the power of resisting it."

Feeling at once "the whole burden of his sin," David tore off robe and crown "and wandered through the wilderness wrapt in simple woollen garments, and pining with remorse." His penitence continued three years, during which he "shed more tears . . . than all humankind before him." "His skin fell from his face and the angels in heaven had compassion on him, and implored for him the mercy of Allah." At the end of the three years David returned to Palestine, recovered in health and appearance so that no one knew what he had undergone. Meanwhile, Absalom had seized the throne and had to be deposed — which was accomplished, by Allah's help, without war.[13]

Similar legends in Jewish rabbinical tradition, perhaps more accessible to Christian writers of the Middle Ages, may be summarized as follows. David asked God why he was called the God of Abraham, Isaac, and Jacob, but not the God of David, and the answer was that they had been tempted and proved by God. "Prove me, then," David prayed. The answer was a choice of kinds of temptation, and David chose unchastity as his means of testing. God sent Satan in the shape of a bird, which sat on a wicker canopy under which Bathsheba was washing. David shot an arrow, missed the bird but shattered the canopy, beheld Bathsheba, and "was at once violently enamored of her. . . . He spent twenty-two years in repenting this sin . . . ; and he also was stricken with leprosy for half a year, during which time he was abandoned not only by his own court, but by the Holy Spirit, in punishment for his sin." Still more severe punishment was Absalom's revolt.[14]

These stories shift the emphasis from the sins of adultery and homicide to that of pride. Other rabbinical writings go so far as to deny that David sinned at all. The Old Testament had provided the basic characterization of David as "a man after [God's] own heart" (1 Samuel 13:14), who "did that which was right in the eyes of the Lord . . . save only in the matter of Uriah the Hittite" (I Kings 15:5). The Christian Middle Ages considered him a saint.[15] The Talmud credited him with being able, by prayer, "to bring things from heaven down to earth"; said that the reason he was not permitted to build the temple was that if he did it would be indestructible; and added that evil inclinations had no power over him. The sin with Bathsheba was "only as an example to show the power of repentance. . . . Some Talmudic authorities even assert that David did not commit adultery," since the custom for soldiers going to battle, like Uriah, was to provide their wives with divorce papers. "Similarly David must not be blamed for Uriah's death, since the latter had committed a capital offense in refusing to obey [the king]."[16]

Evidently, David's sin was an embarrassment to commentators. Christian writers usually emphasized the adultery, but even Augustine, who appears to have originated much of the interpretation that later authors copied, draws a hair-splitting distinction: David was "not lustful, though he fell into adultery," but was instead "carried away by the heat of passion and by temporal prosperity." Rebuked by Nathan, he

"wiped out his sin in deep penitence." Lust "did not take up its abode
with him, but was only a passing guest." Augustine goes on to interpret
Nathan's parable in fine detail: the rich man, of course, stands for David,
the pauper for Uriah, and the sheep for wives; the guest, for whose
dinner the poor man's lamb was slain, "is illicit love, which feasts on
copulation with a woman." But lust was only "a guest with David,"
whereas "with Solomon it truly held sway."[17]

The next segment of the story, David's repentance after hearing
Nathan, engendered many comments and narrative accretions. Medieval
writers make much of the promptness, openness, and completeness with
which he accepted the prophet's rebuke, "Thou art the man." Unlike
Cain, Pharaoh, Saul, and Judas, all of whom said *Peccavi* but "spake it
not with a true harte,"[18] David was recognized immediately to be sin-
cerely contrite. Thus an accepted motto for the emblematic scene of
David and Nathan was *Corde, non voce*[19]—a sentiment perhaps going
back to Nicolaus of Lyra's gloss on 2 Samuel 12:13, "*Ore et corde.*"

Narrators would of course describe such a climactic scene in full,
freely inventing any details that the original did not supply. The account
in 2 Samuel 12:7-14 concentrates entirely on the dialogue. Nathan re-
cites the divine accusation and discloses the judgment: "The sword shall
never depart from thine house. . . . I will raise up evil against thee out of
thine own house, and I will take thy wives before thine eyes, and give
them unto thy neighbour . . . before all Israel, and before the sun."
David replies, "I have sinned against the Lord." Then Nathan remits
David's self-imposed death sentence, transferring it to the child born of
the illicit union. But the visual details of this scene are left to be
imagined—and writers and artists abundantly took the cue. Obvious
enough are the "pious tears" mentioned by Cassiodorus (c. 490-585)[20]
and many others, and David's descent from his throne to humble himself
before the prophet. So firmly established is the latter detail in the
iconography of this scene that, with few exceptions, a picture that shows
David seated or standing is sure to depict an earlier moment—Nathan's
approach, parable, or rebuke—and not the moment of penitence. In the
late poetic version of Sir Thomas Wyatt (1503-42) there are additional
details, betokening humility as well as emotional stress:

> Lyke hym that metes with horrour and with fere,
> The hete doth strayte forsake the lyms cold,
> The colour eke drowpith down from his chere,
> So doth he fele his fyer maynifold.
> His hete, his lust and plesur all in fere
> Consume and wast, and strayt his crown of gold,

"How Nathan the prophet reproved David for his sin which he had committed and promised him vengeance; and David descended from his seat and lay upon the earth and repented greatly and acknowledged his sin before all the people, praying God for mercy."

His purpirll pall, his sceptre he lettes fall,
And to the ground he throwth hym sellff withall.[21]

In illuminations, the prostrate David often still wears his crown, but in some instances is bareheaded. Wyatt goes on to describe David's physical appearance, in terms suggestive of the allegorical iconography of personified abstractions. "Repentant humblenes" has put down the king's "pompous pryd"; "thynner vyle cloth then clothyth poverty" barely suffices to "hyde . . . his nakednes";[22] his white beard no longer conveys "reverent gravite" but, now "ruffeld," is an acknowledgment of "his wykednes." In sum, "More lyke was he the sellff same repentance/ Then statly prynce off worldly governance."[23]

Artists and writers imported some details of this scene from other parts of David's story. When Cassiodorus has David prostrate himself before Nathan, he is probably borrowing from the next scene, where, in prayer for his sick child, "David fasted, and went in, and lay all night upon the earth" (verse 16); the same visualization is evident in the last line of the stanza (quoted above) from Wyatt. Other items that sometimes were transferred from the story of David's praying for his son are the seven nights' duration and the fasting, as in the passage from Gottfried with which we began. One homilist explicitly places the fasting "after the sin" and says that David obtained forgiveness by it; for authority he relies on Psalm 35:13, "I humbled my soul in fasting."[24] An earlier writer, Jerome, incorporates several of the foregoing details: "If holy David, meekest of men, committed the double sin of murder and adultery, he atoned for it by a fast of seven days. He lay upon the earth, he rolled in the ashes, he forgot his royal power, he sought for light in the darkness."[25]

The paragraph heading in Jerome identifies this scene as an example of "public penitence," and this is another idea that is frequently encountered.[26] An illustration of Queen Mary's Psalter (fourteenth century) shows a crowd behind Nathan and explains (beneath the picture) "How Nathan the prophet reproved David for his sin which he had committed and promised him vengeance; and David descended from his seat and lay upon the earth and repented greatly and acknowledged his sin before all the people, praying God for mercy."[27] In the art, the presence of others might be attributed simply to realism in depicting a court scene, but when writers too insist on it, we realize that a deliberate point is being made. Perhaps Nathan's words "before all Israel," which applied to a portion of David's punishment that would be fulfilled much later, are transferred by the commentators to the scene of his penitence.

Thus by drawing both on 2 Samuel 12:11 and on verses 16-18 to expand the narration of David's response to Nathan, the developing iconographic tradition has economically condensed three sequential events into a single, visualized moment.

There is still a fourth event in the David story from which, over the centuries, this scene of penitence has seemed, magnetlike, to draw narrative details. The final chapter of 2 Samuel tells of David's other great sin, his self-glorying insistence on taking a census of his subjects. In several specific details this story closely resembles the other. (1) Both times David is moved by conscience to confess "I have sinned" (2 Samuel 12:13, 24:10, 17). (2) God sends the prophet Gad to pronounce judgment, as he had the prophet Nathan in the earlier incident. (3) The punishment in both cases is not limited to David's private life but involves severe hardship for the whole nation, which is viewed as his flock (2 Samuel 24:17). (4) If we supplement 2 Samuel 24 with the version of the same story in 1 Chronicles 21, we note the use of identical imagery for both incidents. In one account the metaphor of a sword is used for the divine punishment of pestilence, while in the other "the sword" is used by metonymy for the evil strife that will mar David's reign as a part of the decreed punishment.[28] (5) David must undergo humiliation or ritual observance in public (2 Samuel 12:11-12, 24:18). (6) God's mercy produces a mitigation of the penalty (2 Samuel 12:18, 24:16, 25).

In addition, 1 Chronicles 21:16 contains details which, while not actually a part of the earlier repentance scene, are, as we have noted, assimilated to it: David falls prostrate and covers his body with the ritual signs of penitence ("sackcloth," cf. "ashes" in Jerome). The prominence of an angel in the later incident may also be compared with the displacement of Nathan by an angel in some medieval accounts of the earlier incident. And still one more detail in the latter incident eventually entered the iconography of the former. The Lord has Gad offer David three possible punishments, of which he must choose one: famine, helplessness before enemies, and pestilence. It is the seer who offers these choices, but a common artistic portrayal was an angel in the clouds, holding a skull or emaciated person or death figure, a lance, and a scourge, to indicate, respectively, David's three options. For the scene with Nathan, meanwhile, a superficially similar iconographic detail had emerged, an angel brandishing a sword.[29] It is easy to see how an artist might fail to distinguish between these two angelic figures.

Such confusion is documented in an eleventh-century poem describing the paintings then extant in Mainz Cathedral. In one painting David "prays to be restored by means of the threefold divine rod."[30] The scene is unquestionably Nathan's rebuke, for Nathan is named and praised for the "Socratic" stratagem by which he "makes the king confess," yet the "threefold rod"—here, interestingly, more an instrument of restoration than punishment—is an equally clear reference to the judgment pronounced by Gad. By the sixteenth century the triple-threat angel had become a mere iconographic cliché. Wyatt's *Psalms* reflects this confusion of the two separate incidents in David's life, for he says of Nathan's rebuke, "He shewth hym ek from hevyn the thretes," and he has David complain of God's "arrows . . ./Of sword, of sekenes, off famine" which "stikkes diepe in me."[31]

The locale and duration of David's penance received freer embellishment than most parts of the narrative. We have noted the possible biblical basis for Jerome's "seven days," but the three years of Muslim legend and the twenty-two years of rabbinic tradition must surely be independent accretions.[32] Whether derived from those legends or elsewhere, the idea of David's leaving his palace and going out into the wilderness to do penance had a strong appeal. To Petrarch it symbolized the incomparable value of the solitary life of contemplation. He describes how David, when "overwhelmed with the terror of death and with fear and trembling," fled from "the dangerous and ill-omened city" which had been the place of his downfall and sought "safety and happiness in solitude." Remembering the triumphs in the wilderness in his earlier life—victories not only over enemies but "over his own spirit, than which there is no victory more splendid"—he "remained in the wilderness awaiting the Lord, who saved him from the tempest of his mind."[33]

In the *Triumph of Love*, David is one of a whole procession of figures who have fallen victim to this treacherous god, and Petrarch has him driven by remorse to a dark cave, where he regains the divine favor in solitude[34]—just as Saint Mary Magdalene was reported to have done during thirty years of penance in a cave near Marseilles which Petrarch visited as a youth.[35] The cave, to Petrarch, is more than just a conveniently isolated refuge in a picturesque setting. To enter the cave is to "penetrate to the hidden recesses of the solitary life." What would be the point, he asks, of a mere physical journey to the wilderness without the proper spiritual orientation? "What advantage . . . if wherever I go my mind follows me, the same among the woods as in the city? It is the mind that I must lay aside before all; it is the mind, I say, that I must leave at home, humbly imploring the Lord to make my heart pure within me and to establish an upright spirit in my body" (*The Life of Solitude*, I.iv.6; ed. cit., p. 142)—thus closing this passage by paraphrasing from David's psalm of penitence (Psalm 51:10).

Wyatt takes up the cave imagery and, with Aretino's help (see note 21), gives it a different meaning which is related more closely to David's penitence. He has David "withdraw," upon hearing Nathan's judgment, "into a dark Cave/Within the grownd wherin he myght hym hyde,/ Fleing the lyght, as in pryson or grave" (lines 60-62). It is a place of "dark horrour" (64), a fitting emblem for the secrecy of his sin and for his own blindness (31-32). It is a place of isolation from the community (415-18), more in keeping with the spirit of the rabbinical account than with that which emphasizes public confession before the congregation. In this cave, David expresses his spiritual and physical agony in the Seven Penitential Psalms. After the first of these, his spirit has already undergone a change. The dark cave "semyth horrible no more," but rather like a shrine or a refuge; yet it still is referred to as "the grave" (201-5). The first phrase of Psalm 130, the sixth of the penitentials—"Out of the depths"—is expanded by Wyatt to the following:

> Ffrom depth off sinn and from a diepe dispaire,
> Ffrom depth off deth, from depth of hertes sorow,
> From this diepe Cave off darknes diepe repayre.   [664-66]

Later Psalm 143:3 offers him another opportunity to refer indirectly to the cave, when David complains that his enemy "in the dust hath foyld my lustynes" and "hath me forst as ded to hyd my hed" (741, 743). The corresponding biblical text reads, "hath smyten my lyfe downe to the grounde, he hath layed me in the darckenesse, as the deed men of the worlde."[36] With strong hints from his biblical source, then, Wyatt has exploited the symbolism of the cave as tomb—which is no mere casual identification based on superficial physical resemblance, but expresses deep-seated fantasies encountered in many different cultures.[37] In his Christian interpretation of the Psalms, the process of David's repentance and restoration is a form of death and resurrection. David's cave is the place where he dies in order to live.

A similar idea seems to underlie one of the most curious variations among all the portrayals of David's penitence. One of the many books of hours in which the pictures that accompany the Seven Penitential Psalms form a series on David's repentance is a thirteenth-century manuscript illuminated in England by W. de Brailes. The second of these paintings shows David, buried waistdeep in the ground, praying and about to receive relief from a heavenly figure which bends down toward him. The caption reads, "David put himself into the ground until God called him back."[38] The reason for this extraordinary behavior is clear from the preceding scene (fol. 66ᵛ), a picture of Nathan accusing David, which has the caption: "The prophet asks David for a judgment on a rich man who had fifty sheep; his poor neighbor possessed only one, which the rich man seized. What would the oppressor's sentence be? David says, 'Bury him alive.' The prophet says, 'You are he.'" Thus the version here followed makes a special point of applying to David his own sentence on the offender in Nathan's story—mitigated, to be sure (as in verse 13 of the biblical account), in that he is only partially buried.

That the burial is a part of David's penance for his sin is clear from another account of the same event, written in the fifteenth century or earlier and picked up from a traveling companion by William Caxton, who incorporated it in his printed version of the *Golden Legend* (1483). Caxton, who augmented the well-known compilation of saints' lives with stories from the Old Testament, follows the biblical account of David's sin and Nathan's rebuke fairly closely to verse 15, in which Nathan returns home. Then Caxton drops the story of the child's sickness and death, which is so prominent in 2 Samuel 12. In its place he writes, "For this synne david made this psalme Miserere mei deus, whiche is a psalme of mercy. For David dide grete penaunce for thyse synnes of advoultrye and also of homycyde." And then Caxton relates the story he had heard:

> [David] dalf hym in the ground standyng nakyd unto the heed so longe that the wormes began to crepe in his flesshe, and made a verse of this psalme Miserere, and thenne cam out, and when he was hole therof, he wente in agayn, and stode so agayn as longe as afore is said and made the second verse, and so as many tymes he was dolven in the erth as ben verse[s] in the said psalme of Miserere mei deus, and every tyme was abydyng therin tyl he felte the wormes crepe in his flesshe. This was a grete penaunce and a token of grete repentaunce. For ther ben in the psalme xx. verses. And xx tymes he was dolven.[39]

The behavior of the king of Israel has been refashioned in terms of the ascetic piety of a quite different age—a time when a Saint Neot of Cornwall could be credited with the recitation of the entire psalter daily, immersed to the neck in icy water.[40]

Yet another adaptation of the scene of David's penitence occurs in the legend of the Holy Cross, according to which the wood of the cross came from a tree which could be traced to Adam himself. Under this tree David often sat and prayed; here he did penance, composing the Psalter to expiate "the sunne of lecherie/And manslaught," and it was forgiven him more readily for the sake of "that holi tre so swete."[41]

A dramatic version develops this part of the story with great fullness. Written in the fourteenth century and still performed in the seventeenth, the Cornish *Ordinalia* cycle devotes one pageant to the role of

David in the legend. In this play it is not Nathan but the angel Gabriel who comes to David with the story of "a man who had a hundred sheep" but steals his neighbor's single one.[42] David judges the criminal worthy of death; Gabriel then identifies the offender, and instead of the elaborate sentence we find in 2 Samuel, says simply, "Suffer thine own judgment." David, now descended from his throne, pleads with God for forgiveness. Then, according to the stage direction (Nance and Smith, p. 11), beneath the holy rood tree "he begins the Psalter"—and his next speech is the opening of Psalm 1. Apparently the legend would have him compose all 150 psalms, in order, but the play mercifully permits one psalm to stand for all and proceeds. After asking his counselor how to atone for his transgression, David is advised to "order the building of a temple," and there is much bustle of servants and stonemasons until God himself comes down and puts a stop to it:

> David, thou shalt not make me a house,
> Certainly, ever.
>   To be a man-killer is grievous;
> Thou hast destroyed, verily,
> The likeness to my face,
>   Uriah, who was a trusty knight.[43]

This is a considerable adaptation of the biblical account, which says that God forbade David to build a temple because "thou hast shed blood abundantly, and hast made great wars" (1 Chronicles 22:8). Perhaps in deference to medieval doctrines condoning war, the basis of David's disqualification has been changed to the murder of Uriah the Hittite.[44] Thus the powerful story of David's sin and repentance draws into its orbit one more quite separate fragment of the myth.[45]

Two other remarkable features of the Cornish play call for our attention. One is the displacement of Nathan by the angel Gabriel, in which the similarity to the Muslim legend cited above, even to the point of identifying the angel by name, raises some interesting questions about the transmission of folklore during the Middle Ages (questions we cannot here attempt to answer), though the angel may be partially explained by association with the common iconography showing the penitent David confronted by a threatening angel, or the heavenly figure bending to succor David in works like that by W. de Brailes.[46] Another similarity, both to the Muslim legend and to Brailes' version, is the stress on David's being punished according to his own judgment (cf. *Cursor Mundi*, line 7938; II, 458).

The other point is the idea that the Psalms are a product of David's penance. We have seen this already in the *South English Legendary*, as well as the Cornish *Ordinalia*, and it appears elsewhere in the rood-legend versions. *The Story of the Holy Rood* (Morris, *Legends*, p. 78) puts it quite plainly: "And so he made his mis to mende/The sawter buke right to the ende." But to bring in the whole Psalter at this point is unusual and scarcely credible.[47] Far commoner is the attribution of the Seven Penitential Psalms to this part of David's life. In attempting to fit them into the narrative framework of David's penitence, Wyatt, around 1540, was entering a centuries-old tradition. Psalms 6, 32, 38, 51, 102, 130, and 143 were probably first grouped together in the fifth century as a collection of Psalms especially suited for penitents.[48] No doubt the sacred significance of the number seven helped to define and establish them as a set.[49] The fourth of them had long been identified as the response of David to Nathan's rebuke, a title to that effect having been handed down as part of the text.

Given the traditional Davidic authorship of the entire Psalter, it was natural to try to fit each psalm into his biography, and once the grouping of Seven Psalms had been established, though on a quite different basis, they were soon assigned to their obvious place as a part of David's great repentance. These texts, in turn, furnished additional details for the expanding narrative tradition, especially with their many references to severe sickness (e.g., Psalm 38:3: "There is no soundness in my flesh") and to enemies. It must be admitted that not all seven fit the biographical situation equally well, and in fact the ascription of all seven to David's penitence for the sin with Bathsheba was by no means universally accepted. Commentators might bring in Absalom's rebellion (Psalm 143, Vulgate title) or the rebuke by Gad, after the sin of numbering, as alternative occasions for some of the seven, or might even attribute them to other authors altogether, for example, Jonah for Psalm 130 or a Hebrew exile in Babylon for Psalm 102.

Among the commentators on the Seven Penitential Psalms, whose large number points to the important role these psalms played in medieval devotion, some related all seven to the Bathsheba episode while others were content to link only Psalm 51 to David's biography. Humanistic scholarship in the sixteenth century tended to greater caution vis-à-vis supposed biographical association.[50] On the other hand, it was the humanist Aretino who undertook a harmonizing task that called for special ingenuity, fitting the Seven Psalms *in order* into a narrative framework of David's penitence. But Aretino's psychological insight in tracing this spiritual process is smothered by his verbosity. It remained for Wyatt, in his much tauter poetic version, to accomplish the task convincingly.

It is important to notice just what story Wyatt tells. Earlier traditions had shown David composing psalms as a work of penance by which to complete the penitential process as it had come to be understood in Catholic doctrine: contrition, confession, and satisfaction. (We recall that it was in the rood legends of the thirteenth century, when the Third Lateran Council had just given great impetus to the refinement of penitential theology, that David's role as a psalmist began most clearly to be tied to his repentance.) But in Wyatt's version the psalms convey, almost in stream-of-consciousness fashion, the stages through which David's mind goes from the first implosion of Nathan's rebuke until he finally gains assurance of forgiveness and reconciliation. Wyatt has given us "a fully worked-out drama," but one "of repentance rather than of penance"[51]—that is, a drama within David's mind rather than one that can be fully understood from outside. In a sense, the movement toward the Elizabethan soliloquy has begun.

We now consider a side of our topic not much emphasized, David as a *model* of repentance, and in so doing we can appreciate another aspect of Wyatt's achievement. A little calculation indicates that the Seven Penitential Psalms were probably recited millions of times over the years, and it would be absurd to claim that those who said them were always, or even often, conscious of following David as a model. The Seven Penitential Psalms had various liturgical and devotional uses, all associated, in one way or another, with the confession and forgiveness of sins.[52] A rather mechanical association of the Seven Psalms with the Seven Deadly Sins became popular in late medieval devotion. Each psalm was said to be a remedy against one of the sins, but since the order of listing the sins varied, while the psalms always came in the same order,[53] the connection obviously had no intrinsic basis in the psalms. Handbooks for the confessional often prescribed recitation of the Seven Penitential Psalms as a penance for certain kinds of sins—sexual sins[54]—but, even here, any regular association with David and his adultery is doubtful. Many writers were content with the more general idea of the Seven Penitential Psalms as an aid to self-examination and penitence. Still, the figure of David was not forgotten.

An Old English metrical paraphrase of Psalm 51 has an epilogue in which the poet prays to be forgiven as David was.[55] Bishop John Fisher said that David's purpose in writing was threefold: to excite sinners "by a swete melodye" to learn virtue, to encourage great sinners not to despair, and to provide for the penitent ready-made "letters of supplycacyon and spedefull prayers." David is, in fact, an exact model for us; according to

Fisher, the penance he performed consisted not of composing these psalms but "ofte saynge" them until "anone he was made perfytely clene." Prior use having proved their efficacy, he urges their frequent use in acts of penance.[56]

Fully to follow David meant not merely to recite the Psalms but to meditate on them, so as to draw out their meaning and retrace in one's experience the process of penitence they embody. Fisher's treatise was but one of many that offered guidance for such meditation in the form of extensive commentaries on the Seven Psalms. A century before Fisher's work, Cardinal Pierre d'Ailly had written *Devotae meditationes circa septem psalmos penitentiales*, which circulated widely in manuscript and, from about 1485, in print. It was sufficiently popular to be included in an anthology of 1555, from which the following summary is given.[57] For Ailly, each of the Seven Psalms is a rung on the ladder of penitence, by which a sinner can ascend to the "Vision of peace." His tract is worth brief attention, not only because of its author's place as a teacher of the art of meditation[58] but also for the pains he took to use material from the text of each psalm, taking them in their regular order, in his exposition of the "ladder."

The first step, "fear of punishment," appears clearly in the first verse of Psalm 6, the first Penitential. The second, sorrow for sin, gives rise, according to Ailly, to the opening observation of Psalm 32, "Blessed is he whose transgression is forgiven"; this sorrow results in confession, and remission follows (32:5). "Hope of grace" is the third step, but it is preceded by fear—which explains why the third Penitential Psalm begins like the first—and sorrow ensues, as seen in 38:8. After this, hope truly follows (38:15).

Next is "love of purity." Since this comes not by man's righteousness but by God's mercy, Psalm 51 opens with an appeal for mercy, and the love of purity appears in verses 2 and 10. The fifth step is "a longing for the heavenly fatherland"; the opening verse of Psalm 102 shows that the singer has been thinking of heaven. First must come "contempt for the present life" as "smoke" and a "shadow" (vv. 3, 11), and "consideration of the divine eternity" (12, 27), after which follows "desire for the dwelling-place above," which Ailly finds in verse 28. The sixth step of the ladder is "distrust of one's own strength" and "confidence in the divine mercy" (cf. 130:1, 3), which is "plenteous" (v. 7).

With Psalm 143 the ascent is completed, in the "exultation of spiritual joy." Through "faithful prayer" (cf. v. 1) and consideration of God's works (5), the soul ascends into contemplation of God, as shown in the exulting conclusion of the psalm, especially verse 10. Therefore, Ailly concludes, anyone who seeks the heavenly Jerusalem ought to meditate on these psalms with faithful devotion.

While Aretino and Wyatt do not follow Ailly's exposition of the Psalms in detail, they propound in common with Ailly the idea of reading the Seven Psalms as successive stages in a spiritual process. But Wyatt goes a step further—or rather two steps—demonstrating the art of meditation not only in the reader's approach to the psalms but also in the poet's recasting of them, which is an interpretive process,[59] and beyond that in the composition of the psalms by David himself. Many artistic representations in *Horae* and the like show David at prayer, facing upward toward a benign deity, in a posture which seems closer to meditation than to anguished contrition. Wyatt's David begins in anguish (as he must) but soon attains a calmer demeanor that allows him to be meditative (cf. lines 317-24). Then, in the prologues of the later psalms, we are shown David giving himself more and more to meditation, as conveyed by such words as "turn," "pause," "ponder," "weigh," and also by summaries of the process of his thoughts, until finally, "as in a traunce," he has a vision of heaven and eternal life (cf. lines 516-33, 640-61, 695-725). Thus Wyatt takes the traditional idea of meditating on the Seven Psalms and gives it new vitality by offering David himself as a model for such spiritual activity.

This survey has shown the great pictorial and narrative variety that entered into the reshaping and embellishment of a biblical story—changing according to the emphases of piety and general culture in each age. But through all the changes remains the constant theme that the repentant and restored David, now spiritually stronger than ever,[60] stands as an encouragement and guide to ordinary sin-prone men and women.

Three

Two Views of the Evangelical David: Lefèvre d'Etaples and Theodore Beza

Edward A. Gosselin

*A*n admittedly selective reading of patristic, medieval, Renaissance, and Reformation Psalm commentaries yields some interesting perceptions into the changing exegetical mythology of David.[1] The various images of David in the Psalms literature are due in part to the hermeneutic principles assumed by each commentator. For example, a portrayal of David as a prophet, simply prophesying about Christ and Christian doctrine, can be seen as having been largely the result of a hermeneutic which employed an allegorical or "spiritual" understanding of the *gesta et verba Davidis*. On the other hand, a portrayal of David as a moral, theological, or political model for Christians was largely the result of a historical or literal interpretation of David and his times. These two approaches to David and the Psalms played a major role in determining whether the David, as portrayed, was a prefiguration or prophesier of Christ or a man who existed on some kind of moral or theological par with Christians (and was not, therefore, merely a *signum tantum*).[2]

In the pre-Renaissance period, the commentaries of Saint Augustine and Nicolaus de Lyra offer us rather striking examples of the results of these two scriptural approaches. Augustine, though he insisted that "scriptural interpretations could not be built upon air" and that the historical sense must be sought out,[3] employed an allegorical hermeneutic which removed the "veil" that clouded the Old Testament and revealed behind that veil the activities of Christ and the teachings of the New Testament.[4] Intricate as his exegesis often was, Augustine's *Enarrationes in Psalmos*[5] destroyed the literal/historical meanings of the Psalms and valorized the Christian meanings he read into them.

Augustine's abandonment of the Old Testament event for the New Testament reading may be seen in the following, rather typical example. In explicating Psalm 143, Augustine points out that the historical event which prompted the psalm's composition was the battle between David and Goliath. Quickly shedding the Old Testament ambience, Augustine explains that David is really Christ, Goliath Satan; that the five stones with which David armed himself were the Pentateuch, while the one stone which David hurled at Goliath was the New Testament. Thus, says Augustine, the Law of Moses was made efficacious by the grace of the New Testament, which killed Satan and sin.[6] Implicit in this discussion of the battle between David and Goliath is a judgment on the faith of Old Testament Jews. Just as the river's current rushed over the stones, so did the Jews, who had received the law, pass it by. The law itself was imperfect until it was united with the grace of the gospels.[7] This valorization of New Testament event and doctrine, at the expense of Old Testament event and morality (i.e., those very things which constituted its historicity), rendered nugatory the faith of David and other Old Testament Jews, except insofar as it could be said that their faith was spoken of in the Old Testament in order to adumbrate the true, living faith of Christians.

On the other hand, Nicolaus de Lyra's interpretations of David were built upon the schema of *typos*, categories which made David a model for Christian prelates (lay and ecclesiastical), monks, saints, and sinners. For example, Lyra tells the reader of his *Postilla litteralis et moralis super Psalterium* that Psalm 100 is a prayer in which David vowed always to be a good prelate over his people. Thus, says Lyra, his prayer should be earnestly recited by the fourteenth century prelate who would emulate David's pastoral concern.[8] The noteworthy point about Lyra's exegesis of this psalm is not only that David is the figure of the prelate who will fulfill the prophecy by perfecting himself and his curial entourage (for Lyra tells us that David vowed to restore the religious community of Israel to its holy state), but also that Lyra suggests that David *himself* fully exhibited the qualities of a good and holy prelate. David's prayer, then, demands emulation, not fulfillment, in a future time. In a larger sense, Lyra clearly shows respect for the pastoral integrity and morality (and thus the historicity) exhibited in the Old Testament, signs of a moral faith the equal of Christianity's. Lyra's David is a good and holy man, neither simply an adumbration nor merely a prophesier. All he lacks is theological equality with Christians. This fact, however, does not detract from the *imitatio Davidis* preached by Lyra in his *postillae*.

In our examination of the concepts of David in the commentaries of Lefèvre d'Etaples and Theodore Beza, we will find that spiritualizing and historizing approaches to David yield similarly marked differences in attitudes toward and understandings of this Old Testament king and prophet. Yet, as we follow in this paper these two sixteenth-century commentators' strategies in employing these approaches to the Psalms, we will see that there are some important differences between them and their precursors.[9] In the first case, Lefèvre needs only briefly to refer to the historical settings of the psalms (as Augustine had done), for Lefèvre's David is but a cat's-paw; in the second case, Beza presents a David who is not only worthy of ethical emulation (as Lyra had suggested) but is, above all, a theological and political teacher of sixteenth-century Huguenots. We hope to show by selected examples from their commentaries the interpretational differences between Lefèvre and Beza. At the end of this *florilegium Davidicum*, we will attempt to put our analysis into a larger thematic context.

The differences we shall find between Lefèvre's David and Beza's are particularly poignant since both commentators were busy fostering the quickening of religion as "evangelicals": Lefèvre as a Roman Catholic and Beza as a Calvinist.[10] Both participated in that broad sixteenth-century movement which sought to revitalize religious life. But not surprisingly, their definitions of what was necessary to accomplish this task were quite dissimilar. Lefèvre's concerns seem to have revolved around the concept of *renovatio*, Beza's around *reformatio*. The differences between these two concepts are responsible, we think, for the differences between the Lefèvrian and Bezan understandings and uses of David.

Encouraged by his patron Guillaume Briçonnet (then the abbot of Saint-Germain-des-Prés), Jacques Lefèvre d'Etaples published his *Quincuplex Psalterium* in 1509. A retired university professor and an Aristotelian humanist, Lefèvre was also drawn to the medieval mystical tradition.[11] Part of that mystical tradition was the Psalter. That Lefèvre thought the Psalms could aid men in lifting their minds and hearts mystically to God is made clear in his prefatory epistle to the *Quincuplex Psalterium*, where he tells the reader that he has visited several monasteries and found the monks no longer caught up in pious theological studies. The monks, he finds, are no longer in love with the "sweetness" that comes from these studies of the word of God, and so "devotion dies out, the flame of religion is extinguished; spiritual things are traded for earthly goods, heaven is given up and earth is accepted—the most disastrous transaction conceivable."[12] Lefèvre further explains that this degeneration of the monks' religious sensibility has been caused by their attempts to understand the psalms literally and historically—as Lyra had done—and thus their failure to taste the sweetness of the Psalter, their loss of heart, and their disconsolation.[13]

The trouble with the monastic devotional life, Lefèvre avers, is in large part due to the literal/historical hermeneutic which, while it might make David a model for contemporary religious types, tends to exclude the Spirit and Christ from the psalms. He therefore argues in favor of a hermeneutic which would pronounce the spiritual meaning of the psalms—which Lefèvre calls the true literal meaning—and would replace David with Christ as their subject. The *true* literal meaning is the *prophetic* meaning; it is really the Holy Spirit who speaks through David, for, without the Spirit, David could not have risen above the dullish religious consciousness of his contemporaries. And the Holy Spirit, speaking through his mouthpiece David, speaks about Christ.[14]

For Lefèvre, as seen in his *argumenta* in the *Quincuplex Psalterium*, David is primarily the prophetic *typos* of Christ. When the Old Testament event is mentioned, the Spirit is really talking of the events of Jesus' life. David, betrayed by his son Absalom, is *really* Jesus betrayed by Judas.[15] David's triumphant return to Jerusalem after the suppression of Absalom's rebellion is really, *in spiritu*, Christ's glorious emergence from the tomb on Easter Sunday.[16] Lefèvre makes clear that these readings are not to be thought of as allegories; rather, they are the true literal meanings of the psalms.[17]

Throughout Lefèvre's cryptic commentary in *Quincuplex Psalterium*, David remains—and always on the literal level of the psalms—Christ in disguise. David's change of countenance before Ahimelech, the Old Testament event which occasioned Psalm 33, is but a facade for the false face Christ put on before his fellow Jews when he masked his divinity beneath the cloak of humanity and poverty. David's manner is literally, Lefèvre informs us, a prophecy of the way in which Christ would conduct himself before the Old Testament chosen people.[18] Not only David's actions but his words can be prophecies of Jesus' words. Lefèvre tells us, for example, that David's words in Psalm 62:1, "*Deus, Deus meus,*" are, in the Hebrew, the very words Jesus uttered to the Father from the Cross at about the ninth hour (Matthew 27:46). He continues:

> In Hebrew, Psalm 62 begins, "ELOHIM ELI"; ELOHIM is plural, ELI singular, meaning "my God." [The Holy Spirit speaks prophetically through the mouth of David, and He uses] the singular and the plural to prophesy the secret of the Trinity and the mystery of the Triune God, thus distinguishing Their persons and asserting Their consubstantiality.[19]

Once again we see David as able to anticipate Christ's words and the subtleties of the Christian doctrine of the Trinity; in so doing, David's identity is fused into the personality of Christ. He thereby loses his own identity and individuality as a man of faith and becomes a ventriloquist's dummy. And thus he remains in those psalms where he speaks, *in spiritu*, for the Christian faithful.

In Psalm 24, for example, David says, "May innocence and uprightness protect me." He is not speaking for himself, Lefèvre tells us, for "the prophet prays, *in spiritu*, bearing the person of the faithful."[20] David as a holy man, as a man of faith in his own time, is submerged once again—and throughout Lefèvre's comments in the *Quincuplex Psalterium*—beneath Lefèvre's concept of David the prophet as one who speaks antecedently for others.

Evidently, Lefèvre believed that David's acting out a Christological dumb show, with the narration emanating from the Holy Spirit, was an appropriate figure to dissipate the clouds which shrouded the spiritual fortunes of the monks at Saint-Germain-des-Prés and elsewhere. However, before we can summarize what it was about this David which promoted, according to Lefèvre, the quickening of the monk's spirituality, we need to examine a Psalm commentary written by Lefèvre fifteen years after the publication of the *Quincuplex Psalterium*, with a brief discussion of the events which led to the publication of this Psalter.[21]

In 1521 Lefèvre joined his patron, Guillaume Briçonnet, formerly abbot of Saint-Germain and now bishop of Meaux. In Meaux, Briçonnet gathered together, with Lefèvre, several other renowned biblical scholars (such as François Vatable, Gérard Roussel, Pierre Caroli, and Guillaume Farel). Their purpose was to help Briçonnet reform his diocese, invigorate the clergy (whose rather wastrel ways had left almost sole responsibility for the care of the diocesan flock to the Franciscans), and revitalize the spiritual life of the lay community. We find that these scholars, involved in the reform movement at Meaux, produced large numbers of biblical commentaries and editions of biblical texts in the French vernacular.[22] As was true of Lefèvre's reformatory endeavors at Saint-Germain, he once again tried to make the Psalms a vital tool in the reforming activity.

In reading his 1525 *Psaultier de David*, we find that Lefèvre still holds the opinion that, rather than David, it is the Holy Spirit who on the literal level of the psalms speaks through David:

> And these praises are made by the Spirit speaking through David nearly one thousand years before the coming of our Lord Jesus Christ. . . . Therefore, these praises made so long before His Advent contain [prophecies of] His coming, His birth, His adoration by the Magi, His conversation on earth, His deeds, the plots and conspiracies made against Him, His death and passion, His resurrection, His ascension, His seating at the right hand of God His Father, the sending of the Holy Spirit and the apostles throughout the world, the salvation of all accomplished by [Christ], and other divine mysteries.[23]

The true, literal sense of the Psalms is still the *sensus propheticus*. However, we find a change in the manner in which Lefèvre conveys to the reader the prophetic meanings of the psalms. No longer mentioning the base, Old Testament contextual meanings of the psalms (as he had done in the *Quincuplex Psalterium*), Lefèvre's even more cryptic descriptions of their meanings almost totally fail to mention David. No longer does Lefèvre say that "David speaks *in spiritu*"; rather, he says (to give only a few examples):

Ps. 1.   Pseaulme de la beatitude de Jesuchrist.

Ps. 2.   Des assemblees des roys et princes des Juifs contre Jesuchrist.

Ps. 3.   Des persecutions de Jesuchrist, de sa mort et resurrection.

Ps. 22.   Du peuple fidele mys a la pasture de Jesuchrist, laquelle est la doctrine evangelique donnant vie eternelle.

Ps. 24.   Priere en esprit du peuple fidele de la primitive eglise; et de son esperance en Jesuchrist.

Ps. 54.   Oraison et prophetie des afflictions et contradictions faictes a Jesuchrist, mesmes par Judas son familier. Et de leurs punitions.[24]

Certainly, David is lurking here as the organ of the Holy Spirit,[25] but his presence is not necessary for Lefèvre's purposes in his glosses on the Psalms in 1525. Lefèvre has almost completely evangelicized the Psalter: whether the subjects of the psalms deal, as we have just seen, with the beatitude of Jesus, the persecutions he suffered at the hands of the Jews, his betrayal by Judas, or the eternal life he gives to his faithful, we see that Lefèvre no longer has even to refer to what he called the "base" historical sense of the psalms. The Psalter teaches the New Testament *tout court*, and David is but a step in the evangelicizing of this Old Testament text.

In sum, whether he was intent upon revitalizing the spirituality of the monks of Saint-Germain or the larger ecclesiastical and lay community of Meaux, Lefèvre saw the means of achieving renewal (*renovatio*) as lying in the turning of Christians' eyes from this world and its historicity to the "truer" world of the Gospel and to the eternal, timeless world promised by the New Covenant. David himself had a presence and an importance for Lefèvre that was due only to the fact that he was the organ of the Holy Spirit, the physical hand and mouth that wrote and sang the Psalms. By 1525 Lefèvre had found that the *verba* in the Psalms were not David's but the Spirit's, and that the *gesta* of David need not even be mentioned. The New Testament and Christ were present in the Psalms without the mediation of David.

Theodore Beza had a different goal in his treatment of David and the psalms, comparable to that of Luther, Melanchthon, and Calvin.[26] David serves *reformatio*—that is, literally, the *re-formation* of the Christian church and tradition. This emphasis helps explain not only the differences between the Lefèvrian and Bezan Davids but the reasons for these differences. The Protestant David[27] enjoys a historicity which allows him to extend from the reality of his Old Testament time to the sixteenth century in order to instruct the faithful in the venerability, antiquity, and hence the *authority* of Reformed doctrines, as well as in the necessity and credibility of the faithful's various callings in a hostile world.

The Bezan David has a living faith which makes him the theological equal of Christians. David is a member of the "true Israel," the body of true believers who in every age have borne witness to true evangelical doctrine: "The prophet exhorts the true Israel to take courage, also, since we know that Christ has come and has accomplished everything necessary for our salvation."[28]

The suggestion here is that the only thing which divides David and other ancient members of the "true Israel" from sixteenth-century Calvinists is the incarnation. Because he is a member of the "true Israel," David therefore knows the Protestant doctrine of salvation by faith alone: "David intends to speak here of that part of the Word of God which is the Gospel, and . . . he preaches here of the gratuitous pardon of sins."[29] Indeed, remarks Beza, "One would say that [David] speaks more as if from near at hand as an Evangelist than from afar as a prophet."[30]

More than this, David was surrounded by enemies who mightily contended with him and tried to besmirch his reputation and take his life.[31] Thus, as we have seen, the fully developed Protestant David, as found in Beza's commentary, exhibits the closest possible relationship to the contemporary members of the Reformed Church, i.e., the contemporary "true Israel." David's faith, his allegiance to the same evangelical doctrines in which Protestants believed, his probity in the face of countless slanders and trials, and his ultimate success in his struggles against his enemies revealed to Beza that the kingdom of David would be reinstituted in France, the New Jerusalem.

This Protestant David is not a prefiguration of Christ, not a prophetic but otherwise dullish teacher of New Testament doctrines, not a tropological model to be emulated on the level of a more perfect faith, and not a key to the mystical religious life. Philip Melanchthon had previously spoken of David the evangelist: "These words [in Psalm 28] deplore his impurity and recognize the just wrath of God. . . . Saul, Judas, and innumerable others have succumbed in such griefs as these, but David, Ezechias and others, sustaining themselves in the thought of the Promise or *of the Gospel*, know that remission of sin is promised."[32] Beza's remarks about the evangelical David are but a natural continuation of the concept of *David theologus evangelii* which is explicit in this quotation from Melanchthon.

However, Beza goes beyond the concept of David the evangelist. As we shall see, Beza's David justifies French Huguenot revolt against the Catholic Valois monarchy. The theological basis for this Davidic sponsorship of revolt can be found in the fact that, according to Beza, David's royal calling nurtured his concern that true doctrine be "purely" preached and that the faithful be defended and raised up when he became king. As Beza says,

> David then declares . . . that he will guard himself from all persons . . . to whom true virtue is foreign. . . . To . . . calumniators . . . he will mete out capital punishment. . . . He will as much willingly avail himself of the counsel of men of goodness and virtue, carefully seeking them out, as he will banish far from him or will cast down entirely all men of cunning and guile.[33]

By implication the moral opposite of Saul and the Valois Kings, David will establish order in his kingdom:

> He tells of what order he will give to the running of his house . . . and how he will acquit himself in public of this royal charge and dignity. Following this, in the second verse [he begins] to set up a good government by his own person and, in so doing, [he shows] that he is completely unlike those who do not themselves do what they command of others.[34]

The reader of Beza's commentaries on the psalms cannot help but notice a historical parallelism erected by Beza between Davidic times and his own. Just as Huguenot chieftains (such as Condé, Coligny, and Henri de Navarre) had to sustain calumnies and attacks at the royal court and yet remained faithful to their religion, David "witnesses in this psalm that even though he had all the [same] difficulties to bear in the court of Saul, he will persevere in his calling."[35]

David, Condé, Coligny, Navarre: these are what Beza calls the *gens de bien*. They suffer the same trials, the same adversities, at the hands of those who hate and persecute them. They defend the word of God and true religion against Saul, the Guises, Catherine de' Medici, Henri III, and all those who hate "true religion."

This connection between Davidic and sixteenth-century times, as well as between David and his kingdom and the Huguenot leadership and France, is not simply static. It is a dynamic relationship. The reality of David's holy character, the fulfillment of his calling, and his imposition of a theocratic government upon Israel were all, according to Beza's perception, components of the promise which God, having once fulfilled in the case of David, would fulfill again. The historical parallelism which Beza made between David and the Huguenots saw David gaining the throne and restoring true religious worship to Israel, just as the Huguenots, by the grace of God, would attain control of France, cleanse it of deceitful and impious rulers and courtiers, and restore the same "true religion" which David had imposed upon his kingdom.

It is at this point of the fulfillment of God's promise that Beza introduces, in every sense of the word, a revolutionary usage of David. It is David himself who justifies that *re-formation* of state and church that is necessary for the success of the "true" Reformed religion. Previously, in his political writings, Beza had discussed the role of David in righteous *resistance* against an unjust monarch. Beza's political theory, as it is found in his 1574 *Du droit des magistrats*,[36] advocates godly resistance against tyrants. However, it is only in his commentary on the psalms that Beza advocates *revolt*. And it is David—whom no one before could link with aggressive revolt[37]—whom Beza uses to justify Huguenot revolt against the Valois monarchy.

In Psalm 109 David beseeches God to crush his enemies. Speaking in terms that could only call to mind the late sixteenth-century French situation, David talks of what could be interpreted as a persecuting king, his widowed wife, and his fatherless children, and he prays that the widow and her children be despised, cut off, and remembered forever as felons. Commenting on this psalm, Beza reminds his readers that David never bore personal anger against Saul; rather, he says, these words denote holy indignation and a desire for the restoration of the health of the kingdom which God had promised him.

With this in mind, Beza then reminds his readers that they also know men who band themselves against the church and ceaselessly inflame kings against its servants. (Here he is thinking of the Guises and Catherine de' Medici, who exerted so much influence on Charles IX and Henri III, as well as such atrocities as the Saint Bartholomew's Eve Massacre.) David's prayer thus becomes the call to all-out revolt against the Valois, the call to commit regicide and to establish the new *regnum Davidicum*:

> Would that, I say, such people know, although the Church does not *explicitly* use this psalm against them, that nevertheless neither they nor theirs may fare better than is represented in this psalm, *indeed even in this life*, if God does not give them the grace to repent and cease such wickedness, which would be much more desirable. However, that which one can see even now to have befallen some, indicates very well what those who so maliciously attack the innocent can expect.[38]

The modern-day David, Henri de Navarre—the future King Henri IV—will be God's agent in casting down the wicked and reconstructing a godly realm in France. This having been achieved, no one could legitimately advocate the overthrow of Henri, who, because like David he had supposedly been elected by the healthiest part of the kingdom,[39] would be *de facto* and *de jure* king and the beloved of God. Henri's right to the throne devolved precisely from the fact that he was to play the same evangelical role that David, another leader of real faith, had played over two millennia before.

Having seen the different ways Lefèvre d'Etaples and Theodore Beza construed and employed the evangelical David, let us conclude with a few thoughts on the ontological status of their respective Davids.

For Lefèvre, David's filiation comes from the text of the Psalms through the Holy Spirit. Without the Spirit speaking through him, Lefèvre's David would lack religious interest and would therefore be completely devoid of historical reality and interest. Both in the 1509 *Quincuplex Psalterium* and even more in the 1525 *Psaultier de David*, Lefèvre's aim is to lead the reader to an immediate apprehension of the divine. Thus, as we have seen, Lefèvre is able in 1515 to guide the reader to New Testament teachings without the mediation of David; the New Testament and Christ are present in the *Psaultier instanter*. Lefèvre thus is able to move from the Old to the New Testament without historical mediation, collapsing one into the other. Since Lefèvre looks at the psalms and David without memory of their past, his David only vaguely remembers his homeland. He is a-temporal, for he has no temporality of his own. Not centered in his own origin, his origin being really the Holy Spirit, he does not represent something in time, and is timeless.

For Beza, on the other hand, David's filiation is through his actions and the perceived meaning of his prayers. Though he is presumably one of the elect and a member of the perennial faithful remnant who compose the "true church," though he is sanctified by the Holy Spirit, he is not merely the spokesman of the spirit. Beza thus looks at the Psalms and David with memory of their past. David, seen as a *priscus theologus*, is a teacher of the evangel, but his historical being is not totalized into the New Testament. Beza's David remains, then, a man in his own right, and when David rides in tandem into Paris with Henri IV, Beza remembers that he had once ridden into Jerusalem in triumph. Though that triumph was ultimately God's, David was as much a man as his latter-day brother Henri.

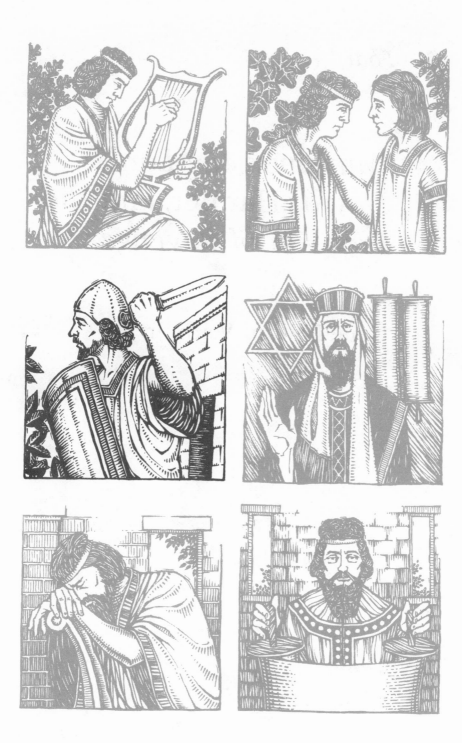

Four

"*Wait upon the Lord*": David, Hamlet, *and the* Problem of Revenge

Gene Edward Veith, Jr.

A young man, with a right to the throne, is set in conflict with a king who alternately flatters him and tries to kill him. The young man feigns madness. He comes upon his enemy, helpless and oblivious of his presence, but forgoes the perfect opportunity for revenge. This partial outline of the plot of *Hamlet* is also that of the biblical story of David, which likewise includes a ghost, fratricide, incest, and a dissembling avenger who invites his enemy to a feast so that he might be killed, unsuspecting and unprepared. This is not to say that the books of Samuel are any kind of source for these motifs, many of them repeated in various forms throughout Renaissance drama and literature.[1] Although it can be shown that Shakespeare and his contemporaries were very familiar with the David narrative, its influence was more likely unconscious and indirect, perhaps as a sanction reinforcing or adding resonance to motifs in secular sources. The story of David is analogous to *Hamlet* as myth, in Northrop Frye's sense of the term, when he comments on the pervasive presence and influence of the Bible on the Western consciousness and imagination.[2]

The Bible, of course, is often more than myth; Western culture has seen it frequently as a supreme index to spiritual and ethical values. In the Renaissance, and most emphatically with the Protestant Reformation, the Bible was revered as the word of God, uniquely reliable in all matters of religion and ethics.[3] Thus it is significant that the story of David deals, in what must have been an authoritative and illuminating fashion, with the ethical problem that animates *Hamlet* and much of Renaissance tragedy—the problem of revenge.[4] The story of David, in addition to more specific similarities to revenge tragedy, illuminates the tension between the legitimate desire for justice and the sense that personal retaliation is somehow a moral outrage. The story of David dramatizes the more general biblical teachings in regard to revenge, realizing in concrete narrative form the complexities of human justice with its desire for retaliation and its need to act in relation to the justice of God, who requires mercy.

Revenge tragedy as a specific art form was popular in England throughout the Renaissance. Deriving from Seneca, the plot of revenge helped the early dramatists achieve unity of action and integrate character and plot,[5] as well as keep the audience entertained with exciting action of suspense, intrigue, and violence. The moral issues also proved inexhaustible. The first full-blown revenge tragedy, which was to prove enormously popular and influential, was Thomas Kyd's *The Spanish Tragedy* (c. 1588). (According to William Empson, the motive for revenge in that play, and thus the crime that provokes the succeeding series of revenges in English drama, was the arranged killing of a man in battle who stood in the way of a royal marriage; that is, the story of David's plot against Uriah the Hittite.)[6] Despite the sensationalistic appeal of many of these dramas, the older theme of God's action in punishing evil often merges with the humanistic focusing on the individual's struggles and emotions. The biblical sanctions against revenge are in full view in the great majority of these plays, as Eleanor Prosser shows,[7] and provide a backdrop to the audience's often conflicting sympathies.

The story of David—with its incest, violence, fratricide, attempted parricide, and revenge—fits in well with the Senecan tragic formula, then in vogue, and it is little wonder that it was adapted for the stage. George Peele's primitive but interesting *David and Bethsabe* (1593), following *The Spanish Tragedy*, unifies its largely episodic plot by focusing on the theme of revenge.[8] David, in his dealings with his sons, consistently avers that "to God alone belongs revenge" (906). Although "David's heart is free from sharp revenge" (952), Absalon is turned into the stereotyped revenger, dissembling his hatred for his half-brother Ammon—his sister's rapist—and casually planning a feast at which he hopes to send his enemy to hell. David is made to parallel his sons in his own lust and murder, but the similarities in his sin throw into higher relief the differences in his response. David refuses to take revenge because he is highly aware of his sinfulness, seeing the disasters that befall him as little more than he deserves. Absalon, on the other hand, is proud, continually justifying his own actions. Though her humiliation calls for justice, his revenge of his sister Tamar is treacherous, and Absalon is led into ever greater sins, including the incestuous rape of his father's concubines—essentially the crime for which he slew his brother.

Citing the play as exemplifying the Renaissance attitude toward revenge, Eleanor Prosser observes that David "becomes a model of patience, who follows the pastoral injunction to look first at his own sin and leave revenge to God. In contrast, Absalon is the man who takes revenge and is destroyed."[9] Peele's play illustrates how the David material was seen as pertaining directly to the theme of revenge and to the exploration of that theme in the theater, perhaps serving as an intermediate step between the scriptural narrative and any sublimation of the David myth in dramatic form in *Hamlet*.[10]

David is a shepherd and poet (the combination was especially gratifying to Renaissance lovers of the pastoral)[11] who has taken on the additional role of warrior; his devotion to the king and to God has resulted only in the jealous King Saul's trying to murder him. David, anointed by the prophet Samuel as the rightful king chosen by God (I Samuel 16), eventually flees the country into Philistia, the land of the Hebrews' enemies, where he again finds himself in the court of a potentially hostile king.

> And the servants of Achish said unto him, "Is not this David the King of the land? Did they not sing unto him in dances, saying 'Saul hath slain his thousand, and David his ten thousand'?"
> And David considered these words, and was sore afraid of Achish, the King of Gath. And he changed his behavior before them, and feigned himself mad in their hands, and scrabbled on the doors of the gate, and let his spittle fall down upon his beard.
> Then said Achish unto his servants, "Lo, ye see the man is beside himself, wherefore have ye brought him to me? Have I need of mad men, that ye have brought this fellow to play the mad man in my presence? Shall he come into mine house?" [I Samuel 21:11-15][12]

David is in danger because he is potentially a danger to the Philistines. He employs madness as a disguise in much the same way as in Belleforest's "Amleth," which cites David as a precedent.[13] To be sure, Shakespeare complicates the device so that the debate still rages over whether Hamlet is really mad. After Hamlet's encounter with the ghost, who charges him with revenge, he resolves "to put an antic disposition on" (I.v.172).[14] His "crafty madness" (III.i.8) enables him to make fools of the court, which excuses his profound and often scurrilous satire on the grounds that he cannot know what he is saying. Although his apparent lunacy ironically increases the attention of the king and the court—"Madness in great ones must not unwatch'd go" (III.i.189)—the device allows him to speak, as Polonius says, with "a happiness that often madness hits on, which reason and sanity could not so prosperously be delivered of" (II.ii.9-10). The disguise of madness, of course, fades into the real turmoil in Hamlet's mind. In Renaissance drama the convention of madness was a means by which the passions of a character could be externalized and thus realized dramatically.[15] Combined with the desire for revenge, which, as Eleanor Prosser shows, was widely held in the Renaissance to result in the actual deterioration of the mind,[16] the simple subterfuge in Samuel and in Belleforest becomes for Shakespeare a means of exploring and complicating character.

Sent away from the presence of King Achish, David, in a precedent for the Robin Hood theme of folklore and romance,[17] establishes himself in a cave. "And there gathered unto him all men that were in trouble and all men that were in debt and all those that were vexed in mind, and he was their prince" (I Samuel 22:2). Saul, in the meantime, whose struggle with actual madness that occasionally breaks all bounds is brilliantly depicted, massacres the priests of the Lord as allies of David.

> Then Saul took three thousand chosen men out of all Israel, and went to seek David and his men upon the rocks among the wild goats.
>
> And he came to the sheepcoats by the way where there was a cave and Saul went in to do his easement: and David and his men sat in the inward parts of the cave.
>
> And the men of David said to him, "See the day is come, whereof the Lord said unto thee, 'Behold, I will deliver thine enemy into thine hand, and thou shalt do to him as it shall seem good to thee.'" . . .
>
> And he said unto his men. "The Lord keep me from doing that thing unto my master the Lord's Anointed, to lay mine hand upon him: for he is the Anointed of the Lord."
>
> So David overcame his servants with these words and suffered them not to arise against Saul: so Saul rose up out of the cave and went away. [I Samuel 24:3-5, 7-8]

Saul has just slaughtered 85 priests and their wives and children because they were David's friends, and is scouring the countryside with 3,000 men to find David, who is hiding in a cave. David, "slayer of ten thousand," who thinks nothing of delivering 200 Philistine foreskins as a wedding present (I Samuel 18:27), with motive, opportunity, and even the apparent sanction of Providence, which has delivered his enemy into his hand, refuses to retaliate against Saul. That David exemplifies the more general biblical teachings against revenge will be treated later in more detail, but the radical ethic by which he spares his enemy in the cave in Engedi is particularly striking.

Hamlet, of course, is given the very same opportunity for a safe, quick, easy revenge, an opportunity which, as it is rejected, serves as an important index of character and values. Hamlet comes upon Claudius as he is praying, agonizingly trying to repent of his murder of Hamlet's father. Claudius, like Saul, is alone, unknowing, helpless—"Now might I do it pat" (III.iii.73). Yet Hamlet spares him, not from mercy, but from a most chilling malice, lest, in killing the king at his prayers, he send his enemy's soul to heaven, and preferring instead to "trip him" into hell.[18]

Structurally, the episodes in I Samuel and *Hamlet* are identical and the characters behave in exactly the same way, although Hamlet's malice is thrown into higher relief when set against David's generosity. In both stories the device of the rejected opportunity for revenge serves as a sort of touchstone, as if to show how the characters, if given the opportunity they seem to crave, will react. This incident of David's sparing a helpless, oblivious king is repeated, some scholars say as a more decorous version of the Engedi incident,[19] but the elaborations particularly parallel *Hamlet* and are especially significant for the theme of revenge:

> So David and Abishai came down to the people by night: and behold, Saul lay sleeping within the fort, and his spear did stick in the ground at his head: and Abner and the people lay round about him.
>
> Then said Abishai to David, "God hath closed thine enemy into thine hand this day: now therefore, I pray thee, let me smite him once with a spear to the earth, and I will not smite him again."
>
> And David said to Abishai, "Destroy him not: for who can lay his hand on the Lord's anointed, and be guiltless?"
>
> Moreover David said, "As the Lord liveth, either the Lord shall smite him, or his day shall come to die, or he shall descend into battle and perish."
>
> "The Lord keep me from laying mine hand upon the Lord's anointed: but, I pray thee, take now the spear that is at his head, and the pot of water, and let us go hence." [I Samuel 26:7-11]

Both David and Hamlet conclude their musings with a catalogue of possible deaths the king might suffer if he is spared.

> Up, sword, and know thou a more horrid hent.
> When he is drunk asleep, or in his rage;
> Or in th'incestuous pleasure of his bed;
> At game, a-swearing, or about some act
> That has no relish of salvation in't—
> Then trip him. . . .
>
> [III.iii.88-93]

Compare this with David's "either the Lord shall smite him, or his day shall come to die, or he shall descend into battle and perish." Hamlet hopes for a more appropriate setting for his revenge, one that will catch Claudius unprepared for death, perhaps in a state of mortal sin. Although both Hamlet and David imagine their enemies under the judgment of God, the difference is crucial. Hamlet addresses his sword, imagining himself as the agent which will deliver Claudius into the punishment of a passive God. David, similarly wanting his enemy dead, insists that "the Lord shall smite him," and dissociates his action from the inexorable punishment that is the responsibility of God alone.[20]

The scene of Claudius at his prayers, trying to repent—especially when contrasted with Hamlet's cruelty—presents even the "villain" of the piece as a tragic figure.[21] Saul too is portrayed sympathetically and tragically; his downfall, encountered by David's rise, anticipates the best tradition of *De casibus* tragedy, the fall of princes through the vicissitudes of fortune or their own vices.[22] Like Macbeth, the greatest protagonist of *De casibus* tragedy, Saul consults a witch, who, after conjuring up an ambiguous ghost, predicts his doom (I Samuel 28:7-20).[23] In the ensuing battle with the Philistines the Israelites are scattered and the forsaken king (like Brutus) begs his armor bearer to run him through, then falls on his own sword. The story of Saul ends in self-destruction, providentially engineered, in which David, though active and and craving justice, does not participate.

A major critical issue in interpreting revenge plays is the probable response of the original audience to the issue of revenge. Most critics have assumed that blood revenge, however distasteful to modern sensibilities, was held to be a sacred duty, according to the conventions with which the playwrights were working. Thus Hamlet's "delay" becomes the central problem of the play and of Hamlet's character; many critics have even wondered why he would be so weak and vacillating as to not kill Claudius at his prayers, when he had the perfect chance.[24] Lily Campbell, Fredson Bowers,[25] and Eleanor Prosser (as well as others) have shown, however, that revenge was *not* held to be a sacred duty in the Renaissance and, in fact, was consistently condemned throughout Renaissance writings. But without exaggerating the audience's disapproval of revenge, it is safe to say that the average spectator of a revenge play "was probably trapped in an ethical dilemma—a dilemma, to put it most simply, between what he believed and what he felt,"[26] a dilemma usually shared by the tragic revenger himself. Revenge is an impulse for justice, but—however just—revenge is also criminal. The very concept "suspends" nobility of motive by a tragic flaw that is inherent in the action—making, potentially, for the highest tragedy. Blood revenge has been an option in many cultures, and even in England until surprisingly late. Opposing the impulse for revenge, while sharpening the concept of justice, was the Bible, the final basis for the Elizabethan condemnation.[27] This biblical view of revenge, more complex than usually realized, is dramatized in the story of David, which illustrates how the ethical teachings on revenge might be realized dramatically, with the same tensions and conflicts that we see in *Hamlet*.

David, like analogous cultural heroes, is depicted as a superhuman warrior—a "slayer of ten thousand" who collects Philistine foreskins like scalps, a giant killer. The fact that he is a man of blood disqualifies him from building the temple (I Chronicles 22:8). Yet the Hebrew writer focuses most of his attention on David's restraint rather than on his violence, finding the fact that David spares Saul at least as impressive as the fact that he slays Goliath. Indeed, it has been observed that David provides the most explicit model outside the New Testament for turning the other cheek, returning good for evil, and loving one's enemy.[28] David, both as fugitive and king, is put into situations where he must choose between retaliation and forbearance; sometimes he makes the wrong decision, but the individual's relationship to the justice of God, the connection between personal vengeance and God's vengeance, is explored in authoritative detail.

After David spared him in the cave, Saul, soon realizing what had happened, "lifted up his voice, and wept, and said to David, 'Thou art more righteous than I: for thou hast rendered me good, and I have rendered thee evil'" (I Samuel 24:17-18). Saul's repentance is only momentary, it turns out, but the value that he perceives in David's action becomes a central teaching in the Sermon on the Mount, repeated, often practically in Saul's very words, throughout the New Testament (Matthew 5:43-44, I Thessalonians 5:15, I Peter 3:9). David's answer to Saul is instructive: "The Lord be judge between thee and me, and the Lord avenge me of thee and let not mine hand be upon thee" (I Samuel 24:14). David craves vengeance in the sense of vindication, of satisfaction for injustice, yet he refuses to take revenge himself, leaving judgment and vengeance to God. Saint Paul directly echoes both Saul and David in his teaching on revenge in Romans 12: "Recompense to no man evil for evil," "Overcome evil with good," but also "Vengeance is mine; I will repay, saith the Lord." David must restrain himself from taking his own revenge, but, as his enemies learn, as in the corollary to the "Vengeance is mine" saying in Hebrews, "It is a fearful thing to fall into the hands of the living God" (Hebrews 10:31).

These principles of the individual, restraining his impulses for revenge in order to let God act, are illustrated in the very next episode, in the fate of Saul. David and his retainers, apparently in return for guarding his flocks, are denied food by the wealthy Nabal. "He hath requited me evil for good" (I Samuel 25:21)—the converse of David's ethos—and David and his men are bent on revenge until they are suddenly halted by Abigail, Nabal's wife, who meekly urges David "from avenging thyself with thine own hand" (I Samuel 25:26). Nabal, in the meantime, is so happy that he celebrates, to the point that he gets drunk and suffers a paralytic stroke when Abigail tells him what she has done. "And about ten days after, the Lord smote Nabal, that he died" (I Samuel 25:38). David refuses to avenge himself "with his own hand," but the vengeance is nevertheless providentially arranged, Nabal's sickness being seen as a punishment from God: "the Lord smote Nabal," but David did not. Similarly, Saul's death is a vindication of David. Yet what is interesting in David's feelings for Saul throughout the narrative is that, however much he might desire vengeance against Saul, he nevertheless at the same time literally fulfills the biblical injunction to love one's enemy. In his eloquent lamentation over the death of Saul—"The beauty of Israel is slain upon thy high places: how are the mighty fallen!" (II Samuel 1:19)—David, as poet, undercuts any personal or moralistic satisfaction that might be found in Saul's fate.[29]

David, though bloody in battle or in arranging the death of Uriah the Hittite, is remarkably consistent in his rejection of retaliation, of not repaying evil for evil; even after he becomes king—an office which, however, requires him to be a revenger, to execute the wrath of God against evil—his tendency is to forbear, though the vengeance of God follows close behind, often to David's discomfiture. After Saul's death, civil war breaks out between Judah, David's kingdom, and Israel, held by the factions surrounding Ishbosheth, the heir of Saul—a civil war heightened by the old kinship codes of blood revenge. In a battle, Abner, Saul's former general, reluctantly kills the brother of Joab, David's loyal but often unscrupulous general (II Samuel 2:12-32). The escalating retaliations are halted when Abner, focusing on the destructive futility of any vendetta, eloquently raises the question, "Shall the sword devour forever?" (v. 26), and the weary survivors go home. Later, dishonored by Ishbosheth, Abner goes over to David's side, an action decisive for the ending of the conflict. The accord proceeds smoothly, as does the narrative, until the casual mood is startingly broken: "And when Abner was come again to Hebron, Joab took him aside in the gate to speak with him peaceably, and smote him under the fifth rib, that he died, for the blood of Asahel his brother" (II Samuel 3:27). David is horrified, the treachery threatening to demolish his gains of unifying the nation. Disclaiming before God and the people his complicity in Abner's death, David neither accepts Joab's kinship obligation of blood revenge nor punishes his invaluable general as a murderer. Rather, he characteristically leaves retaliation to God: "Let the blood fall on the head of Joab, and on all his father's house, that the house of Joab be never without some that have running issues, or lepers, or that leaneth on a staff, or that doth fall on the sword, or that lack bread" (II Samuel 3:29).

Once David is secure on his throne, the kinship patterns of blood revenge, which he is to repudiate as king, assert themselves within his family. After the well-known incident with Bathsheba and the slaying of Uriah the Hittite (II Samuel 11), Nathan prophesies rightly that "the sword shall never depart from thine house" (II Samuel 12:10). Next is the account of Amnon, David's son, raping Tamar, David's daughter and Amnon's half-sister, and afterward casting her out in revulsion (II Samuel 13:1-19). Rape and incest, according to the law, were "abominations" punishable by death (Leviticus 20:17, Deuteronomy 22:25-29), but David, though angry, is forgiving. Absalom, Tamar's full brother, is not. Consoling his sister, Absalom dissembles his true feelings: "'Hath Amnon thy brother been with thee? Now yet be still, my sister: he is thy brother: let not this thing grieve thine heart!' So Tamar remained desolate in her brother Absalom's house . . . . And Absalom said unto his brother Amnon neither good nor bad: for Absalom hated Amnon, because he had forced his sister Tamar" (II Samuel 13:20, 22). Two years later Absalom, like so many later literary avengers, plans a celebration at which, "when Amnon's heart is merry with wine" (II Samuel 13:28), Tamar is avenged. This outrage (fratricide within the royal family) also demands punishment, but again David is forgiving. Absalom had immediately fled the country, but Joab, three years later, conspires for his return by arranging for David to explicitly and judicially set aside the principle of revenge and the remaining function of the *goel* ("revenger of blood"). Joab tutors a woman of Tekoah to plead before the king. She tells him that she is a widow with two sons, one of whom killed the other. Now the family is clamoring that she deliver her only remaining son to be killed by the *goel.* "Then said she, 'I pray thee, let the king remember the Lord thy God, that thou wouldest not suffer the revengers of blood to destroy any more, lest they destroy my son," (II Samuel 14:11). Her plea is that David "remember the Lord thy God," from which the judicial outlawing of revenge should follow. Moved, the king grants her petition, whereupon she points out that her case parallels David's, and that by his ruling he should also not punish Absalom. David recalls his son.

Illustrating how one sin, unpunished, leads to ever greater sins, Absalom rebels.[30] Having built popular support, Absalom drives his father from Jerusalem, crowns himself king, and publically rapes his father's concubines (II Samuel 15-16). David, still forgiving, accepts his humiliation as the will of God (II Samuel 16:5-13). Absalom comes with an army to kill his father. In the ensuing battle, David orders his men to "deal gently" with his son, who, having been providentially ensnared in the oak, is dispatched as a traitor by the pragmatic Joab. Then follows one of the most touching episodes in the Old Testament: David mourning the death of Absalom, who, despite the enormity of his crimes, was still his son whom he loved. "And the King was moved, and went up to the chamber over the gate, and wept: and as he went, thus he said, 'O my son Absalom, my son, my son Absalom! Would God I had died for thee, O Absalom, my son, my son!" (II Samuel 18:33).[31] The pathos, the sublimity of David's radical forgiveness, his deeply felt love for his enemies, is profound but dangerous. The people are confused and demoralized, and Joab bitterly accuses David of loving his enemies but of hating his friends (II Samuel 19:6). The victory is spoiled and David refuses to act as a king, so devastating are the effects on the secular world of David's radical forbearance.

David's heroism comes not from deeds of war but from his heroic mercy.[32] Forced to choose between justice and mercy, David consistently opts for mercy, and although his leniency is often problematic, it never seems sentimental or weak. David's heroic mercy is sustained and kept intact through his faith in a God who alone is just, whom he can trust to punish the evil he faces. Saul, Nabal, Amnon, and Absalom all receive mercy from David's hand, but the "accidents" that befall them and their ultimate destruction are all seen as the judgment of God.

The story of David suggests the paradox that all evil must be punished, but it is heroic to refrain from punishing. Critics of Hamlet's revenge, who tend to emphasize either one point or the other, must remember both horns of the dilemma. Some unquestioningly accept Hamlet's desire for revenge as a conventional duty and wonder why he does not act more decisively. Others decry his bloodthirstiness and question whether he should act at all. Both sets of critics, of course, are essentially right: Claudius *does* need to be punished; Hamlet *is* wrong to want to murder him. Emphasizing one pole of the paradox minimizes Hamlet's, and David's, tragic dilemma. For David and, as will be shown, for Hamlet, resolution of the dilemma comes in trusting a just, holy, and active God, leaving judgment and their own actions open to his will.

As Lily B. Campbell observes in her survey of Elizabethan writings on the subject,

> It must be noted . . . that the teaching of the Scriptures seemed to the Elizabethans to include both a command and a promise; not only did God forbid man to recompense evil for evil; he also proclaimed vengeance as his own prerogative, and he proclaimed the everlasting truth that he would repay. No consideration of the attitude toward

revenge can, then, be complete which does not see the complementary nature of these two principles which must forever govern man's
attitude toward revenge. . . . *"I will repay, saith the Lord."* This was the
threat, this the promise.[33]

God punishes through apparent accidents and disasters, whether
public or private, through guilt and bad dreams, through madness and
suicide, through the threat and the reality of hell.[34] The medieval *De
casibus* tragedies, which traced the rise and fall of great men, originally
were studies of the fickleness of fortune, but soon came to illustrate
God's punishment for sin, so that the concept of fortune gave way to the
concept of providence.[35] Applied to the rise and fall of kings and nations,
the theme of the disasters that befall sin comprehends practically all of
Renaissance tragedy.[36] "God's revenge is the general theme dominating
all the tragedies of the period; the revenge play is concerned with one
variant of this theme, that of private revenge in its relation to God's
revenge."[37]

The David story, with its particular attitudes to the workings of
justice, may help to adjust the emphasis in the last scenes of *Hamlet,* in
which this wronged prince seems to attain a faith similar to David's.
Hamlet, though thirsting for revenge, is stymied in his actions and, like
David, exiled[38] (in the Bible, sojourns in the wilderness are always of the
greatest significance in determining direction and purpose). One night
Hamlet, on the ship to England, strangely unable to sleep, impetuously
pilfers some documents and finds they are orders for his execution.
Hamlet comments on his impetuousness, which, though experienced as
free will, he now perceives as being guided:

> Praised be rashness for it—let us know,
> Our indiscretion sometime serves us well,
> When our deep plots do pall; and that should learn us
> There's a divinity that shapes our ends,
> Rough-hew them how we will.   [V.ii.7-11]

He changes the orders with as little regard for Rosencrantz and
Guildenstern as David had for the Philistines. Horatio asks how he was
able to counterfeit the official seal on the orders.

> Why, even in that was heaven ordinant.
> I had my father's signet in my purse.   [V.ii.48-49]

Hamlet has discovered that "heaven is indeed ordinant," that there
is an overriding "divinity that shapes our ends," regardless of our own
"deep plots" and "indiscretions," which requires that Hamlet be back,

alive, in Denmark to fulfill its purpose. In light of this, "is't not perfect conscience/To quit him with this arm? And is't not to be damned/To let this canker of our nature come/In further evil?" (V.ii.67-70). Seemingly, Hamlet is to be an instrument for God's justice. Nevertheless, though he only has a short time before Claudius hears the truth about what happened in England, Hamlet plots no vendetta, makes no plans, and takes no course of action whatsoever toward fulfilling his purpose. The fencing match is announced, and Horatio rightly suspects a trap.

> *Hor.* If your mind dislike anything, obey it. I will forestall their repair hither, and say you are not fit.
> *Ham.* Not a whit, we defy augury: there is a special providence in the fall of a sparrow. If it be now, 'tis not to come; if it be not to come, it will be now; if it be not now, yet it will come—the readiness is all. Since no man owes of aught he leaves, what is't to leave betimes? Let be. [V.ii.209-17]

Though speaking of his own death, the words relate as well to the death of his enemy. Hamlet has surrendered his earlier frenetic sense of responsibility to a trust in the providential control of God. The allusion to the teaching of Jesus, the "special providence in the fall of a sparrow" (see Matthew 10:29-31), signals the ethic of faith in God which surpasses, though it contains, the ethic of retribution. Hamlet is resigned and passive. Final justice, when it comes, is practically an accident, effected by the king's plot to murder Hamlet and the providential mix-up of swords. Though the final catastrophe, coming at a celebration—a feast, play, or game—became conventional in revenge tragedy, such stratagems were usually planned by the revenger, such as Hieronimo in *The Spanish Tragedy*, or Absalon. *Hamlet*'s variation is crucial: Claudius plans the avenging revels; Hamlet plans nothing. Though Hamlet wields the poisoned rapier, Laertes' dying comments set the true emphasis:

> Why, as a woodcock, to mine own springe, Osric;
> I am justly kill'd with mine own treachery.   [V.ii.298-99]

Compare the "Psalms of David":

> The heathen are sunk down in the pit that they made: in the net which they hid is their own foot taken.   [Psalm 9:15, KJV]

> The wicked in his pride doth persecute the poor: let them be taken in the devices that they have imagined.   [Psalm 10:2, KJV]

Laertes underscores the ironic justice by which the king has been killed and removes, by forgiveness, at least part of Hamlet's culpability:

He is justly serv'd:
It is a poison temper'd by himself.
Exchange forgiveness with me, noble Hamlet.
Mine and my father's death come not upon thee,
Nor thine on me!   [V.ii.319-23]

Justice comes not through premeditated murder, but in the complicated course of "purpose mistook/Fall'n on 'inventors' heads" (V.ii.376-77). In the tragic spectacle of death, final judgment is consigned to heaven (324).

Hamlet, like David, eventually assigns vengeance to the Lord, who providentially—in what might seem accidents—brings justice to pass.[39] The similarities between the story of David and the tragedy of Hamlet—feigning madness, sparing a helpless enemy, a dissembling revenger who surprises his enemy at a reconciliation banquet, and the more general structural and thematic analogues—show not so much a genetic relatedness but suggest how universal issues, sensitively and truthfully explored, tend to realize themselves in similar forms—that is, in myths. David, perhaps, can serve as an index by which Hamlet can be judged and his problem of revenge better understood. When David and Hamlet spare their royal enemy, their motives are as different as their personalities, but both see the king in terms of the judgment of God, to whom they ultimately consign their cause.[40]

Five

David as Epic Hero: Drayton's David and Goliah

Anthony Allingham

*T*hough Michael Drayton (1563-1631) ended, as he began, a biblical
poet—*David and Goliah* (1630) is one of his last works—he surely
transcends his Elizabethan heritage in this poem and shows himself an
artist with seventeenth-century sensibilities. The novelty of Drayton's
treatment of David lies in his telling the story in a baroque epic style.
Goliath's approach, for example, is viewed with the eye of an artist:

> the free Sunne
> That t'wards the noonsted halfe his course had runne,
> On the Philistian darting his cleere rayes,
> His bright refulgent Armes so sundry wayes
> Reflects the beames, as that he seems to all
> Like that in painting we a Glory call,
> And from his Helmet sharpning like a Spyre,
> He lookt like to a Piramid on fire.[1]

The assembled Israelites and Philistines could not have seen him so,
and Drayton gives the imagined onlookers the benefits of his own trained
eye and the sophisticated projective arts of his period. The happy result
of this sophistry is to glorify David's coming of age—his "proving his
manhood" upon Goliath—and to assert his vitality as a folk hero in the
seventeenth century.

A major problem for the poet in taking up epic conventions is that
the character of the biblical David defies them. Considered in isolation,
Goliath is an epic figure in his armour-clad bulk, but the incident in the
war between Israel and Philistia shows him brought to earth by unor-
thodox and unheroic means. As the stripling slayer of a giant, David is
not easily represented as heroic. Strictly speaking, there is no contest
between the two, for Goliath dies without making either an offensive or
a defensive movement, defeated by cunning, not skill. Under Drayton's
handling, David and Goliath become epic figures in whose opposition
aesthetic and artistic sympathies are much engaged. To achieve this
transformation, Drayton redesigns his material and resets the scene,
giving David, the hero of folklore, consistent heroic elevation.

Drayton begins by representing all of "Ishay's" (Jesse's) seven sons
as goodlier than other men. Each is given some superlative attribute:

> Nature prepar'd forth goodly fruit to bring:
> So comely all, that none in them could read
> Which one of them should any one exceed,
> If he exceld for loveliness of face,
> Another for his person and his grace
> Match'd him at full, as nature meant to show
> Her equal bounties how she could bestow.
> There he beholds one brother tall and straight,
> Another that was wanting of his height,
> For his complection and his curious shape,
> Well neare out went him, nature let not scape
> Ought she could doe, in them each limbe to fit
> To grace the other that was next to it.   [152-64]

Even so, their glory is less than David's: "All those rare parts that in his brothers were/Epitomiz'd, at large in him appeare" (181-82).

In his zeal for heroic ennoblement, the poet robs Saul and Absolom to pay David. In the Bible, Saul inaugurates the reign of Israel's comely men. He also was a nonpareil when chosen by Samuel, "a choice young man, and a goodly: and there was not among the children of Israel a goodlier person than he: from his shoulders and upward he was higher than any of the people" (I Samuel 9:2). Drayton reports Saul as merely "comely" (27). Absolom is described in II Samuel 14:25-26: "In all Israel there was none to be so much praised as Absolom for his beauty . . . there was no blemish in him." His hair grew so luxuriantly that he weighed it every year "at two hundred shekels after the king's weight." In Drayton's poem, David's hair is singled out for praise: "His curled Tresses on his shoulder hung,/To which the dewes at Morne and Eve so clung,/To the beholders that they did appeare/As nature threded Pearle with evry hayre" (56-60). As he advances toward Goliath, the youthful warrior's hair wins the hearts of the watching soldiers: "his locks of hayre/ As he came on being play'd with by the ayre/Tost to and fro, did with such pleasure move,/As they had beene provocatives for love" (711-14). As the biblical basis for David's appearance is simply "Now he was ruddy, and withal of a beautiful countenance, and goodly to look to" (I Samuel 16:12), it is evident that Drayton has embellished his hero with a lavish hand.

The status of *David and Goliah* as legend or epic has been debated. In Kathleen Tillotson's view, "The narrative of 1 Samuel xv-xvi provides the ground plan, and Drayton has not troubled with its historical or moral values: he has recognized in his story the eternal fairy-tale of the youngest son, the simple shepherd-boy, who becomes a hero. Only a few of the poet's additions can be ascribed to non-Biblical sources."[2] Lily

B. Campbell, with more of an eye for the epic qualities, notes that "the story observes the order of events in time rather than plunging into the midst of things, but it is clearly a heroic poem, whether it be called legend or epic."[3] Much may be said for both points of view; as I hope to show, however, *David and Goliah* is an epic poem in more than its manner of introducing theme and invocation.

Though (as Tillotson says) Drayton keeps most of the biblical account and adds little to it, he subtly reorders some details and expands others, and his handling of two details shows the tendencies of this comprehensive modification. In I Samuel 17:28, David's eldest brother, Eliab, reproves him for coming to the camp "that thou mightest see the battle"; David gives the brief and confused reply, "What have I now done? Is there not a cause?" Drayton augments David's aggrieved reaction—he is "somewat mov'd/To heare himself thus scornfully reprov'd"—and gives him a spirited speech of a dozen lines (523-35) in which he turns the rebuke back on Eliab. David may appear "humble" and "meeke"—"This holy Youth so humble is" and "He with a meeke smile boldly doth reply" (192, 555)—but heroic boldness and greatness of mind prevail in his character.

A second telling departure reflects Drayton's attempt to link the two parts of the story. In the Old Testament, the tale of the shepherd boy who became Saul's armor bearer and expelled his evil spirit by playing on the harp (I Samuel 16:21-23) is sharply divided from the tale of the boy who came to see the battle and stayed to fight Goliath. The journey to court, the gift of food, and the meeting with Saul are apparently duplicated in I Samuel 16:20-21 and 17:17-20; Saul's memory seems short, for although he seeks "a man that can play well," the youthful David is also recommended to him as "a mightly valiant man, and a man of war, and prudent in matters, and a comely person." Drayton passes smoothly over these textual difficulties by focusing on David throughout and by anticipating developments.

In the original, for example, David saves his anecdote of the lion and the bear until Saul questions his capacity to fight Goliath, and then he narrates it to great effect (I Samuel 17:34-36). Drayton prefers to have David perform the feat early in the poem, so that it is later available for telling to Saul, thus emphasizing the heroic qualities David possessed even before he became a warrior:

> if a Beare opprest
> With cruell hunger, hapned to molest
> His feeding flocks, he with such bangs him plyde,
> That with the prey even in his teeth he dyde;

> Or if a Lion as his faire flock graz'd
> Hapt to assayle it, he no whit amaz'd
> At his sterne roaring, when his clutches caught
> At this brave Sheepheard but such blows him raught
> Till by the beard that kingly beast he shooke,
> And from his jawes the trembling Wether tooke.   [43-52]

Furthermore, the calling of shepherd is far from a peaceful and peaceable occupation. To the catalogue of the bear and the lion that prey upon the sheep, Drayton adds other chance "vermine"—wolves, foxes, and eagles. David's only weapons are his sling and sheephook, or, in the case of the lion, his bare hands. For the eagle, only the sling will serve: he "downe from the clouds would fetch her as she flew" (56). His skill with the sling allows him to hit an even smaller moving target. Occupying himself with daydreams of glory, he practices wargames while the sheep rest:

> Sometimes againe, he practised a fight,
> That from the Desart, should a Dragon light
> Upon his Sheepe, the Serpent to assayle,
> How by cleere skill through courage to prevaile.
> Then with a small stone throwne out of his Sling
> To hit a swallow on her height of wing.   [95-100]

Drayton's David uses a martial hand even while making music. He competes with it, and birds break their hearts and die of grief that they cannot rival his music. It disarms the fierce and puts spirit into the meek:

> What wondrous things by Musick he had done,
> How he fierce Tigars to his hand had wonne,
> Had layd the Lion, and the Beare to sleepe,
> And put such spirit into his silly sheepe,
> By his high straines, as that they durst oppose
> The Woolfe and Fox, their most inveterate foes.   [243-48][4]

In addition to his marked resemblance to Orpheus in this passage, David resembles Adonis as the cynosure of nature. He is, like the lovely youth of Shakespeare's early epyllion, *Venus and Adonis*, a fantastic red and white creature from a distorted mythology:

> The Bees, and Waspes, in wildernesses wilde,
> Have with his beauties often bin beguild,
> Roses and Lilies thinking they had seene,
> But finding there they have deceived beene,
> Play with his eyes, which them that comfort bring,
> That those two Sunnes would shortly get a spring;

His Lippes in their pure Corrall liveries mock
A row of Pales cut from a Christall Rock,
Which stood within them, all of equall height.   [61-69]

And so to war. When David finally sets out to see fighting, he goes
eagerly. Along the way he visits Eliab in camp and has the delight of a
young boy in the prospect of seeing his ideal heroes:

From his brave thoughts, and to himselfe he told,
The wondrous things that he should there behold.
The rare Devices by great Captaines worne,
The five-fald Plumes their Helmets that adorne.
Armours with stones, and curious studes enricht,
And in what state they their Pavilions pitcht,
There should he see their marshalling a warre,
The iron-bound chariot, and the armed Carre:
As where consisted either armies force,
Which had advantage by their foot or horse:
The severall weapons either nations beare,
The long Sword, Bow, the Polax and the Speare:
There the Philistian gallantry, and then
His Israels bravery answering them agen:
And heare them tell th'adventures had bin done,
As what brave men had greatest honour wonne.   [421-36]

This passage reveals quite explicitly Drayton's motivation for transforming the David story. He wrote of the encounter with Goliath in terms of
the history he knew and loved best: English military history of the
medieval period, transformed by the romantic imagination.

When, following this daydream of martial glory, David arrives to
play the harp for Saul, he achieves no mean triumph. Music is a weapon
in the hand of Drayton's David, and there is clear anticipation of his
conquest of the monster Goliath. At first, Saul is another freak of nature,
another tangent to David's balance and physical perfection. Melancholy

craz'd his wits,
And falling then into outrageous fits,
With cramps, with stitches and convulsions rackt,
That in his pangs he oft was like to act
His rage upon himselfe, so raving mad,
And soone againe disconsolate and sad;
Then with the throbs of his impatient heart,
His eyes were like out of his head to start,
Fomes at the mouth, and often in his paine,
O'r all his Court is heard to roare againe.   [209-18]

Fortunately, there are among Saul's courtiers "some whose soules were ravished more hie,/Whose composition was all harmony,/Of the'Angels nature and did more partake" (229-31). Having heard of David's conquests as a musician—over the swains, the birds, "the sluggish Sheepheardes," the "vermine," the very sheep themselves—Saul's susceptible courtiers persuade him to have his fits treated by music. Drayton describes David's playing as a heroic act:

> His quavering fingers he doth now advance
> Above the trembling strings, which gin to dance
> At his most cleere touch, and the winged sound
> About the spacious Roome began to bound,
> The Aers flew high, and every dainty straine
> Betters the former. . . .
> ·
> The Wyery cords now shake so wondrous cleere,
> As one might thinke an Angels voyce to heare
> From every quaver, or some spirit had pent
> It selfe of purpose in the Instrument;
> The harmony of the untuned'st string
> Torments the spirit which so torments the King,
> Who as he faintly, or he strongly groanes,
> This brave Musitian altreth so his tones,
> With sounds so soft, as like themselves to smother;
> Then like lowd Ecchoes answering one the other;
> Then makes the spirit to shift from place to place,
> Still following him with full Diapase.   [281-86, 293-304]

Saul's attendants are so enthralled as David plays "that they heare not/ Sauls sad complaints, and suddainly forgot/To lift or stirre him" (287-89)—a well-observed, imaginative detail.

David's triumph as Orpheus is complete. His fight with Goliath can now clearly be seen as Adonis-like, as a struggle between beauty and ugliness. In the biblical version of the fight, Goliath has the conspicuous advantages of size, maturity, protective covering, and experience; David, a mere youth, puts off the armor because he has not "proved" it, and is a shepherd, not a soldier. Drayton gives Goliath the further advantage of skill with his weapons: "And this vaste man, beside his wondrous might,/No man as he, so skilful is in fight;/Expert in all, to Duels that belong,/Train'd up in Armes whilst yet he was but young" (575-78).

Drayton carries the opposition a good deal further, and makes it total, not so much in the area of religion as aesthetics. Goliath is belabored with the epithet "uncircumcised dog!" (588), but Drayton also requires him to offend the reader's sensibility. To David's beauty—what Saul perceives as "high valour mixt with truth"—the Philistine opposes beastliness and monstrosity. The suggestion carried by his defiance of David—"Am I a dog, that thou comest to me with staves?" (I Samuel 17:34), a reference to the short staff of the sling—and by David's allusion to the bear and the lion as his earlier opponents, allows Drayton to represent Goliath as David's aesthetic opposite, who offends by unnatural proportions. David is the perfect man, by whose every limb "one might try,/Or give true lawes to perfect Symmetry" (72); he longs to try his manhood on the monstrous Philistine. Goliath offends him to the soul as "this huge Beast" who has more in common with animals than men. "Hee's but a Dogge" (486); his voice rumbles like a lion's and offends against the canons of harmony: it is harsh and unmusical, like "an unbrac'd Drum" (680). In armor, he is a metallic and mechanical man whose weapons are extra limbs. David's defiance presents his enemy to the eye as a monstrosity clad in brass: "That for thy shape, the monster art of men:/Thou thus in brasse com'st thy arm'd into the field,/And thy huge Spears of brasse, of brasse thy Shield" (746-48). Even as he dies, Goliath strikes a jarring note; as he falls, "His brazen armor gave a jarring sound like a crackt Bell" (780-81). For Drayton, the essential conflict between David and Goliath is between the beautiful and the ugly. David represents order, proportion, and harmony, Goliath the disorder of nature without the civilizing arts.

It is not surprising, then, that Drayton finds traditional poetic means for discussing such a contrast. Cacophony confronts harmony on his battlefield. In one of the poem's handful of epic similes, Drayton discriminates the sound of Goliath's voice: his angry frown, "like a cloud, when it like Pitch appeares,/And some sterne tempest in its bosome beares" preludes a rumbling voice which seems to "grumble within the earth" (374-75). Hoarse and hollow, it produces a storm of sound rather than articulate speech, its quality "so strong,/As when you heare the murmuring of a throng/In some vaste arched Hall" (377-79)—a sound consistent with the muffled rolling of thunder. The image says much more than that Goliath has a voice like thunder, however. Drayton appears to anticipate Milton here, who with precision conveys such vocal qualities as pitch, timbre, and volume. Milton discriminates in much the same way in representing "the murmuring in a crowded hall." The hall is, of course, Pandaemonium, and the throng the host of fallen angels assembled to hear Satan's pronouncement:

> but chief the spacious Hall . . .
> Thick swarm'd, both on the ground and in the air,

> Brusht with the hiss of rustling wings. As bees
> In spring time, when the Sun with Taurus rides,
> Pour forth thir populous youth about the Hive
> In clusters; they among fresh dews and flowers
> Fly to and fro, or on the smoothed Plank,
> The suburb of thir straw-built Citadel,
>   . . . expatiate and confer
> Their state affairs.[5]

Goliath also falls in the heroic tradition; leaning on his spear, he sways and falls at last "like an o're-growne Oake,/His huge Roote hewne up by the Labourer's stroke" (777-78). As a narrative poet, Drayton does not abound in lengthy or elaborate images that would impede the action, yet two or three similes are characteristic of the fully developed epic. Joan Grundy considers that "the sympathies between [Drayton] and Milton are perhaps the profoundest of all those exerted by the Spenserian poets."[6] In his aesthetic sensibility, Drayton mediates between Spenser and Milton.

Drayton found the fight between David and Goliath a narrative with the folk or fairytale elements of the youngest son: the killing of a giant, the marriage of a princess, and the gaining of a kingdom. He gilded it with baroque artistry. His David, far from a simple shepherd boy, is a glowing heroic figure of *jeunesse d'orée*, with as great a debt to the mythological Adonis or Orpheus as to the biblical model of the comely man, David's son, Absolom. As Mrs. Tillotson says, "As a piece of descriptive writing, the poem ranks high among Drayton's works, and admirably illustrates both his vigour and mellifluousness of style."[7] As a precursor, Drayton might have given hints to Milton; the heroic *David and Goliah* heralds the epic *Paradise Lost*.[8]

Six:

Cowley's Davideis *and the Exaltation of Friendship*

Ted-Larry Pebworth

*T*he late Renaissance was fascinated by the David story. Between 1500 and 1700, over one hundred poems, plays, and prose works with Davidic subjects were published in western Europe in English, German, French, and Latin.[1] The most popular episodes in David's career during that period, judging by their frequency of treatment, were the slaying of Goliath, the love affair with Bathsheba, and the revolt of Absalom. Few treated the friendship of David and Jonathan at any length. In England, only Peter Martyr, Francis Quarles, Abraham Cowley, the earl of Orrery, and Milton's young Quaker friend Thomas Ellwood explored the relationship between the two young warriors. Peter's commonplace book entry does not advance much beyond application of classical friendship theory to the biblical materials;[2] Orrery's *The Tragedy of King Saul* is a deservedly forgotten, pedestrian play;[3] and the efforts of Quarles and Ellwood are little more than uninspired and uninspiring paraphrases of biblical passages.[4] But Cowley's treatment of the friendship of David and Jonathan is an artistic achievement of consequence.

In 1656, Abraham Cowley published the first four books of his epic *Davideis, A Sacred Poem of the Troubles of David*, all that he was to complete of the twelve books originally projected. Two years before that publication, the poem's first recorded critic, the youthful Dorothy Osborne, sent a manuscript copy of a portion of the work to her future husband, William Temple. Too shy and well bred to refer to her feelings for her fiancé as "love," she characteristically used the terms of "Platonick" friendship then fashionable; and she found a pattern for her feelings in *Davideis*. Significantly, that pattern was not the David-Michol but the David-Jonathan love story. She remarks to Temple, "heer are some Verses of Cowly's, tell me how you like them. tis only a peece taken out of a new thing of his, the whole is very longe & is a discription of, or rather a paraphrase upon the friendships of David and Jonathon, tis I think ye best I have seen of his, and I like ye subject because tis that I would bee perfect In."[5] Even in its unfinished state, *Davideis* includes much more than the friendship of David and Jonathan. But that relationship is important to a major theme of the poem: Cowley's concern that man discover and live in harmony with the divine plan. And while many other aspects of *Davideis* have received critical attention,[6] that part of the poem which so moved its first critic has been accorded scant consideration.[7]

Cowley's representation of the friendship between David and Jonathan is much more than a paraphrase of its biblical source. It is more, even, than a rehearsal of the Neoplatonic doctrine which was popular in western Europe in the sixteenth century and which was given new impetus in England in the 1630s by Charles I's French queen, Henrietta Marie.[8] In *Davideis*, Cowley synthesizes several theories of friendship and love. To the Neoplatonic concept of love as developed by such Renaissance humanists as Marsilio Ficino and Pietro Bembo, he joins elements of the classical theory of friendship as derived from Plato, Aristotle, Cicero, and Seneca; he adds four *"Effects of Love,"* drawn from the *Summa Theologica* of St. Thomas Aquinas; and he raises the love of these two friends into the sphere of that divine love which first created and now sustains all things.

In *Davideis*, Cowley intended to tell David's story from its beginnings to the point just before the young man is proclaimed king at Hebron, concluding the epic "with that Poetical and excellent elegie of David's upon the death of *Saul* and *Jonathan*" (Preface, p. 11).[9] The poem begins, *in medias res*, during a lull in Saul's jealous persecution of David (I Samuel 19:6-7); and, in its unfinished state, it breaks off during David's exile in Moab (I Samuel 22:3-4). In this brief portion of the biblical narrative, Jonathan is shown protecting David from Saul's wrath and aiding his friend's escape from the king's murderous pursuit. But Cowley's poem, through interpolations, also recounts the first meeting of David and Jonathan (II.28-41) and the swearing of their covenant of love (III.625-38; cf. I Samuel 18:1-4). Moreover, the first of these interpolations, one of the most powerful and beautiful sections of the poem, provides Cowley with the opportunity for *"a digression concerning the nature of* Love" (II.42-91, and Contents, p. 283).

Cowley intended *Davideis* to be a "classical" epic, "after the patern of our master Virgil" (Preface, p. 11), but one that used Judaeo-Christian materials. A prominent feature of most classical epics is emphasis on male friendship; and in arguing the superiority of biblical subjects over classical myths and legends as poetic and dramatic raw materials, Cowley asks, among other rhetorical questions, "why is not . . . the friendship of *David* and *Jonathan* more worthy celebration, then that of *Theseus* and *Perithous*?" (Preface, pp. 13-14), thus explicitly linking the David-Jonathan relationship to the long classical tradition. The superiority of the friendship of David and Jonathan over the pagan pairings of Damon and Pythias, Orestes and Pylades, Scipio and Laelius, and Cicero and Atticus had been argued almost a century earlier by Peter Martyr (*Common Places*, part III, pp. 258-59). And Cowley found, just as Peter had before him, that most of the details of the David-Jonathan relationship in I Samuel are compatible with classical ideals of friendship.

Most of the ancient authorities had advised, directly or indirectly, that friends be of equal social rank; and all agreed that true friendship can exist only between good and virtuous persons. These classical theorists argued that there must be complete trust between friends; and they emphasized that between friends there must be total agreement in aims, ambitions, and attitudes. The ancients denigrated a friendship entered into by one of the parties with the hope of selfish gain; but they counseled that once a relationship has begun for the right reasons, a friend should willingly sacrifice himself and all that he possesses for his companion.[10]

All of these classical ideals of friendship are expressed in *Davideis*. For instance, Cowley emphasizes the social equality of the two young men. Although Saul and his elder daughter Merab haughtily forget that Saul was not born a king, that his forebears are no more distinguished than David's, Cowley asserts that between Jonathan and David "No weight of *Birth* did on one side prevaile,/Two *Twins* less even lie in *Natures Scale*" (II.96-97). Equal in birth, they are also equal in virtue. Both are shown as courageous in battle, generous, merciful, and pious. And both strive for the same goal, the deliverance of Israel from its enemies. Of these friends, Peter Martyr had earlier remarked, "in both of them there was a perfect likeness of age, of religion, of godlinesse, and of care towards the common weale; both of them also put their life in danger, to deliuer the common weale from the Philistines. This likeness procured betweene them a most neer friendship. . . . This friendship was stedfast and firme; for it was founded vpon loue towards their countrie, and pietie towards God" (*Common Places*, part III, p. 258). Whether Cowley knew firsthand these comments of Peter on David and Jonathan, *Davideis* emphasizes exactly those aspects of their friendship stressed by the sixteenth-century humanist.

There must be implicit trust between friends joined by virtue. Persecuted and hounded by Saul, David places his safety in the hands of Saul's son. It is to Jonathan whom David goes for protection, and Jonathan proves himself completely worthy of that trust: "Not all that *Saul* could threaten or perswade,/In this close knot the smallest looseness made" (III.639-40). Cowley writes admiringly of Jonathan: "His own lifes danger sheltered oft his *Friend*" (III.642).

Cowley follows the ancients in despising friendship entered into primarily for gain, remarking, "pity this base world where *Friendship's* made/. . . a *Trade*" (II.118-19); but he obviously agrees with Aristotle that for the sake of a friend one should be willing, if necessary, to "throw away both wealth and honours and in general the goods that are objects of competition."[11] This element of the classical friendship tradition is one of the most striking features of the relationship in *Davideis*. For love of David, Jonathan willingly gives up any hereditary rights he has to the throne of Israel. And while Saul finds such devotion to a friend incomprehensible and even traitorous (II.385-408), Cowley leaves no doubt as to the correctness of Jonathan's position, exclaiming:

> Ah wondrous *Prince*! who a true *Friend* could'st be,
> When a *Crown Flatter'ed*, and *Saul threatned* Thee!
> Who held'st him dear, whose *Stars* thy birth did cross!
> And bought'st him nobly at a *Kingdoms loss*!
> *Isra'els* bright *Scepter* far less glory brings;
> There have been fewer *Friends* on earth then *Kings*.   [II.120-25]

In the classical tradition, the ultimate goal of friends should be to rise to the selflessness of "one soul in bodies twain."[12] Such a merger of souls is also a step—not the ultimate goal—in the kind of ideal love envisioned by the Neoplatonic theorists of the Renaissance. Ficino, Bembo, and others saw the union of two souls as a penultimate state, followed—if the love be pure and strong—by a merger with the Godhead. According to most of the Neoplatonists, human love progresses from love of a person's physical beauty to love of that person's virtue, and finally to love of pure virtue—or in Christian terms God. And the most idealistic Neoplatonists thought it desirable that, as the couple move upward, they cast off physical desire and self-love, ultimately achieving a pure, incorporeal union.[13]

At its core, Neoplatonic love is essentially antisexual. In its idealized form, all sexual relationships are devalued, as physical attraction finally yields to the love of abstract virtue. Although their conception of love derives from the Platonic dialogues concerning the love of males for males, Neoplatonists as early as Plotinus abandoned "the homosexual associations of *eros*."[14] But if overtly physical homosexual attachments are denigrated, so are explicitly physical heterosexual ones. Although most Renaissance Neoplatonists concentrated on the male-female relationship, others (preeminently Michaelangelo) reapplied the theory to the love of males for each other. And in Cowley's day there was a group of Neoplatonic dramatists who, while stressing the male-female bond, paid considerable attention to male friendships, admitting that spiritual union was possible in such pairings. William Cartwright, William D'Avenant and, later, the earl of Orrery are the best known of these; and in their plays one finds male friends who are "one in mind and sense" and who "think with each other's thoughts, hear and see with each others ears and eyes."[15] If in Renaissance Neoplatonic literature there is little evidence of overt homosexuality, men who loved men nevertheless found, articulated in its underlying theory, an ideal of love as applicable to them as to heterosexuals.

In *Davideis*, Cowley has David and Jonathan initially attracted by each other's physical beauty (II.30-37, III.472-73) and virtue (II.38-41, III.473-535), the first and second steps in the Neoplatonic progression of love; and in one of the most beautiful passages of the poem, Cowley describes the merger of their souls and their ultimate ascension to the Godhead:

> They mingled Fates, and both in each did share,
> They both were *Servants*, they both *Princes* were.
> . . . .
> Never did *Marriage* such true *Union* find,
> Or mens desires with so glad violence bind;
> For there is still some tincture left of *Sin*,
> And still the *Sex* will needs be stealing in.
> Those joys are full of dross, and thicker farre,
> These, without matter, clear and liquid are.
> . . . .
> O ye blest *One*! whose *Love* on *earth* became
> So pure that still in *Heav'en* 'tis but the same!
> There now ye sit, and with mixt souls embrace,
> Gazing upon great *Loves* mysterious Face.   [II.98-99, 104-9, 114-17]

The souls of David and Jonathan become one, and the reward of their perfect love for each other is the eternal contemplation of God in the person of primal, absolute love.

Just as classical friendship and Neoplatonic love theories share several particulars, enabling Cowley to synthesize them in his treatment of David and Jonathan, so Neoplatonic and Thomistic concepts of the love of friends are compatible and admit of synthesis. In his *"digression concerning the nature of* Love" (II.42-91), Cowley lists four effects of love: "*Union, Inhaerance, Zeal,* and *Extasie*" (73)—citing as their source the *Summa Theologica* (II, n. 7).[16] The compatibility of the union and the inherence (mutual indwelling) of souls with the Neoplatonic concept is evident; and Aquinas defines zeal and ecstasy in such ways that they too are consistent with Neoplatonic theory. "Zeal," he argues, "arises from the intensity of love" (p. 333) and "from love of good" (p. 334); and "a man is said to be zealous on behalf of his friend, when he makes a point of repelling whatever may be said or done against his friend's good" (p. 333). To be ecstatic, according to St. Thomas, "means to be placed outside oneself" (p. 331); and since "love makes the beloved to dwell in the lover's mind" (p. 332), ecstasy in this form is another name for mutual indwelling. Furthermore, Aquinas notes, "in the love of friendship, a man's affection goes out from itself . . . because he wishes and does good to his friend, . . . caring and providing for him, for his sake" (p. 332).

It is in this "*digression on the nature of* Love" that Cowley raises to preeminent importance the relationship of David and Jonathan, for he sets their love within the context of divine, generative love:

> What art thou, *Love*, thou great mysterious thing?
> From what hid stock does thy strange *Nature* spring?
> 'Tis thou that mov'est the *world* through every part
> And holdst the vast frame close, that nothing start
> From the due *Place* and *Office* first ordain'd.
> By *Thee* were all things *Made*, and are *sustain'd*.   [II.42-47]

To this last line, Cowley appends a note: "*Power, Love*, and *Wisdom*, that is, the whole *Trinity* (The *Father, Power*; the *Son, Love*; the *Holy Ghost, Wisdom*) concurred in the *Creation* of the World; And it is not only preserved by these *Three*, the *Power, Love*, and *Wisdom* of *God*, but by the *Emanations* and *Beams* of them derived to, and imprest in the *Creatures*. Which could not subsist without *Power* to *Act, Wisdom* to *direct* those *Actions* to *Ends* Convenient for their Natures, and *Love* or *Concord*, by which they receive mutual necessary assistances and benefits from one another" (II, n. 3). In raising the merged souls of David and Jonathan into union with that love which first created and now orders the world, Cowley has truly exalted human friendship.

Robert Hinman has defined "Cowley's lifelong central theme" as the search for and the exposition of "divine order, knowable and beneficial to man, but contemned by him" (p. 227). And Hinman sees *Davideis* as focusing on "happy men who find no discontinuity between God and His creation," and on their opposite, "miserable men who break the chain of being" (ibid.). David is one of the happy ones; he "so completely participates in the love that created the universe that he experiences more perfect concord in human relationships than most men imagine. He and Jonathan realize the Renaissance ideal of friendship, the earthly duplication of divine love" (p. 265). It is no coincidence that the most beautiful and most moving passages in *Davideis* are concerned with poetry and music and with the friendship of David and Jonathan. Cowley believed that all creation has an underlying harmony; and he saw poetry, music, and friendship as manifestations of that harmony. In creating his picture of ideal love, Cowley harmonizes the classical friendship tradition with Neoplatonic and Thomistic concepts of love, imposing a poetic order on seemingly disparate philosophies. And one can agree with A. H. Nethercot that in "the description of the love of David and Jonathan for one another," Cowley achieves the "high seriousness of Milton" (p. 50).

Dorothy Osborne was not alone among Cowley's contemporaries in responding to the compelling power of the friendship motif in *Davideis*. In the late 1650s, Baron Broghill (who later was created earl of Orrery) praised the poem and its author in verse,[17] paying particular attention to the treatment of the David-Jonathan relationship. Broghill, who had already written a Neoplatonic prose romance in the French fashion and who was later to write heroic plays in which friendship was emphasized and celebrated, was much moved by Jonathan's extraordinary sacrifice in the name of friendship:

> Greate *Jonathan* in whome such freindship shone,
> That we, like him, prize it above a Throne.
> Yet know not which in most esteme to hold,
> The freindship, or the freindship soe well told.
> His Character ne're reach'd its just Degree
> Unless when sung by *David* and by Thee.
> He is a freind (such Acts can freindship doe)
> The Crowne did yeild, and kept the freindship too.
> Which cleerely prov'd he for a Crowne was fit,
> If but because soe well he yeilded it.   [21-30]

Not only does Broghill praise both Cowley's noble conception of friendship and his realization of that conception in poetry of a high order, he concludes that only one who was capable of such friendship could have written so well about it:

> where thou mak'st him [David] *Jonathan* commend,
> Thou shew'st thy selfe greate Poet, and greate friend.
> For of a brave freind none could write so much,
> But such a Writer as is highly such.   [69-72]

While we may not wish to go as far as Broghill in denying the possibility of imaginative invention, it is clear that this Irish peer considered the David-Jonathan friendship in *Davideis* a reflection of deeply felt emotion in Cowley.

All too frequently, modern critics have dismissed Cowley as a poet who, though highly talented and clever, ultimately fails to engage the reader's emotions. They label him a poet of thought rather than of feeling, as, for example, Ruth Wallerstein does when she concludes that "intelligence more than poetic fury possesses his work. His intelligence . . . coolly used his poetic feeling as a tool, rather than becoming itself the instrument of that feeling."[18] Wallerstein arrived at this conclusion by measuring Cowley's erotic poems against Donne's. But Cowley's heart was probably not engaged when he wrote the poems published as *The Mistress*. He seems never to have had a deep romantic attachment to a woman and, undoubtedly, he wrote love poems only because a major poet was expected to do so. It should therefore come as no surprise that such productions are often merely exercises in a wit uninformed by feeling. But in works that treat of a friendship which is complete and profound enough to be called love, Cowley completely fuses thought and emotion, creating true and powerful poetry.

Even Wallerstein recognizes the greatness of Cowley's ode "*On the Death of Mr*. William Hervey" which celebrates Cowley's Cambridge friendship with a fellow student and mourns that young man's early death. There are striking similarities between Cowley's picture of Hervey in this elegiac ode and his delineation of Jonathan in *Davideis*. Regardless of when his religious epic was actually written, Cowley conceived the poem during his stay at the university.[19] Its loving emphasis on the David-Jonathan friendship was undoubtedly inspired by and intended as a tribute to the poet's relationship with Hervey; and in *Davideis*, as in the earlier ode, the poetic force with which friendship is treated is as passionate as it is intellectual.

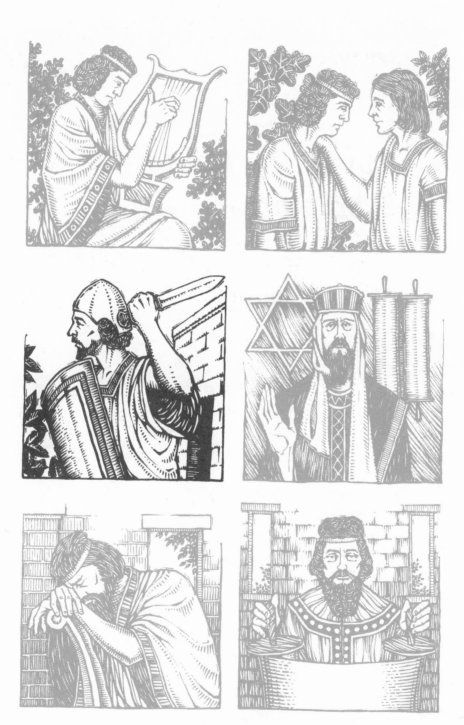

Seven:

David, the Military Exemplum

Marie L. Ahearn

*I*n puritan sermons of the seventeenth and early eighteenth centuries, David's lamentation for Saul and Jonathan and the fallen fighters of Israel (2 Samuel 1:17-27) was used as a text to encourage soldiers, urge military preparedness, and justify war. The sermons were delivered on the training days of honorary, voluntary military companies, first in England and later in New England. Such an occasion for the sermon of the Puritan minister signalized the importance of the military day and provided high sanction for the martial exercises. Quite often the text for the sermon was taken from some exploit or action of David, specifically from his role as warrior and military leader; the text was then developed, deriving themes from David's martial example and applying them directly to the citizen-soldier auditory.

At first glance, use of David's funeral elegy for Israel's slain warriors as a text for the encouragement of soldiers and the justification of war seems to be incongruous, for such a text would appear to be more appropriate in encouraging peaceful attitudes and pursuits, wherein there would be no further occasion for the slaughter of soldiers in warfare. However, the sermons emphasized one verse from the funeral elegy, the eighteenth, which provided quick insight into David's practical reaction to Israel's loss: "Also he bade them teach the children of Judah the use of the Bow."[1] Even amid the solemn lamentations for death, this verse demonstrated David's concern for military preparedness and training; it also indicated the intent of waging war in retaliation for injuries suffered. From this action of David, the military leader, the sermons argued that military training was a laudable exercise and that all prudent rulers should take steps to ensure that their people were instructed and trained in military endeavors.

In 1629 the Reverend John Davenport preached a sermon from 2 Samuel 1:18 to the "Captains and Gentelmen of the Honourable London Artillery Company," titled "A Royall Edict for Military Exercises." The artillery was an elite and somewhat social company of prosperous London merchants and artisans who were interested in the martial arts and engaged in military exercises in their Artillery Garden; their voluntary endeavors were similar to the trained bands (militia) of the City of London and some members of the Artillery Company served as officers in the bands.[2] In Davenport's sermon the royal edict demanding military training came from David's concern for military preparedness; and David's counterparts in the present day should heed the lesson of his directives: "it is a care well beseeming Kings to provide that their subjects may . . . be trained up to warres."[3] Davenport argued that the very fact of David's warrior example, in itself, justified war, for "how shall that be recorded to David's praise, which beseemes not other Kings?" (p. 11). But David's example was by no means limited to kings and their responsibilities, for the minister made clear that it spoke to the ordinary soldier as well. A man ought to come forward for military exercises voluntarily, willingly to train and be fitted for warfare. Davenport set out for his auditory the example of David and "the worthies" of his army:

> David knowes how to mourne for evils past, so as to take a course for prevention of the like for time to come: not to be afflicted after such a losse in Israel had been stoicall apathy; to have beene so afflicted for the losse of Saul and Jonathan, as to neglect the people's good had been base pusilanimity: therefore David at once actes divers parts, of a good subject, and patriot, in lamenting the losse of his King and Country, and of a gracious Soveraigne, in providing for the safety of his subjects. For as he mourned, with this lamentation, over Saul, and over Jonathan his Son," So also he bade them, etc.
>   He bade them Not by way of counsale only, but by way of Command also. So that these words seeme to containe an edict, or a law of David, injoyning the people the use of the Bow. [p. 2]

Not only did the sermon emphasize the duty incumbent upon every man to be trained in warfare, it also celebrated the man who was trained and skilled in the martial arts: a soldier was praiseworthy. Indeed, just as a (Military) Company of such worthy citizens was the lustre of Israel, so also will it be the lustre of London and England. And the shining model of the London Artillery Company composed of such worthy citizens engaged in martial exercises will encourage all the trained bands throughout the city of London and the countryside of England (pp. 12-14). At the close of his sermon, Davenport addressed the company in rhetorical reminders of duty and the glory of their high calling:

> [Conduct yourselves] that every one may say, these are the Lords Worthies, Christian Souldiers indeed. So shall you be valiant in fight, victorious in battle, and in these militarie Exercises, the head and glory of all the Artillery Gardens in the whole world. [p. 26]

When the English Puritans immigrated to New England, they brought with them not only their religious beliefs but also their accustomed and approved civic rituals. (Indeed, they would demonstrate a unique ability to intertwine religion with civic concerns.) The sermon on the day of military training was to become even more prominent in New England, where the need of every man to be a willing soldier was not theory but ever present fact. Again, the occasion of a sermon before a voluntary military company provided the opportunity to invoke the example of David. The Reverend John Richardson of Newbury, Massachusetts, in a sermon to an Artillery Company of the Massachusetts Bay Colony in 1675 used the text of 2 Samuel 1:18 to demonstrate that military skill and exercises "do well become and truely belong to a Christian Commonwealth."[4] Richardson, like Davenport, found the text a mandate for war and a directive for study in the martial arts:

> We have here an example of David's Kingly Care and Prudence, who (from the overthrow of Saul etc) doth Command his Subjects (for the safety of themselves and preventing the like defeat) to excercise themselves to the skilful managing of that weapon the bow; now every good example is binding. David as King accounting it his place of Duty to look after the Ordering of that Armie, sheweth it to be a Duty incumbent upon all Christian Rulers in Place of like Authority or Power; and they that are Rulers over others, are chiefly accountable for any neglect in this great Duty. [pp. 3-4]

War is the usual means whereby God defends and works the deliverance of his people, and thus to be able to fight according to art gives much glory to God.

David's actions and example, moreover, ought to give encouragement to the colonial citizen-soldier—the militiaman. Specifically, David's directive ordering Judah to learn the use of the bow should hearten military leaders to be good teachers and to be "careful, diligent and conscientious" in the performance of their instruction of the military arts (p. 11). In turn, the designated training days should find the militia soldier serious and diligent in his study and practice of warfare. Richardson exhorted the assembled part-time soldiers to take David as their model:

> Be much and as often as you can upon these Exercises; Use makes perfectness or Expertness: Thou canst not be too exact in this Art military, make David thy pattern, never leave till thou hast it *adunguem* at thy finger ends, as we may inferr from those words of his, Psal. 144.1. [p. 13]

Sermons before the Ancient and Honorable Artillery Company of Boston, Massachusetts, an honorary and voluntary military company patterned on that of London, provided a prime ceremonial occasion in

New England wherein the minister could use the David paradigm as encouragement to the soldier and incitement to military preparedness.[5] While there were frequent references to David's military career throughout the many sermons delivered before this company, a discourse by Oliver Peabody in 1732 reiterated the argument and demonstrated the continuance of the Puritan military exhortations drawn from the model of the biblical hero. Again, Peabody's sermon was based upon the familiar text from 2 Samuel 1:18 and was titled "An Essay to Revive and Encourage Military Exercises, Skill and Valor Among the Sons of God's People in New England." In addition to a call to manifest a more vigorous martial spirit, Peabody provided an extensive and knowledgeable examination of the effectiveness of the New England militia and its mode of training, and offered guidelines for future military readiness.

Peabody asked the New England militiamen to learn the skills of war that might be most successful in combating their particular enemies. In this call, the minister once again took as his model the action of David, who ordered the men of Judah to be taught the use of the bow, which was the weapon of their enemies, the nomadic Amalekites. David recognized the enemy's expert martial skills and superior weapons, and therefore he ordered his allies to familiarize themselves with the methods of their adversaries. To be formidable in battle, David's soldiers had to meet the aliens on their own terms. In like manner, Peabody asked that groups of young men be given specialized training in Indian methods of warfare, so the New Englanders would be better able to combat the unfamiliar methods of Indian fighting.[6] The traditional European style of military drill was insufficient amid new conditions and strange adversaries. At the same time, however, Peabody remained flexible and farseeing in his recommendations for military preparedness; he did not demand that New England totally abandon training in traditional methods of European warfare (p. 34). Following the wisdom of David's instruction to acquire familiarity with new methods of fighting, Peabody urged New England to produce a versatile soldier, ready for all possible wars, whether provoked by Indian enemies or European invaders. The New England citizen-soldier ought to be able to handle every contingency of battle:

> He must be a *finished* soldier, that can find, fight and conquer his enemies in the thicket of the woods; and immediately fall into a marshalled and regular Army or into a disciplined Troop, and fight and overcome in open Field; and also excel again on the Mighty Deep, fighting on the Sea. [p. 26]

Peabody received special reassurance from the spirit and tone of

David's elegy. The funeral elegy, Peabody felt, was "entirely Military" and therefore designed by David to fire "the Ambition of the Militia of Judah" (p. 7). Throughout the sermon the minister often repeated his assertion that "this was the chief design (or meaning or import) of our text, and of this elegy, (as all agree) even to stir up a warlike spirit, emulation and valour and quicken to teach and learn the Art of War among the Sons of Judah, as was before observed" (p. 35). When the elegy is recounted, then, it should also stir up among the sons of Judah in New England—the Puritans—a vibrant martial spirit and strengthen the zeal of the militia for their mandated training days. The actions of the "valiant and expert David . . . the Captain-General of the standing forces of Israel" and great master of the art of war were clearly pertinent to New England's situation, a Bible commonwealth precariously situated between wilderness, ocean, and Indians (pp. 10ff.). Peabody compared the Indians and their provoking border attacks to the Canaanites in the Bible: just as the attacks of the Canaanites served to teach Israel war, the Indians provided the same usefulness to the people of New England (p. 31). Considering the vulnerable situation of God's people among enemies, it would behoove the Puritans to study David's example, noting that his actions ever exemplified a ready martial spirit. Although a vigorous martial spirit should be the first requisite, soldiers must also be taught and trained in all parts of warfare because the safety and happiness of a people, under God, is dependent upon the skill and discipline of a brave militia. Again, David set the example, as the text—"Also he bade them teach the children of Judah the use of the Bow"—underscored the requirement of God's people to study and train in the art of war.

Of course, the minister was well aware of abuses on the mandated military training days. While military drill and defense fell as a duty upon every man in New England, too often the designated training days had become lackadaisical occasions, without any manifestation of true martial spirit, and in some instances they had even lapsed into days of frivolity and overmuch conviviality. David's words and actions, as invoked by the minister in military sermons, sought to inspirit the citizen-soldiers, exhorting them to perform their military obligations willingly and with serious purpose. The sermons should make clear to the military audience the biblical imperatives of David's example: it is laudable and countenanced by God for the New England farmer or merchant—the militiaman—to be an accomplished and committed soldier.

The Reverend Oliver Peabody's sermon before the Ancient and Honorable Artillery Company of Massachusetts in 1732 disclosed his awareness of and appreciation for another, very popular sermon that had been printed a few years before: *Lovewell Lamented* by the Reverend Thomas Symmes of Bradford, Massachusetts. This sermon had been printed in 1725 upon the occasion of the fall of Captain John Lovewell and his company in an engagement with the Indians at Piggwacket (now Fryeburg), Maine, in May of 1725. Symmes was familiar with sermons on military themes for he had also been honored by being asked to deliver the Artillery sermon in Boston in 1720. On that day, he had praised the militiaman, urged readiness and training, and declared the calling of the soldier to be acceptable and good in the eyes of God.[7]

With the sad outcome of the attack upon Captain Lovewell's company of volunteer Indian hunters, Thomas Symmes' sermon eulogizing the slain fighters turned to David's elegy for its text, and specifically to verse 27: "How are the Mighty fallen, and the Weapons of War perished!" As the lament asserted that the beauty of Israel had been slain upon the high places, so must New England recognize its parallel loss. And Symmes, like David, even in his lamentations for the deaths of brave New England soldiers, took pains to point the lesson of the importance of military readiness among the people. He emphasized that the famous elegy must be considered a "martial poem" in which David grieved for heroes, "considered in their military character."[8] Symmes underscored the lesson to be learned from David, who teaches us "not to be so overcome with grief, on such sorrowful occasions, as to forget our duty and neglect the means for our own or our countrie's safety" (p. 7).

According to Symmes, David had two main purposes for his elegy: not alone to perpetuate the memory of Saul and Jonathan but also "to stir the ambition of his contemporaries and successors, to seek to excel in chivalry; and to fire them also with zeal to prosecute the war against the barbarous Philistines and to avenge the death" (p. 9). Symmes made clear his same purpose in the elegy for Lovewell: he trusts that good use might be made of his sermon, "to provoke all among us, of a military character, to inure themselves to the use of the gun, and all such exercises as may accomplish them for service in the doleful war, we're unhappily involved in" (p. 10). For those who were trained soldiers, the news that brave men had been killed in battle should neither "daunt" nor "terrify," but whet their courage and make their blood boil. They should be roused by such an occasion "to rally forthwith, and come to March with utmost expedition" to rescue their brothers and mete out retaliatory punishment for the injuries inflicted by the enemy (p. 29).

In addition to the funeral song's insight into David's actions and reactions, other qualities of this biblical warrior were delineated in the military sermons of colonial New England. Most frequently celebrated and extensively described was the young and untried David in his combat with the Philistine giant, Goliath. In this confrontation and overcoming of a seemingly overwhelming, superior adversary there was much instruction for God's people in the wilderness settlements. There could be no question that Goliath was vastly superior in strength, military skill, and arms, while David relied only on the name of the Lord to strengthen his weak human resolve and talents. Yet David was not frightened by the strength and fearful ability of his foe, and because he maintained his courage and his faith, he was triumphant. This was the lesson emphasized in Mather Byles' 1740 sermon before the Massachusetts Artillery, which took its text from 1 Samuel 17:45: "Thou comest to me with a Sword, and a Spear—But I come to thee in the Name of the Lord of Hosts, the God of the Armies of Israel." In his sermon, Byles provided his version of the famous combat:

Attend then to the Voice of my text. The words are a gallant Speech of young David, rushing to encounter the tall Giant of Gath. Long had the huge Monster daily strode towards the camp of Israel, and roared his challenge over the Campaign, to the Ears of the frightened Army. An universal Panick run through the Ranks, chilled their Blood, and shook their Fabrick. Not a man, not a Captain bold enough to issue from their Ports, and engage the brawny Champion: they all shrunk behind their Entrenchments, and retreated from the thundering Defiance. Thus it was that David by Accident in the Host, heard the menace of the godless Giant, and a generous Indignation fired his Breast. Away goes the blooming Hero to the intimidated Monarch, and demands the combat with Goliah. The King is surprized at the daring Genius that glowed in a heart so young, and undisciplined to the Dangers and Art of War, and hardly consents to the unequal Fight. "Thou art but a Youth, my son, and he, a Man of War from his Youth." "Why," replies the Rosey Warriour, "why may I not venture? These unpromising Arms of mine, tender as they seem to you, are not unused to rugged Encounters. I am the Stripling, that have wrested a Kid of my Flock from the Paw of a Bear, and from the Rubid jaws of a Lyon; and my God shall alike deliver this Philistine into my Hand." Astonished, Saul gives a faint consent; and David with a Sling, and a few Pebbles, runs out to the glorious Expedition. Goliah saw; and in a transport of Disdain, curst the little Adventurer by his Gods; "Come hither, Youth, and by Dagon, will I scatter thy Limbs Prey to the Beasts of the Field, and to the Fowls of the Air." To this boasting Period, the Words of my text are the ardent Reply: Thou comest to me with a Sword, and with a Spear, and with a

Shield; but I come to thee in the Name of the Lord of Hosts, the God of the Armies of Israel, whom thou has defied. . . .

More than this had been unbecoming the manly Genius of a Warriour. Actions and not words must decide the Dispute. The mighty Philistine hasted onward, and David rushed to meet him with undaunted Eyes, while the Sling in his Hand whirled round, and away sung the Victor-Stone towards the broad Front of the Enemy. It strook, it crushed, it sunk, and down fell the proud Boaster thundring to the Plain.

This was the Courage, and this the Success of David; and Devotion and Religion was the Spring and the Basis of all. A Zeal for the God of Israel inspired his glowing Breast, and a firm trust in Him animated him, undaunted in the Undertaking, compounded of Religion and Enterprize.[9]

David's devotion and his religion "was the Spring and Basis of all" and from them flowed courage, action, zeal, and success. This was the lesson to be learned from any recounting of the famous combat between the youth and the fearsome warrior. This was the lesson, moreover, that had special significance for the soldiers of the new English Israel that was New England. Certainly the militia forces of the Bay Colony were young and untried, insufficiently armed for the strange combat with savage Indians, and lacking in comparative strength and skills. David's example must speak clearly to New England's citizen-soldiers, who, like him, must put their trust in God and also say to their enemy: "Thou comest to me with a Sword, and a Spear—But I come to thee in the Name of the Lord of Hosts, the God of the Armies of Israel." David's strategy was the true way of overcoming.

In 1739 Samuel Mather had also based his Artillery sermon upon the youthful David's going forth to battle. In this sermon Mather devoted four pages or more to a colorful description of the scenes leading up to the combat with the Philistine champion. Mather provided David, the shepherd boy who is not a trained soldier, with a speech that stated the source of his future military success:

I allow that I am but a Learner in the Art of War: But in the present Case I have an unshaken Reliance, not on my own Power and Skill, but on the Recruits and Aids of Divine Power and Grace: the audacious, godless Giant has reproached our God, who therefore must be his Enemy: And, when this our God is my Friend, I have no Doubt but that He will be my potent Auxiliary and crown me with Victory and Triumph.[10]

The Puritan military sermons repeatedly insisted that religious faith and trust were the necessary first virtues of the soldier. The goal was a Christian soldier — a praying, religious, fighting man. And David was the preeminent exemplar of such qualities, as Samuel Mather made clear in his sermon.

> We ought not to confide in an Arm of Flesh and the Force of Military Weapons: But while we are improving the Instruments of War we are to place our Trust in the Principal Agent: So David would not trust in his own Sword or Bow or faithful Sling: But he trusts in God, and blesses him as teaching his Hands to War and his Fingers to fight, as in Psalm CXLIV.1: Where, an ancient Writer observes, David alludes to Moses's lifting up his Hands for the Conquest of the Amalekites: And it is very probable the Psalmist's Meaning was, that God had taught his Hands to fight in Prayers, as well as with Arms. [p. 14]

Moreover the godly Puritan citizen-soldier could be heartened by the illustration of David, the shepherd boy, leaving his pastoral duties to become the heroic warrior. For was not this a parrallel situation to the New England militia? In every way it was plain that the paradigm of David fit New England's circumstances. And there was much to be learned from the combat of David and Goliath. Samuel Mather enunciated a doctrine he drew from the text and his explication of the David-Goliath story. Three things can be concluded: first, the lawfulness of going to war; second, arms as a requisite for those who go to war; and third, men should not go to war "but with such arms as are provided" (p. 8).

While every man would deplore the damage and death proceeding from war and its conditions, still, Mather asserted, there may be times when war is requisite and necessary. War is necessary for the recovery of what is "unjustly taken away, and for the vindication of some wrong sustained," as well as for "procuring and establishing desirable Peace" (p. 10). Furthering this argument for the occasion of justifiable war, Mather declared:

> that a People, as such, have their just Rights and Claims, that they may and should assert and maintain these, and in so doing, repel the Violence used against them with their best Forces. [p. 11]

The many passages in Scripture in favor of going to war comprised a considerable argument. Mather took as one example the eleventh chapter of Hebrews, concerning David and other "ancient Worthies" and their war efforts; because their war endeavors were made in the "Exercise of Faith," they were permissible. Altogether, abundant scriptural proofs attested to the lawfulness of going to war. In considering his doctrine that arms are requisite for those who go to war, Mather pointed out that even David had his sling, and according to the Jewish historian Josephus, he wore a breastplate as his defensive piece of armor. Like David, soldiers must acknowledge God and put their trust in him. Also like David, they are allowed to use ordinary means and instruments — that is, to take up weapons of "Defence and Annoyance." Finally, it is not only necessary to have arms for war, it is also important "to have fit and chosen ones, and such as are both suitable to the times and adapted to the persons that wear them" (pp. 12-15).

Again Mather turned to David for his example, and to the words of the sermon's text in which David, returning the gift of a warrior's armor to Saul, said "I cannot go with these; for I have not proved them" (1 Samuel 17:39). David needed arms with which he was comfortable and could use well. From this gesture of David, Mather drew the importance that militiamen undertake training to produce "Complete Soldiers" — to learn the use of all kinds of arms because they have exercised and proved them (pp. 19 ff.). Then and only then will the "Complete Soldier" have emulated the example of David and be ready for justified war.

Time and again the militiamen mustered for their training day, heard the minister's sermon or prayers, and listened to some exemplum drawn from David's military career. David's courage and religious virtues were the spark to fire the militia into becoming true soldiers and patriots. It was imperative that, like David, these soldiers and patriots put their trust in God and duly recognize him as their strength. Having done this, who or what could stand against such a godly soldiery? If the sermon did not center upon a text from David's martial career, as do the sermons cited thus far in this essay, there was at least some reference or anecdote to illustrate his martial spirit and to recommend it as the perfect model for the militiaman. And the paradigm of David continued to inform the military sermon throughout the eighteenth century.

For example, a sermon delivered in Brooklyn, Connecticut, to the military company under Captain Israel Putnam on the 13th day of April 1757 by James Cogswell was titled, *God the Pious Soldier's Strength and Instructor*. Taking as its text Psalms 144:1, "Blessed be the Lord my Strength, which teacheth my Hands to War, and my Fingers to Fight," Cogswell's examination of David's words in this psalm led to assertion of the doctrine that in some cases it is a duty to make war. Cogswell also recommended emulation of David's courage to the militia, and in his sermon he discussed in detail the nature of true courage:

This courage is not a fool-hardy Presumption. . . . Tis not a blind
Rage, . . . But 'tis a calm, deliberate Resolution, enflamed or cooled
by Reason, governed and conducted by Discretion, which will pru-
dently face the greatest Dangers and press for Victory. And the
Christian Hero, whose Courage takes its Rise from a just confidence
in God, the Justice of the Cause he is engaged in, and a Love to God
and his Country, who aims at the Recompence of Reward; not a
Crown of fading Laurels, but of unfading Glory, which thro Christ
he hath secured a title to, is of all Heroes the most valiant. With such
a prospect as this, which Christianity only can give, and which comes
from God, Men may safely mock at Fear, and defy Danger, and not
give Ground tho the Quiver, the glittering Spear and the Shield
rattles against them. Such a Temper and Conduct as this is the Gift of
God too, and what we should look to Him for. So did David that
valiant Soldier, that powerful Monarch and pious Saint. Thro God
shall we do valiantly; for it is He that shall tread down our Enemies.[11]

The presentation of David as military paradigm was not confined to
Boston or New England. Abraham Keteltas preached to the soldiers of
Elizabeth-town, New Jersey, in 1759; his sermon centered on the military character of David and was titled "The Religious Soldier." With a
text drawn from 2 Samuel 17:8, Keteltas declared that to inquire into the
military character of David is "equivalent to showing what is necessary
to constitute a good soldier." The sermon provided a thorough elucida-
tion of every facet of David's military character for the edification of the
assembled soldiers. Keteltas' sermon investigated and discussed at length
nine qualities exemplified by David, and the following is a summary.

1. David was endued with natural courage and valour. His heart was
as the heart of a lion, bold, intrepid and dauntless; he was an inter-
prising and fearless man from his youth. . . .

2. David was entirely acquainted with every branch of knowledge
that related to his duty as a soldier. . . . David was the most celebrated general of his age, for his skill in military affairs. . . .

3. David was a regular and obedient Soldier; he obey'd commands,
and follow'd the direction of his superiors, without the least hesitation; and to the great peril of his life. . . .

4. David's breast was animated with a fervent love to his country; he
was deeply concerned for its honour; and more especially as the true
Church of God, as pure and undefil'd religion, existed in it. . . .

5. David was a loyal soldier, and true to his King. . . .

6. David, tho a brave soldier, was not of a violent disposition: he was

not inclined to take away the property of his countrymen by force of arms, without asking their consent, and contrary to reason and law. . . .

7. David was an hardy, watchful and active Soldier. . . .

8. David was a compassionate and humane Soldier. . . .

9. He was a virtuous and religious Soldier; he loved and feared God, and cheerfully obey'd his commandments; he was eminent for the purity of his heart; the warmth of his devotion, and the holiness of his life; he undertook and executed all his warlike operations in a humble dependance on the divine power and Assistance; he put no trust in an arm of flesh, abstract from his Creator's blessing. . . .[12]

In his sermon, Keteltas urged each soldier and officer to be another David: they were to identify with and recapitulate his martial spirit in their endeavors. The minister addressed the soldiers, urging them to take David as their exemplar.

Brethern, I have proposed, for your imitation, the example of a very religious and accomplish'd soldier, a man of distinguish'd piety, and under the infallible direction of God's holy spirit: Therefore let there be an emulation amongst you, who shall resemble it most; let there be a generous strife, who shall make the nearest approaches to THE MILITARY CHARACTER OF KING DAVID.[13]

The sermons of Cogswell and Keteltas were delivered to military companies involved with the English expeditions against Canada during the French and Indian Wars. The assembled English soldiers were largely volunteers from various American colonial militia companies, and it was to these soldiers that David was put forward as the paradigm of the heroic warrior.

The military sermons' vigorous recommendation of the martial David as exemplum served to sanctify soldiers and warfare. Because of the prestige of their biblical counterparts, the minister could accord high honor and praise to godly colonial militia soldiers. Sermon appeals to emulate David's martial spirit sought to promote a bellicose attitude and provide reasons for a ready and aggressive, albeit godly, militia. David, the biblical warrior, was a key figure in the achievement of this rhetorical argument, to influence the hearts and minds of colonial America to approve and support soldiers and warfare.

Eight

"Blest Light": Christopher Smart's Myth of David

Thomas F. Dillingham

*C*hristopher Smart's career is generally perceived as a paradigm of professional disorder, a kind of poetic junk shop littered with odd bits of undergraduate humor, Miltonic fustian, Grub Street hackwork, and only occasionally enriched with the poetic jewels in the creation of which Smart, as Robert Browning observed, "pierced the screen/'Twixt thing and word, lit language straight from soul."[1] The disorder of Smart's life is undeniable and can be seen by all in any of several more or less sympathetic biographies, as well as permanently impressed in the minds of any who read Boswell's report of Johnson's sometimes inaccurate but always affectionate remarks about his irregular friend. The incoherence of Smart's poetic output, however, is not as certain, although it is widely assumed.

Certainly there is variety, certainly there is inconsistency; there are probably more bad lines than good. The major division by theme and genre—the division, that is, between his secular and his religious or devotional poems—seems also to provide the line between good and bad. The poems we most value are those in which Smart makes us forget that language is an artfully manipulated veil between ourselves and the phenomenal world—those in which he achieves the orphic effect, persuading us that the mentioned objects leap and dance before us, enlivened by the poet's divinely inspired and empowered words. But Smart was neither a latter-day pagan, dabbling in mysteries, nor a wasteful hypocrite longing to disavow his secular poems or his classical heritage. Rather, he persists in his devotion to a personal myth of the poet as both servant and representative of God, as the voice of prophecy, inspiration, and thanksgiving. This expansive and inclusive myth embraces Orpheus and Horace, Milton and John Gay, religious fervor and sexual innuendo, devotion and dissipation, sublimity and wit. At the center of the myth is the complex figure of King David, the Psalmist whose poetry inspired the most voluminous as well as the best part of Smart's poetic work.

Smart's *A Song to David* celebrates, through description, the figure of the psalmist whose career forms the basis for Smart's myth of the poet, as well as his justification of his own career. While the adequacy of that justification is open to question, it is a mistake to ignore the effort to construct it which occupies Smart at various points in his life and provides some of the best moments of his poetry. The variety of Smart's output and his notorious "madness" have led to the critical fragmentation of his life and work into the stages or periods which take on normative as well as descriptive force. This fragmentation can be avoided if we recognize the persistent role of David both as the inspiration of Smart's best work and the somewhat idealized model of the life Smart would have liked to lead. The poetry and the life are closely linked, in this view, since Smart's myth of David projects a vision of a man whose whole being and every action are, in effect, poetry, and whose poems are only the most inspired, because verbal, expressions of that poetry—inspired by the voice of God himself. In this myth words and actions carry the force of divine will, and the equation gives the poems the peculiar energy we associate with Smart's successes. But Smart extends the authority of his myth beyond his purely devotional or Psalm-like poems in an effort to embrace all the words of all the poems he has written and all the poets he admires, thereby sanctifying poetry as prayer just as he sanctifies his cat Jeoffrey's antics as a form of devotion or adoration.[2]

After enumerating David's virtues in the opening section of the *Song*, Smart begins his description of the Psalms with a reference to their special healing power:

> His muse, bright angel of his verse,
> Gives balm for all the thorns that pierce,
>   For all the pangs that rage;
> Blest light, still gaining on that gloom,
> The more than Michal of his bloom,
>   Th'Abishag of his age.[3]

These lines, clearly, refer to the special place of the Psalms in David's mature life, to their smoothing, consoling power which mirrors his lost youthful vigor and warms his aged chill. The reference to the "muse" does double duty here, both reminding the reader of the divine inspiration inherent in the Psalms and referring metonymically to the Psalms as they affect the listener or reader who comes after. That the "Blest light" is "still gaining" on the surrounding gloom is welcome news to any who might feel oppressed by evil and darkness. It is also Smart's reassurance, both from and to himself (as we shall see), since he offers himself as a "restorer of adoration" in England and yet still needs the sustaining power of his myth in the face of his own afflictions.

In succeeding stanzas Smart enumerates the subject matter of David's songs, then returns to the characterization of the poet and his poems' effects:

Blest was the tenderness he felt
When to his graceful harp he knelt,
   And did for audience call;
When satan with his hand he quell'd,
And in serene suspence he held
   The frantic throes of Saul.

His furious foes no more malign'd
As he such melody divin'd,
   And sense and soul detain'd;
Now striking strong, now soothing soft,
He sent the godly sounds aloft,
   Or in delight refrain'd.

When up to heaven his thoughts he pil'd
From fervent lips fair Michal smil'd,
   As blush to blush she stood;
And chose herself the queen, and gave
Her utmost from her heart, 'so brave,
   And plays his hymns so good.'

[Callan, pp. 354-55]

If stanza XVII emphasizes the reflexive virtues of the Psalms, these stanzas add to the consolatory balm the ability to suppress Satan and soothe the agony of one possessed, to disarm his foes by transforming their perception of him, and even to seduce (in a proper way and with chaste result) a beautiful young wife. Smart attributes other virtues to David as well, but it is these poetic strengths which act most centrally in the myth which unifies Smart's work, from the early Seatonian poems to the late verse translations of Horace and the paraphrases of the Psalms. To soothe inner pain and turmoil, to neutralize malignity and reveal inner goodness, to cement the loving relationship of souls to each other and to God—these are the special powers of the divinely inspired prophet and poet.

The peculiar succession of actions described in the verses just quoted—silencing the powers of darkness, soothing anger, and gaining the love of a good woman—may remind us of another myth of the poet. The songs of Orpheus soothe the guardians of the underworld and gain him, at least temporarily, a wife. That David is more successful is correct only from Smart's Christian viewpoint. Smart himself had made this same association in his Seatonian poem, "On the Goodness of the Supreme Being":

Orpheus, for so the Gentiles call'd thy name,
Israel's sweet psalmist, who alone could wake

Th'inanimate to motion; who alone
The joyful hillocks, the applauding rocks,
And floods with musical persuasion drew;
Thou, who to hail and snow gav'st voice and sound,
And mad'st the mute melodious!—greater yet
Was thy divinest skill, and rul'd o'er more
Than art or nature; for thy tuneful touch
Drove trembling Satan from the heart of Saul,
And quell'd the evil Angel:—in this breast
Some portion of thy genuine spirit breathe,
And lift me from myself; each thought impure
Banish; each low idea raise, refine,
Enlarge, and sanctify;—so shall the muse
Above the stars aspire, and aim to praise
Her God on earth, as he is prais'd in heaven.

[Callan, pp. 240-41]

This euhemerist linkage of the pagan inventor of poetry (especially devotional poetry) with the ancestor of Christ himself, and of all Christian devotional poems, is not unique with Smart. He would have found it in a "life" of David published in 1740 by the Reverend Patrick Delany.[4] Smart, interestingly, turns the Orphic control over inert objects of nature into metaphor, thus reflecting his own faith in language, properly directed toward adoration, as the means of imbuing all creation with spiritual force. By describing and praising God's works, David in effect makes them Godly for the listener and that, in spirit, is the true version of the Orphic myth as well as Smart's plan for his own work and his prescription for any poet who wishes to avoid vanity.

Regardless of the historical merits of the Orpheus-David association, its importance to Smart cannot be overestimated. Smart's educational background, and an important faction of literary opinion in his time, emphasized the primacy of classical poetry and saw the myths of Greece and Rome as the most appropriate subjects and decorative matter for serious poets. There was, of course, a countertradition which asserted the primacy of the poetry of the Bible as better suited to the edification of Christians. For a Cambridge scholar and Grub Street wit such as the young Christopher Smart, the efforts of Bishop Robert Lowth to reconcile these conflicting claims, recognizing the merits of both traditions and asserting the intrinsic value of poetry as a mode of adoration, must have come as a welcome patch for a troubled conscience. In his second lecture, Lowth defends the study of biblical poetry *as* poetry:

It would not be easy, indeed, to assign a reason why the writings of Homer, of Pindar, and of Horace, should engross our attention and monopolize our praise, while those of Moses, of David and Isaiah pass totally unregarded. Shall we suppose that the subject is not adapted to a seminary, in which sacred literature has ever maintained a precedence? Shall we say, that it is foreign to this assembly of promising youth, of whom the greater part have consecrated the best portion of their time and labour to the same department of learning? Or must we conclude, that the writings of those men, who have accomplished only as much as human genius and ability could accomplish, should be reduced to method and theory; but that those which boast a much higher origin, and are justly attributed to the inspiration of the Holy Spirit, may be considered as indeed illustrious by their native force and beauty, but not as conformable to the principles of science, nor to be circumscribed by any rules of art?[5]

Lowth here acknowledges the traditional tensions between artifice and inspiration as a prelude to his effort to demonstrate that they are not necessarily in conflict. The poets of the Bible proceed, as he demonstrates, with due attention to rhetoric and decorum, and he offers a solution to the mystery of Hebrew metrics which remains convincing today. Presumably, Smart needed no reassurance about the artistic excellence of biblical poetry, though he no doubt welcomed Lowth's arguments as a means of advancing the cause of adoration. Smart might well, however, have found Lowth's arguments useful from a different perspective. The reconciliation of inspiration and artifice adds a practical dimension to the association of David with Orpheus. By identifying Orpheus, the fountainhead of classical poetry, with David, the model for Christian adoration, Smart reconciles the two traditions and their combined influence on him, and finds a way around the opposition between "divine inspiration" and "art and nature." He can, as an accomplished and artful poet in the prevailing public mode of his time, nonetheless maintain his inspirational role as "the poet of my God" (Callan, p. 227). David is not, then, merely a personal myth (or mania, as some might say) but embodies the terms by which Smart can proceed as a poet in both the secular and the devotional modes.

When Smart invokes David's help, it is not supernatural power he wants but the ability "to praise Her [the Muse's] God on earth, as he is prais'd in heaven" (Callan, p. 241). There is in this some of the conventional trope of unworthiness which accompanies most invocations of muses, and if it were an isolated case in Smart's work we might leave it at that. The wish to be able to worship and praise, the impulse to adora-

tion, is so frequently expressed in Smart's work as to be a central part of
his myth of David. In the lines already quoted from "On the Goodness
of the Supreme Being," Smart shows himself conscious of the "worldly"
elements in his own nature which must be "refined" and "sanctified" if
he is to achieve his aim. His plea, "in this breast/Some portion of thy
genuine spirit breathe,/And lift me from myself" is echoed and clarified
in the *Song to David:*

> O David, highest in the list
> Of worthies, on God's ways insist,
>   The genuine word repeat:
> Vain are the documents of men,
> And vain the flourish of the pen
>   That keeps the fool's conceit.
>
> Praise above all—for praise prevails;
> Heap up the measure, load the scales,
>   And good to goodness add.

[Callan, p. 359]

This segment of the poem introduces the sequence of stanzas which
describe the various levels of creation engaged in adoration, and asserts
David's primacy among them:

> For Adoration all the ranks
> Of angels yield eternal thanks,
>   And David in the midst.

[Ibid.]

David's possession of the "genuine spirit" makes it possible for him
to repeat the "genuine word"—a word which is free of the "fool's con-
ceit" that is characteristic of most of the vain productions of the human
pen. Thus it is not the style of the poet which determines his worth but
the purpose for which he writes that assures the perfection of his style.
In this way Smart's myth of David helps him reconcile his quotidian
existence with his religious ideals; like a penitent offering his sufferings
for the glory of God, Smart sanctifies all his activities, all his poems, by
including them in the category "adoration," through which he can most
fully identify himself with David.

The fullest potential implication of Smart's myth of David may be
traced in connection with the concept of the "genuine word" and its
relation to what appears to be Smart's theory of language, as revealed in
his poems and *Jubilate Agno.* Scattered references in the *Jubilate* suggest
that Smart believed in a direct connection between objects or
phenomena and the words which designate them. Further, the words
themselves, when they are the right words, have sacred characteristics.

Two examples from the *Jubilate* should suffice: "For Action and Speaking are one according to God and the Ancients" (B2.562), and "The right names of flowers are yet in heaven. God make gardners better nomenclators" (B2.509).[6] Smart's belief that names bear a direct relationship with their objects may be derived from the many biblical passages which impute active, creative power to God's "word," such as Psalm 119, or the first chapter of the Gospel of John. Smart, in *A Song to David*, paraphrases another such passage, the account from Genesis 1:27 of the creation of man: "So God created man in his own image, in the image of God created he him." In Smart's version an important verbal change takes place:

> Sigma presents the social droves,
> With him that solitary roves,
>   And man of all the chief;
> Fair on whose face, and stately frame
> Did God impress him hallow'd name,
>   For ocular belief.

> [Callan, p. 356]

The substitution of "name" for "image" cannot be dismissed as a bow to the exegencies of rhyme. The passage connects seeing with believing, and since the true names are all, in a sense, God's names, all the words of the poet have the power to evoke God's name by evoking true images of the works of God already impressed with his name. In the *Jubilate*, Smart claims that "my talent is to give an impression upon words by punching, that when the reader casts his eye upon 'em, he takes up the image from the mould wch I have made" (B2.404). Thus the poet's power is likened to the power of God's word, just as David is likened to Adam and to Christ (the Word). In biblical typology, David is the type of Christ; in Smart's myth he is also the type of the poet who engages in adoration, in which tradition Smart places himself: "For all good words are from GOD, and all others are cant" (B1.85), but "For the grace of God I am the Reviver of ADORATION amongst ENGLISH-MEN" (B2.332).

Familarity with the unifying character of the myth of David in relation to Smart's career helps clarify the importance and relevance of certain projects which might otherwise seem departures from his best modes. In particular, the late verse translation of the works of Horace and the paraphrase of the Psalms may be better understood and appreciated when seen in relation to the myth. The notion that Smart's career is "divided" by his madness into periods of shallow secular wit, on the one hand, and religious enthusiasm on the other is, if not dismissed, at least altered by reconsideration in light of the myth.

A recent study of Smart's work by Geoffrey Hartman describes the standard view of the fragmentation caused by his madness:

> Smart's poetic career is emblematic of the fate of enthusiasm. It divides neatly into two parts. Before 1756 he was "the ingenious Mr. Smart," a facile and brilliant practitioner of neoclassic modes of verse. But recovering from a serious fever he began "confessing God openly" by praying aloud whenever the impulse came. "I blessed God in St. James's Park till I routed all the company" (B1.89). He was confined for insanity in 1757-58 and again from 1759-63. During his "illness" he produced two long poems as daring and personal as any the Romantics were to write. The *Song to David* (1763) was dismissed in its time as a "fine piece of ruins" while the *Jubilate Agno* was not published till 1939. Smart's contemporaries saw him as an excellent versifier misled by religious mania, and though he reverted to such modest tasks as translating Horace and composing hymns for children, he never reestablished himself in their eyes.[7]

An understanding of his use of the David myth can show us that Smart himself did not consider his later tasks aberrant or "modest" at all; rather, there is continuity in his ongoing efforts to undermine the conventional opposition between "nature and art," the elements of his best secular verse, and "divine inspiration," the essential prerequisite of his poetry of adoration. Smart sees his translation of Horace's odes as an enhancement of his own powers as a poet and as homage to a poet whom he explicitly identifies with David and, by extension, himself.

In his "Preface" to his four-volume *Works of Horace Translated Into Verse* (London, 1767), Smart remarks that "Genius is certainly that *great witness*, which God never suffered himself to be without even amongst the Heathens" (I, xiii). In a fascinating if mysterious passage, he attributes to Horace that same talent of "impression" which he claims for David and for himself: "*Impression* then, is a talent or gift of Almighty God, by which a Genius is empowered to throw an emphasis upon a word or sentence in such wise that it cannot escape any reader of sheer good sense, and true critical capacity" (I, xii). Not only does Smart come close to claiming divine inspiration for Horace, in spite of his heathen religion, but he further attributes to Horace the virtue he holds in highest esteem: gratitude. He describes Horace as "one of the most thankful men that ever lived," which judgment he derives "not only from the warmth of his language in his Odes and other works, but from the circumstances of his behavior to all his friends of all parties, with whom he always kept himself well to the last" (I, xxx). That Horace's gratitude is primarily directed to his friends, rather than the Christian God, is not necessarily an impossible limitation, since he shows gratitude to God by exercising his genius.

Smart frequently refers to the primacy of gratitude among virtues and the special evil of ingratitude. In *Hymns for the Amusement of Children*, the hymn to "Gratitude" is one of the most charming and contains an explicit statement of the special importance of gratitude to God. The speaker is "Gratitude" personified:

> I in Eden's bloomy bowers
> Was the heav'nly gardner's pride,
> Sweet of sweets, and flower of flow'rs,
> With the scented tinctures dy'd.
>
> Hear, ye little children, hear me,
> I am God's delightful voice;
> They who sweetly still revere me
> Still shall make the wisest choice.

[Callan, II, 984]

In *Jubilate Agno*, Smart explicitly states that "the sin against the HOLY GHOST is INGRATITUDE" (B2. 306), and the theme recurs constantly in the *Psalms*, reinforced by Smart's practice (in the paraphrases) of elaborating on the themes in the originals which most appeal to him. In other words, Smart comes very near to crediting Horace with everything he might need for salvation, except the cross.

Smart's self-identification with Horace, like that with David, focuses on his wish to be a "reviver of adoration." He sees in Horace the same fruitful link between religion and poetry, and between divine inspiration and poetry. He responds strongly to the elements of piety and moral enlightenment in Horace's works, perhaps overemphasizing them. In this way not only Horace's matter but his urbane manner as well can be reconciled with Smart's religious fervor and subsumed under the categories of his myth of David. The crucial link is Horace's *Carmen Saeculare*. In his "Preface" Smart explains: "The Secular-Ode, that brightest monument of the *Heathen Psalmist* and Roman worship, I have laboured with all the art and address I am capable of" (I, x-xi). The appellation "Psalmist" must surely be the highest praise Smart can bestow, as it leads to association with King David. Also, the fact that the original ode was composed at the request of Augustus for a public religious celebration is important. The hymn is designed to be sung antiphonally by a pair of choirs of young boys and girls, precisely the kind of occasion, form, and means of performance for which Smart himself would most like to write. The poem expresses both gratitude and hopeful anticipation, and in its conclusion reflects upon itself as the instrument of thanksgiving and the means of drawing down the favor of the gods. Even in the work of the civilized and skeptical Horace, faith in the special powers of poetry suggests the continuing force of primitive belief in poetry's divine origins, a belief which is most fully expressed in poetic prayer and song. By assimilating Horace to his myth of David the Psalmist, Smart gives an added dimension to the possibilities of poetry, joining "enthusiasm" to artful and witty intelligence.

Smart's paraphrases of the Psalms are another major monument to his personal myth of David, and because they are, I think, generally undervalued where they are not ignored, I will attempt an account of them which may further illuminate Smart's unifying myth. Smart's purposes in writing metrical paraphrases of the Psalms differed importantly from his purposes in translating Horace, in spite of his near identification of the two poets with each other and his complete personal identification with both. The *Horace* is intended as a close translation to catch the spirit and as much of the art of the original as possible. Smart demonstrates his prosodic mastery, using a surprising variety of stanzas and rhythmic patterns to approximate the Horatian forms. The *Psalms*, on the other hand, is intended to replace the versions in the Anglican psalter and to be used in the Anglican service. Because they must be simple and singable, Smart used variations on only three basic stanzas: the standard four- and five-line hymn stanzas and the six-line *Song to David* stanza (similar to the "romance six"), and translated loosely. As the title indicates, Smart's version is *A Translation of the Psalms of David, attempted in the Spirit of Christianity, and adapted to the Divine Service.*

Smart's deletions and expansions in his versions of the Psalms reveal his myth-making power at work, transforming David's vision in the light of subsequent Christian history and doctrine and, in a sense, transmuting David forward in time to union with the gentle soul of his eighteenth-century avatar, Christopher Smart. His most obvious alteration from the biblical Psalms is inserting Christ as a merciful mediator between man and the stern, vengeful Old Testament God who is invoked so often by King David. Christ's mercy and pastoral benevolence temper God's fierce justice. In Psalm 94, for example, the final verse describes God's reward for those who persecute the righteous: "He shall recompense them their wickedness, and destroy them in their own malice: yes, the Lord our God shall destroy them." In Smart's version this becomes:

Foes of their benign Creator,
  Would, as their own malice, fare,
Did not Christ the Mediator
  Plead his merits and his pray'r.

[Callan, II, 621]

But less obvious and more intriguing, from our point of view, is Smart's pervasive intrusion into the poem. His identification with David is so complete that he pours his own sorrows into David's laments. In Psalm 105, for example, which describes the wanderings of the Israelites, verse 14 announces: "He suffered no man to do them wrong, but reproved even kings for their sakes." Although God reproves the kings for tyrannical acts which take advantage of the weakness of the homeless Israelites, no specific examples of tyranny are mentioned. Smart makes the passage more specific and more closely related to his own situation, but also, interestingly, to aspects of David's life:

No man could hurt their goods or lives
  As they their tents remov'd,
And for the virtue of their wives,
  He mighty kings reprov'd.

[Callan, II, 653]

The association of tyrannical seizure of "goods" with the threat of adulterous lust reminds us that Smart, in *Jubilate Agno*, is obsessed with the idea that he has been cheated out of an inheritance, and that his wife has cuckolded him (cf. B1.56-60 and B1.74-76).

Another Psalm which seems to speak clearly to Smart's situation is 120, which begins, in the Prayer Book, simply: "When I was in trouble I called upon the Lord: and he heard me. Deliver my soul, O Lord, from lying lips and from a deceitful tongue." Smart's version shows his tendency to raise the emotional tone of the Psalms by referring to specific situations and inserting more concrete imagery:

When strong calamity pervailed,
  And all my mirth was mute,
By pray'r the topmost heav'n I scal'd,
  And Jesus heard my suit.

Shield me from lips with lies replete,
  Or which their word revoke;
And from the language of the cheat,
  Expert his thoughts to cloak.

[Callan, II, 731]

The psalm is especially poignant in view of Smart's probable state of mind in the madhouse:

> My soul her sorrows overcharge
>   Unto the last extreme,
> For while I still on peace enlarge
>   They question and blaspheme.
>
> I strive to work them up to peace
>   From horror and despair;
> But at the word their bands increase
>   And they their cross prepare.

[Callan, II, 731]

This passage is extraordinary for several reasons. The Prayer Book version reads: "My soul hath long dwelt among them that are enemies unto peace. I labour for peace, but when I speak to them thereof, they make ready to battle." Smart makes explicit the implicit "horror and despair" of his original, but his last two lines jolt us by their deviation from "they make ready for battle." They suggest either that Smart/David sees himself as interceding with Christ's executioners or that Smart sees himself preparing for his own crucifixion as a disciple of Christ, caught in a pagan world. Or in a third, somewhat too ingenious reading, the stanzas may refer to Smart's fellow inmates in the asylum: Smart, trying to bring them out of their horror to share his peace, finds them deaf to his teaching and, by their continuing violence and stubborness, preparing their own continuing crucifixion ("And they their [own] cross prepare"). Given Smart's benevolence and wish to bring all creatures to join in worship, this is not an impossible alternative. We may remember his plea in the *Jubilate:* "For I pray the Lord JESUS that cured the LUNATICK to be merciful to all my brethren and sisters in these houses" (B1.123).

Smart does not merely inflate the Psalms with random associations and ornate words, despite the harsh rejection of his paraphrases by some critics.[8] The extension of the associations makes the poems more immediate to the audience Smart has in mind. The language allows a complexity of meaning for which the Psalmist does not strive, but which is consistent with Smart's notion of singing a new psalm which will be England's own. His ability to fuse disparate images and ideas cements the identification of his own life and beliefs with the ideal forms of the "poet" which he perceives in his past. He places himself in the two traditions—Horatian and "Davidic." As a result of the fusion, he suggests an exciting possibility: the old dichotomy between art and passion need not be an impassable gulf, but the two terms of a dialectic.

Smart's myth of David—the scholar, the poet, the thankful celebrant of his God—is also his myth of himself, his composite picture of the disparate—sometimes tragic, sometimes buffoon-like—qualities of his own poetic personality.

Nine

Faulkner's Absalom, Absalom! and the David Story: A Speculative Contemplation

Stephen M. Ross

O my son Absalom, my son, my son
Absalom! would God I had died for thee,
O Absalom, my son, my son!

II Samuel 18:33[1]

—Henry . . . his father holds his
face between both hands, looking at it.
—Henry, Sutpen says —My son.
—Absalom, Absalom![2]

Although Faulkner knew both Testaments well, and drew on the Gospels for Christian symbolism in works like *The Sound and the Fury*, *Light in August*, "The Bear," and *A Fable*, he apparently preferred the Old Testament to the New. At least he preferred to *read* the Old Testament, listing it among his favorite books. Just as he read Shakespeare, Cervantes, and Dickens every year, so he read and reread the Old Testament for its stories and people, for the pleasure of a good tale—but not, he would explain, for its "message":

> To me the New Testament is full of ideas and I don't know much about ideas. The Old Testament is full of people, perfectly ordinary normal heroes and blackguards just like everybody else nowadays, and I like to read the Old Testament because it's full of people not ideas. It's people all trying to get something for nothing or . . . to be braver than they are—just ordinary everyday folks, people, that's why I like to read that. That's apart from the fine poetry of the prose.[3]

The distinction Faulkner makes here between a Testament of "ideas" and a Testament of "people" is crucial for understanding his rendering of the David story in *Absalom, Absalom!* Whether or not we accept his distinction as a valid description of the Bible, Faulkner clearly valued the Old Testament for its stories, its legends, its narrative, its characters. And though he loved to dissimulate, behind his "Mississippi farmer" mask, just how conversant he really was with "ideas," it is fair to say that Faulkner was a better storyteller than a philosopher. One suspects, too, that he preferred to read the Old Testament because it does not always supply solutions to the complex, even paradoxical moral questions its stories raise. Faulkner overburdens his most extensive representation of Christ's life, in *A Fable*, with philosophizing on the human condition; his most explicit rendering of an Old Testament narrative, his retelling of the David story in *Absalom, Absalom!* derives its very power from mystery, ambiguity, and tragic uncertainties.

The common interpretive strategy in assessing Faulkner's use of the David story has been to set up an analogy between King David and the novel's protagonist, Thomas Sutpen, and then see how the latter fails to achieve the moral stature of God's imperfect but anointed progenitor of kings.[4] Similarities of plot and context indeed support such an analogy, but the nature of Faulkner's respect for the Old Testament should warn us that David is reportrayed in Sutpen not so much because he is a gauge by which we can measure Sutpen's villainy, but more importantly because the two characters participate, in similar but not identical ways, in the tragic contradictions of kingship, pride, and love. Unlike Christ, who can be emulated or symbolized but not repeated, David the earthly king can recur in Sutpen as one of those "perfectly ordinary normal heroes and blackguards" Faulkner enjoyed reading about. That we are far more apt to respect David's *personal* qualities—his spontaneity, his affection, his commitment—than Sutpen's does not necessarily make *moral* comparison a simple matter. Moral causality is not clear even in the David story itself, veering as it does between natural consequence and divine intervention. Causality in *Absalom, Absalom!* is as complicated, if not more so, than in Samuel, and this makes any unambiguous judgmental comparisons suspect. *Absalom, Absalom!* and the David story should be approached as texts which reflect upon each other, not just as "source" and "derived story." King David himself may be better known to us in light of Thomas Sutpen. Considered in what seems to me the proper Faulknerian spirit, the two stories become equally problematic recognitions of human frailty.

First, we need to explore the important parallels between David and Sutpen, though with an eye to seeing why this central analogy does not sufficiently chart Faulkner's recuperation of the entire David legend. Second, we shall examine the sons' rebellions and some patterns into which these rebellions arrange themselves. Third, we shall consider how Faulkner orders the narrative of his novel as an interpretation of its biblical predecessor.

Both David and Sutpen emerge from obscure origins to assume their respective positions as king and cotton baron. In the process, both prove themselves superior to other men according to the standards of the cultures they will lead. The youngest of Jesse's sons, David was nearly overlooked when Samuel came to anoint Israel's future king. Unlike Saul, who even before he was chosen king possessed exceptional stature ("and there was not among the children of Israel a goodlier person than he; from his shoulders upward he was higher than any of the people" [I Samuel 9:2]), David is but a youth, "ruddy, and withal of a beautiful countenance" but not as far as the reader can yet tell superior in those qualities—strength, wisdom, leadership—expected in a good king. Our first impression of David is of a boy, a boy who will prove himself.

The initial physical description of Sutpen is quite the opposite from that of a boy. He looks older than his twenty-five years, "gaunt," with a "short reddish beard . . . a face whose flesh had the appearance of pottery . . . a dead impervious surface as of glazed clay" (pp. 32-33). This is hardly a "ruddy" youth, and even beyond the physical disparity one crucial difference between David and Sutpen is the absence in Faulkner's protagonist of that exuberance, that affection and youthful passion that leads David to dance naked before the ark of God, to sing openly of his grief at Jonathan's death, or lament the death of his son Absalom.

Sutpen's background, however, is no less humble than David's, no less obscure. We know this even before we have the details of his past. Lacking the proper family credentials, this man, who Rosa Coldfield tells us is "not even a gentleman," muscles his way into the plantation aristocracy simply by doing better whatever it is that aristocrats do: "he was like John L. Sullivan having taught himself . . . to do the schottische. . . . He may have believed that [Quentin Compson's] grandfather or Judge Benbow might have done it a little more effortlessly than he, but he would not have believed that anyone could have beat him in knowing when to do it and how" (p. 46). The story of Sutpen's childhood (which is not given until chapter 7) brings forth the symbolic figure of a boy, a figure which in retrospect can be seen to recur throughout the novel. For the youngest child of an Appalachian "white trash" family, the crucial revelation comes at the front door of a Tidewater plantation house where a "nigger" butler orders Sutpen around back to the servants' entrance. Slapped with this realization of his unimportance, the young Sutpen sets out to beat the aristocracy with its own weapons: land, slaves, and heirs. The image of a boy turned away from a door is repeated symbolically in the figure of Charles Bon's seeking recognition at his father's house.[5]

Both boys earn their stature in a man's world. Being chosen by God does not exempt David from a heroic initiation. He slays Goliath, who possesses in exaggerated proportions the prowess of a grown man, in contrast to David's youth and inexperience: Goliath is "a man of war from his youth," so that "when the Philistine looked about, and saw David, he disdained him: for he was but a youth, and ruddy, and of a fair countenance" (I Samuel 17:33, 42). David further proves his worth by purchasing the hand of Saul's daughter (and avoiding the snare Saul sets for him) with twice the required Philistine foreskins. Sutpen fights his Philistines, too, singlehandedly quelling a slave revolt in Haiti. His victory has an even greater aura of mystery and magic than David's killing of Goliath (at least we see how David slew the giant), for Sutpen simply walks into the night and somehow, like a demon, terrifies the slaves to death with his imperviousness. And like David, Sutpen wins a wife, the Haitian plantation owner's daughter. Both youths thus make their claims to kingship legitimate in the terms demanded by their cultures: neither is a rebel nor a reformer, but an extraordinarily successful participant in their society's rites of passage. David, it is true, brings a new spirit of forgiveness to his reign—twice sparing Saul's life, for example—but without question he earns the kingship given him by God. Sutpen's very defense of the slave-holding class tinges his successful rise with the racial ironies which later bring his "design" (his plan for a dynasty) down around his head.

The boy-symbolism plays its role in another way as well, reinforcing the innocence and childish blindness which contribute to both David's and Sutpen's suffering. Neither can see why their wishes should be thwarted. David impulsively takes Bathsheba and disposes of her husband Uriah as if suddenly struck blind to his responsibilities as king, as upholder of God's law. Unlike David, who eventually perceives his error, Sutpen can never comprehend where his design went wrong, believing always that he paid his dues and should be granted his dynasty. "Sutpen's trouble was innocence . . . that frank innocence which we call 'of a child' except that a human child is the only living creature that is never either frank or innocent . . . that innocence which believed that the ingredients of morality were like the ingredients of pie or cake and once you had measured them and balanced them and mixed them and put them into the oven it was all finished and nothing but pie or cake could come out" (pp. 220, 246, 263). With the single-minded intensity of a child going after the one thing it wants, Sutpen "innocently" ignores others. In putting aside his first wife and son, in refusing to acknowledge Bon as his son, in offering Rosa Coldfield the chance to "breed" with him to see if they could produce a male heir—in all these instances Sutpen acts with the same insensitivity (an insensitivity apparently free of malicious intent) that David exhibits in stealing Bathsheba from Uriah.

The single incident which most closely recalls the Bathsheba episode, at least in detail, is Sutpen's seduction of Milly Jones. Wash Jones's granddaughter, the last available female to carry Sutpen's seed, is almost a parody of the beautiful Bathsheba.[6] But Jones himself, who worships the "kernel," rises at the last to a dignity greater than that of the more passively duped Uriah. Jones has allowed Sutpen to seduce Milly because, he tells Sutpen, "I know that whatever your hands tech, whether hit's a regiment of men or a ignorant gal or just a hound dog, that you will make hit right" (p. 284). When he hears Sutpen insult Milly (who has given birth to a girl), he is dumbfounded, then enraged, and he mows the "kernel" down with a scythe like old Father Time. If David can be forgiven his sin with Bathsheba through God's patience and mercy, Sutpen has only Jones's loyalty and inertia to depend upon.

The Bathsheba and the Milly Jones episodes differ in one vital implication which can be drawn from them. David seriously abuses his power as king when he takes Bathsheba and orders Uriah's death, but this is the only time he abuses that power. Sutpen's treatment of Milly, however, is only the last in a series of abusive acts. David falls momentarily from his status as an exceptional ruler, one who usually lets love influence his actions. Sutpen's repeated inhumanity to others grows out of his total acceptance of his culture's worst values. He stands apart from the other slave-owning cotton kings only in his exaggerated version of a fanatical drive for dynastic power, common in the antebellum South. Through Sutpen's behavior—indeed, through the very existence of a racial hierarchy which could induce behavior like Sutpen's—an entire culture indicts itself.[7]

Many of the similarities and differences between David and Sutpen make the latter seem a fallen David, a haughty aristocrat morally inferior to the king of the Israelites. But only if Sutpen is extracted from the context of the total novel can *Absalom, Absalom!* be regarded in such simple allegorical terms. Sutpen is heroic as well as villainous, tragic as well as sinful. He must be if Quentin Compson's fascination with him (and ours, for that matter) is to be justified. The novel weaves a web of causality which entraps Sutpen and threatens to exonerate him *personally* for his failure to live up to "God's law"—much as David is personally forgiven his sin with Bathsheba though his house must suffer the consequences. Demons of fate are at work in *Absalom, Absalom!*, demons which Faulkner's incantatory rhetoric calls forth, which, in the absence of God, almost "forgive" Sutpen his transgressions. At times he seems the victim of a curse inherited from the world around him. What, after all, is "God's law," as Sutpen can know it? No Samuel comes forth to tell him, no Nathan to reprimand him. As a boy, he sees only that whites (some whites at least) are kings and that black blood renders ludicrous any claims to legacy, to perpetuity, to human dignity. The sense of doom and entrapment is at times overwhelming in this book, with the result that we cannot pass the easy judgment against Sutpen which the comparison of him with David would first suggest.

In the end, when we discover (as Quentin Compson has discovered) that "it's the miscegenation, not the incest, which [Henry] can't bear" (p. 358), we have reached a horrific revelation, not a triumphant and smug condemnation of racial injustice. We want to say—Quentin wants to say—that Sutpen's racial fears are wrong, that black blood should not matter to him, that when he discovered the truth about his first wife, or when Charles Bon sought him out, he should have accepted them and not perpetuated the sin. But while the novel does not prevent us from condemning Sutpen, it does not permit us to do so blithely or unambiguously. Quentin and Shreve imagine, as part of the episode in which Sutpen tells Henry about Bon's Negro blood, this reunion between father and son:

> —Henry . . .
> It is the older man who moves first, though they meet in the center of the tent, where they embrace and kiss before Henry is aware that he has moved, was going to move, moved by what of close blood which in the reflex abrogates and reconciles even though it does not yet (perhaps never will) forgive, who stands now while his father holds his face between both hands, looking at it.
> —Henry, Sutpen says—My son. [p. 353]

By evoking, even faintly, David's lament for Absalom, this scene echoes the poignancy of David's grief as well as the ironies of Sutpen's failures. Faulkner carefully reserves this scene until long after we have seen Sutpen's ignominious death at the hands of Wash Jones, so that our last vision of Sutpen affords him a touch of tragic dignity, a dignity we must grant him at the very moment he is committing the error which makes a fratricide out of his son, as David's forgiving Amnon did Absalom.

None of this is to say that *Absalom, Absalom!* exonerates Sutpen; it does not. He is responsible for the values he once put on as unthinkingly as he later donned his Confederate uniform. We can insist, however, that it is a mistake to see Sutpen as merely a pale and fallen imitation of King

David. Faulkner forces us to discover the same paradox of forgivness and moral enforcement, the same contradiction between love and authority, in *Absalom, Absalom!* as we experience in the David story. The same mystery of causality also infuses Sutpen's and David's life—that mystery in which series of events which appear to have natural causes remain somehow inexplicable. Mr. Compson expresses this perfectly when he admits that the information available about the Sutpen history is "just incredible. It just does not explain. . . . we see dimly people, the people in whose living blood and seed we ourselves lay dormant and waiting, in this shadowy attenuation of time possessing now heroic proportions, performing their acts of simple passion and simple violence, impervious to time and inexplicable . . . they are there, yet something is missing" (pp. 100-101).

That "something" which is "missing" from causal explanation in *Absalom, Absalom!* is present in the David story. At one point the young David, still relatively unknown, is described by one of Saul's servants as "cunning in playing, and a mighty valiant man, and a man of war, and prudent in matters, and a comely person, and the Lord is with him" (I Samuel 16:18). The last phrase, "the Lord is with him," fills the gap between David's as yet unearned heroism and his always present (since Samuel's anointment) glory. This is the mystery the narrative constantly moves through. Does David possess the good qualities he is said to possess because the Lord is with him or is the Lord with him because he has these virtues? The question has no answer, of course, nor does it need one in the face of the Lord's will—any more than God's forgiveness of David's sins, but not Saul's, needs "explanation." Divine providence simply *is.* The mystery, but not the divinity, remains in *Absalom, Absalom!* Especially early in the novel, we get a narrative tone of withheld or undiscoverable explanation; we almost expect to see "And it came to pass" in such summaries as this:

> It seems that this demon—his name was Sutpen—(Colonel Sutpen)—Colonel Sutpen. Who came out of nowhere and without warning upon the land with a band of strange niggers and built a plantation—(Tore violently a plantation, Miss Rosa Coldfield says)—tore violently. And married her sister Ellen and begot a son and a daughter which—(Without gentleness begot, Miss Rosa Coldfield says)—without gentleness. Which should have been the jewels of his pride and the shield and comfort of his old age, only—(Only they destroyed him or something or he destroyed them or something. And died)—and died. [p. 9]

What is missing from Mr. Compson's formula is not more information (which *seems* to help but only deepens the mystery) but the divine intervention which can, by fiat, resolve paradox. The only "providence" left in *Absalom, Absalom!* is circumstance plus culture—and in this sense, unfortunately, Thomas Sutpen is not a godless man.

We have thus far been considering the most common groundwork on which comparisons between *Absalom, Absalom!* and the David story have been built, the similarities and differences between Thomas Sutpen and David. As we examine the family relationships in both stories, it might be tempting to stretch the primary analogy between David and Sutpen to include their children; but the analogy simply cannot be extended to other characters. Any one-to-one correspondences between these characters become rapidly entangled in the network of love, incest, and rebellion that is woven through the family histories. Furthermore, relying too much on the David-Sutpen equation has caused critics to misjudge just how thoroughly Faulkner intermingles the *entire* David story, from both I and II Samuel, into *Absalom, Absalom!* [8] It is only in the uses Faulkner makes of I Samuel that we can see what may be his novel's deepest thematic affinity with the David story: portrayal of the inevitable conflict between love and authority, once love has entered a sequence of historical events.

If we *do* extend the David-Sutpen analogy, we would necessarily equate Henry with David's son Absalom, Charles Bon with Amnon, and Judith with Tamar. [9] Such analogies work only with some rather complicated adjustments. The most obvious and simply stated is the substitution of the racial taboo for incest as the motive for Henry's fratricide. Only when he knows Bon is black does the threat of "rape" move Henry to act.

Other adjustments, however, are not so easily made. Bon's role as the Amnon figure, the despoiler of his sister, is complicated by our uncertainty about his motives. Certainly they are never reduced to Amnon's brutish lust; he never literally rapes Judith or even threatens to. If Bon's function as a moral focus for the book's racial theme is to be validated, it would follow that his claim to Judith would need to be "taintless." But Faulkner encourages doubts about Bon's innocence, first by spending considerable space (in Mr. Compson's narrative in chapter 4) portraying Bon as a would-be bigamist, a sybaritic voluptuary come to the edenic wilderness to corrupt the virgin Henry (and Judith, though Mr. Compson sees Bon's interest in Judith as coming only through Henry). When Quentin and Shreve later recast Bon in the role of a romantic hero, gallantly seeking the union with his beloved that is denied him by an intransigent parent, their version fails to explain Bon's determination to marry a woman whom—even the Harvard roommates admit—it is doubtful he could really love. Quentin and Shreve say again and again "but that's not love," as reason after reason fails to free Bon from some responsibility for his own death. When Bon is about to leave the war to return for Judith, he tells Henry that he has no choice but to marry her: he has been waiting the last four years for recognition from his father, and now that it will never come he must force a response. This is hardly Amnon's drunken rape of Tamar, but he *does* push Henry as far as possible, challenging him to act by reminding him "No I'm not [your brother]. I'm the nigger that's going to sleep with your sister. Unless you stop me, Henry" (p. 358). Bon, in a sense, "forces" Henry and Judith.

Henry, like Absalom, kills his half-brother because of the brother's actions against his sister. But Henry becomes like Absalom only in the act of killing Bon. Before that act, Henry is in nearly all ways the reverse of Absalom. Both are in revolt against their fathers but for very different reasons: Absalom kills Amnon because David would not; David then forgives Absalom his revenge, only to see him turn into a political traitor who foments civil war. Henry repudiates his father because Sutpen would "punish" Bon by forbidding the marriage. When he shoots Bon, Henry ceases to be in revolt against his father, for he stops the marriage, the very thing Sutpen wants (whether Sutpen wanted it stopped at the expense of Bon's death we can only guess). Henry has in a way carried out his father's will; he has reacted to Sutpen's instigation not in rebellion but in support of the cultural and racial hierarchy Sutpen so totally stands for.

The father/son/brother relationship in *Absalom, Absalom!* reflects the Saul/David/Jonathan triad in I Samuel more than the David/Amnon/Absalom family of II Samuel. Sutpen himself, in that he instigates Henry's murder of Charles Bon, seems more like Saul than like David: Saul tried to move Jonathan against David, warning him that he would never be king as long as David lived, and ordering Jonathan to kill David. Sutpen places dynasty above moral law, as does Saul. The bond between Henry and Charles Bon mirrors Jonathan's and David's love in I Samuel. Because of his affection for David, Jonathan repudiates his father: "Jonathan arose from the table in fierce anger . . . for he was grieved for David, because his father had done him shame" (I Samuel 20:34). Henry "formally abjure[s] his home and birthright" to side with Bon against his father "in the fierce repercussive flush of vindicated loyalty" (pp. 106, 107).[10]

The importance of this brotherly love, indeed of love in general, cannot be overemphasized in these stories. Just as we are told, simply and directly as a fact that is utterly crucial to what later happens, that "the soul of Jonathan was knit with the soul of David, and Jonathan loved him as his own soul" (I Samuel 18:1), so Mr. Compson begins his attempt to explain the fratricide with the simple but utterly crucial assertion that "Henry loved Bon" (p. 89). Love makes the events more tragic, more poignant; the Sutpen saga especially becomes one of pity and terror precisely "*because* Henry loved Bon" and murdered him.

It would not be unreasonable to interpret the David story as a mythic account of the introduction of love, divine and human, into worldly historical processes. David's greatness lies in his compassionate and spontaneous affection for others, even for those like Saul or Absalom who seek to kill him. With the coming of King David, love (either for David or by David) enters the affairs of kings; love matters. Jonathan's love for David preserves the line of the house of David; David's love for Amnon, his firstborn, may be the reason he fails to punish him; his love for Absalom turns military victory into mourning. Faulkner, too, injects love into the events of history, thereby rendering them tragic. Love, or its failure, contributes to every major turn the events of the Sutpens' history take: Sutpen rejects his first wife and son; Henry comes to love Charles Bon; Rosa "loves" Sutpen and hates him; Sutpen travesties love with his proposal to Rosa and his flippant dismissal of Milly Jones.

We have been speaking throughout our discussion of "the David story," but the many parallels with I Samuel indicate that we should more properly speak of the David *stories*. We are comparing at least three stories: that of Saul, David, and Jonathan; that of David, Amnon, and Absalom; and that of Supten, Bon, and Henry (and perhaps there is a fourth story in the relationships among Mr. Compson, Shreve, and Quentin, a possibility we shall consider later). Such similar multiple texts imply underlying patterns which a structuralist approach might help us to sort out.

John T. Irwin, in *Doubling and Incest/Repetition and Revenge* (Baltimore: Johns Hopkins University Press, 1975), has elaborated a structure in which *Absalom, Absalom!* "participates," a structure that is repeated in the David story, and is identifiable as a version of the Freudian Oedipal triangle. Irwin builds a convincing case for the triad of Father, Brother Seducer, and Brother Avenger as central to Faulkner's imagination, especially in his creation of Quentin Compson in both *The Sound and the Fury* and *Absalom, Absalom!* Irwin speaks of the David, Amnon, and Absalom story as a version of this structure, though perhaps, because of his emphasis on Freudian notions of incest, primal revenge, and repetition, he does not discuss the story of Saul, Jonathan, and David. To account for both I and II Samuel, and thus for Faulkner's recuperation of the Jonathan-David love relationship—which I have argued is essential to *Absalom, Absalom!*—we need to expand the possibilities of Irwin's triad by changing its familial roles from Father, Brother Seducer, and Brother Avenger to Father, Son, and Brother. The "Son" is defined as a role by its relationship to the role of Father, as the Father's heir. The "Brother" is defined by its relationship to the Son. (Note that "Father," "Son," and "Brother" denominate *roles*, not persons; the role of Brother is, of course, occupied by a son of the father, but as a role, "Brother" gains its identity from the sibling relationship.)

Because of acts perpetrated by the person who is the Son, the Brother is driven into rebellion against the Father, in order either to protect or destroy the Son. The Brother can be brought into a state of rebellion against the Father either by usurping his authority (as Absalom does in punishing Amnon) or by renouncing *his own* eventual inheritance (as Jonathan and Henry do).

Such an alteration in Irwin's triad allows love to function as an affective force in the dynamics of succession and rebellion, since Jonathan and Henry each acts out the Brother's role because of their love for their brothers, David and Bon (who, in turn, each occupies the role of Son). Indeed, the major flaw in Irwin's argument is the short shrift given to love as a motivation.[11]

A structuralist perspective like Irwin's, at least as redefined above, can reflect Faulkner's use of his biblical sources by charting similarities and differences not in terms of moral comparisons but in terms of how given characters fulfill their respective roles and move from one role to another. Such a perspective takes us a further step from the David-Sutpen equation, which unduly limits our ability to appreciate how deep the affinities between the David stories and *Absalom, Absalom!* run. Sutpen belongs in a category like "Father" or "King"—as do both Saul and David—instead of in a category like "David figure." Furthermore, seeing Jonathan and Henry as Brothers who act from love reinforces the conflict between love and authority; both Jonathan and Henry were in fact Sons, due to inherit the authority of the Father-King; yet both relinquish that position to their brothers (until Henry reverses his role again and kills Bon). Absalom shifts roles, in the opposite way, by killing the Son (Amnon) and thereby usurping the place of succession as well as David's power to punish incest. Absalom then acts out his new identity as Son by trying to supplant David, driving him from Jerusalem and taking over his concubines. Perhaps Bon's suicidal prodding of Henry, and his stubborn refusal to give Judith up, are more comprehensible as acts of a Son seeking inheritance than as acts of a child seeking only recognition. Henry, by killing Charles Bon, succeeds in regaining his "rights" as Son—and it is a final Faulknerian irony that, of all the Sons we have been concerned with, only Henry survives the Father, returning to Sutpen's Hundred to die.[12]

The redrawing of an Old Testament king in the figure of Thomas Sutpen, the reenactment of filial rebellion, the reshuffling of elemental father-son-brother relationships—these suggest how intimately *Absalom, Absalom!* engages us with the first two Books of Kings. But no assessment of Faulkner's recuperation of the David story would be complete without some attempt to account for the Old Testament quality that *Absalom, Absalom!* somehow invokes—which the comparisons discussed so far cannot fully explain. Like Melville, another American novelist who had little formal education but who read voraciously, Faulkner has the uncanny power to immerse us in a reading process appropriate to but not simply imitative of his sources.[13] He creates in *Absalom, Absalom!* the effect the Bible has on the reader as a narrative, demanding exegesis both retrospectively, after we read (the comparisons we have considered amount to retrospective readings), and incipiently, from the moment we begin to read and as we read. As soon as we have stepped into the narrative flow of *Absalom, Absalom!* we have perforce embarked on a hermeneutic enterprise akin to reading the Old Testament books in their ongoing accretion of knowledge and pattern toward some apocalypse just over the horizon of history. In part this effect results from the sense of history implied by Faulkner's conception of time and reflected in his fictional methods. In part this Old Testament effect derives from the successively renewed discoveries we share with character-narrators, and in part also from the involvement of Quentin Compson in a fourth version of the father-son-brother triad that is central to the David story.

Eric Auerbach's famous description of biblical "realism" (in the first chapter of *Mimesis*) is a convenient context in which to summarize those Faulknerian conventions of time and history which add so much to the 'Old Testament' resonance of *Absalom, Absalom!* Specific scenes in the Bible are given to us, Auerbach says, laden with a depth of implied prior experience that always remains at least partially unarticulated in any depiction of the immediate moment. The biblical stories are "fraught with background," unlike Homeric tales in which everything, present and past phenomena, is brought out into the light of a clear and "complete" foreground:

The human beings in the Biblical stories have greater depths of time, fate, and consciousness than do the human beings in Homer; although they are nearly always caught up in an event engaging all their faculties, they are not so entirely immersed in its present that they do not remain continually conscious of what has happened to them earlier and elsewhere; their thoughts and feelings have more layers, are more entangled. . . . How fraught with background, in comparison [to the Homeric heroes] are characters like Saul and David! How entangled and stratified are such human relationships as those between David and Absalom, between David and Joab![14]

Absalom, Absalom! is "historical" in the same way. When Faulkner introduces Sutpen to us, he evokes an implied, dense history that has the same effect as the biblical "backgrounding" Auerbach describes. Faulkner can render foreground scenes as vividly as any writer, but he always (in *Absalom, Absalom!* at least) inculcates the present with the past, achieving a richness of accompanying heritage similar in its effects to the history of Israel which accompanies the rise of David. Faulkner said once that his sense of time was like "Bergson's theory of the fluidity of time. There is only the present moment, in which I include both the past and the future, and that is eternity."[15] If such a conception values the present, it also enriches it with the inclusion of the past, and in *Absalom, Absalom!* the layering of time causes any single moment to reverberate back and forth in the echo chamber of history.

The book's first chapter initiates the reverberations by placing us with Quentin Compson, who listens to Rosa Coldfield, "talking in that grim haggard amazed voice," summon forth the "long-dead object of her impotent yet indomitable frustration . . . as though by outraged recapitulation evoked" (pp. 7-8). Sutpen "abrupts" onto the narrative scene from out of the past, and entangled with the past, so that Quentin experiences Sutpen's story as an echo: "his very body was an empty hall echoing with sonorous defeated names" (p. 12). The narrative movement, even within single sentences, oscillates between abrupt clarity and evocative, miasmic density. Vivid impressionistic foreground scenes seem to have been pulled from the background like bright stones plucked out of a lump of clay, with bits of clay still clinging to their smooth surfaces. The best example is the beginning of chapter 2, in Quentin's Harvard room, which moves back in time to the summer of Quentin's listening to Miss Coldfield and to his father, when he hears about the Sunday morning in 1833 when Sutpen first arrived in Jefferson—and it is this last moment that suddenly rushes into focus. "And there the stranger was. He was already halfway across the Square when they saw him, on a big hard-ridden roan horse, man and beast looking as though they had been created out of thin air and set down in the bright summer sabbath sunshine in the middle of a tired foxtrot" (pp. 31-32).

Absalom, Absalom! is a novel of "books," of different versions of the same or similar events which, taken in order, accumulate information and constitute a procession of interpretations toward a final revelation. Although the biblical stories tend to repeat and rework types of events, while in *Absalom, Absalom!* the same event is told and retold, we can sense a direction of implication in Faulkner's novel that is analogous to the progression of the biblical narrative. The implications of the separate versions of Sutpen's story reflect the implications of the David story as we read through it from the pre-Samuel Old Testament, through the books of Kings, and even beyond. (By "implication" I mean the total context of history, myth, and values evoked by a story as it is told and perceived.)[16]

Our first version of Sutpen reminds us more of a creation myth than of the David story. The first chapter contains fewer analogies with David than any other. As he listens to Rosa Coldfield, Quentin imagines Sutpen descending godlike upon the Mississippi wilderness and creating his plantation out of chaos, "creating the Sutpen's Hundred, the *Be Sutpen's Hundred* like the oldentime *Be Light*" (p. 9). To Rosa, of course, Sutpen is a "demon," "djinn," "fiend blackguard and devil," so her "creation myth" is a diabolical one; but the implications that her story carries have the same sense of godlike beginning, the start of everything to follow, that Genesis implies for the whole history of man preceding the reign of David.

Chapters 2 and 3 offer a history of Sutpen's rise in Jefferson which paints him as a fated king. He is much like Saul in these chapters, greater in stature than his fellow mortals, tougher, more ruthless—"*Given the occasion and the need, this man can and will do anything*" (p. 46, Faulkner's italics). Chapter 4 describes the Henry-Bon relationship, echoing Jonathan's love for David that is so vital in I Samuel. While we learn that Henry killed Bon, we cannot explain it; so Henry at this point in the novel has not yet become the Absalom figure he later will.

Chapter 5 (Rosa's account of Sutpen's return from the war) and chapter 6 (Shreve's and Quentin's recapitulation of the Sutpen family history) begin the transformation of implication from Saul to David. Sutpen is seen here as an old king, desperate, like Saul, to save his dynasty: an "old wornout cannon which realizes that it can deliver just one more fierce shot and crumble to dust in its furious blast and recoil" (p. 181).[17] We learn how Sutpen dies, though the Milly Jones episode is not yet developed in its full reflection of the Bathsheba incident. In

chapter 7 Sutpen becomes more analogous to David (and, concomitant-
ly, less like Saul), for in this chapter we are given the facts about his
origin, facts which are a main source of specific analogies with David.
We also learn about that innocent blindness which plagues Sutpen all his
life; the boy image is developed fully; and the seduction of Milly Jones is
rendered more completely.

Quentin and Shreve, in chapter 8, concentrate on the love between
Henry and Bon, just as Mr. Compson did in chapter 4. Jonathan's love
for David again reminds us of Henry's love for Bon, but this time there is
a crucial change: we watch Henry turn into the Absalom figure of II
Samuel. The chapter ends with the long scene at the Confederate Army
bivouac in which Sutpen tells Henry of Bon's black blood. Not only is
David's lament for Absalom echoed, but Henry is driven into his
brother-avenger role. We now have a reason, however morally unpalat-
able, for the killing of Charles Bon. Love between the brothers is muti-
lated into fratricide, as in the progression of David's reign the love
between himself and Jonathan repeats itself in reverse in Absalom's
revenge. *Our* discovery of the causes of Henry's act proceeds in a developing sequence analogous to the reading sequence of the David story
from I Samuel (backgrounded by the whole creation myth and history of
Israel) through David's final lament for the dead Absalom. We see love
infused into history by God, by David, by Henry, and by the narrators
of *Absalom, Absalom!* We then see that love fail as it turns into fratricide
and civil war. That Absalom dies in a civil war against his father fits
perfectly with the Civil War that Henry, Bon, and Sutpen fight in.[18]

The final chapter of the novel moves beyond the David story to a
gothic revelation scene in which Quentin Compson finds, at Sutpen's
Hundred, the dying Henry, his "wasted hands crossed on the breast as if
he were already a corpse" (p. 373).[19] This apocalypse is appropriately
personal, for Quentin has been acting out his own story while narrating
and interpreting the Sutpens'. Faulkner regarded Quentin as the "protagonist" of the novel, "so that it [would] not [be] complete apocrypha,"
as if Quentin's *response* to the tale were the most "real" part of the book.[20]
As the same young man who commits suicide in *The Sound and the Fury*,
Quentin has a particular fascination with the romance among Henry,
Bon, and Judith. John Irwin demonstrates at considerable length how
the Sutpen triangle reflects the Quentin, Caddy, Dalton Ames confron-
tations in its potential incest, in its struggle against the "darker brother,"
and in the yearning to protect the sister. Quentin, who has failed to
protect Caddy's (very tenuous) honor and to force Mr. Compson to
punish him for his incestuous desires, discovers in horror that Henry did

indeed play the brother-avenger role but for the wrong reasons, for fear of miscegenation. Quentin thus confronts a distorted double in the corpselike figure he finds at Sutpen's Hundred.

Once we acknowledge Irwin's legitimate claim that the psychic chains that bind Quentin to Sutpen are unbreakable (an acknowledgment that does not *require* that we recall *The Sound and the Fury*, but is enriched by it), we can better understand his narrative role in *Absalom, Absalom!* Quentin's personal feelings are bound up with his sense of history—his own history, the Sutpens', the South's—so that his narrative act places him inside those very processes of history which his own storytelling set in motion. Not only does he provide the crucial piece to the puzzle (Bon's black blood), he also reenacts a fourth version of the David story's essential triadic structure, engaging him in a conflict of "love" versus "authority" that is symbolically equivalent—but now occurs on a hermeneutic level—to the father-son-brother pattern we can find in I Samuel, II Samuel, and the Sutpen story.

The triadic structure works itself through the narrative level of the fiction's discourse in three ways. First, Quentin "rebels" against and finally usurps the "authority" that his father's narration (in chapters 2, 3, and 4) represents: the authority of heritage, information, and interpretation.[21] Second, his collaboration with his roommate Shreve joins him with a "brother" against the father. Third, the collaboration falters occasionally as Shreve replaces Mr. Compson as the antagonist of Quentin's hermeneutic quest.

Mr. Compson cannot explain Henry's murder of Bon, and derides its significance through his stance as skeptical fatalist. He knows that "Henry loved Bon," but he will not allow love to be a satisfying reason for what happened. Quentin, on the contrary, wants love to account for the mysterious murder: at the end of chapter 5 we are told he "cannot pass" the imaginary door that Rosa Coldfield's narration has just flung open on Henry and Judith, "speaking in short brief staccato sentences like slaps" about Bon's death. It is the brother-sister love and fratricide that he must come to grips with.

When Quentin and Shreve collaborate, Quentin is often frustrated and "outraged" because he has heard the story too often from his father, and yet is compelled to tell it again:

> *Am I going to have to hear it all again* he thought *I am going to have to hear it all over again I am already hearing it all over again I am listening to it all over again I shall have to never listen to anything else but this again forever so apparently not only a man never outlives his father but not even his friends and acquaintances do.* [p. 277]

Shreve "sounds just like father" as he at first sardonically questions the incredible tale, only to be caught up in Quentin's search for a romantic interpretation. By chapter 8 the identification of Quentin with Henry and Shreve with Bon is total, and buttresses the narrative version of the father-son-brother conflict: "four of them and then just two—Charles-Shreve and Quentin-Henry" (p. 334).

But the interpretation based on love does not quite triumph. Quentin himself provides the information about Bon's race which will reduce the romance to a racial murder. Shreve, in response, can revert to his cynicism, but Quentin cannot. His love for the South clashes with "authority"—with, that is, the truth about Sutpen. Quentin's frantic protests that he does not "hate the South" signals the dilemma—another version of the David story—he has participated in literally and "hermeneutically."

Ten:

The Words of Their Roaring: Roethke's Use of the Psalms of David

M. L. Lewandowska

*T*heodore Roethke's long *Praise to the End!* sequence is probably best approached through Roethke's own guide to perception: "We think by feeling. What is there to know?"[1] Indeed, it is one of the few long sequences in modern poetry that can be read aloud, dramatically, and erupt into meaning solely by means of its sounds and images. Yet, for those of us who must know as well as feel, the sequence is extremely complex and thus difficult to explicate. Though Roethke insisted he did not "rely on allusion," he suggested many of the ancestors for these poems and among the sources he first mentions is the Bible.[2] He notes one direct quotation from Job, but the more fertile source material is that of the Psalms, especially those traditionally attributed to David. Although their authorship is debated by modern biblical scholars,[3] these songs have for centuries formed part of the mythical and literary reality of that heroic figure, a man who knew triumph and despair, power and persecution, and who ordered his most intense experiences by shaping them with music. It is toward that persona, that popular image of the lyric side of David, that Roethke reaches in his own unique way. The Psalms contain dramatic emotional correlatives for Roethke's protagonist and their rhetoric and images provide the means by which the two voices can blend in their singing.

An immediate link between the Psalms and the *Praise* sequence is suggested by parallels in rhetorical patterns. A great many Psalms begin with invocation: "Hear the right, O Lord," "Plead my cause, O Lord," "Our Lord, Our Lord, how . . . ," "Help, Lord," "My God, my God . . ." The protagonist in Roethke's poems uses similar invocations, "God, give me a near" ("Where Knock is Open Wide"), but the object addressed soon becomes quite different: "Hear me, soft ears and roundy stones" ("I Need, I Need"), "Voice, come out of the silence" ("The Lost Son"). As the sequence progresses, Roethke invokes metaphoric spirits which come from dreams or the unconscious: "You child with a beast's heart," and "Mother of blue and many changes of hay," and "You tree beginning to know" ("Give Way, Ye Gates").

Another example, "Worm, be with me," is a perfect echo of David and the pattern found so often in the Psalms: the address follows, or is followed by, the imperative. "Bow down thine ear, O Lord" (86:1),

"Judge me, O Lord" (26:1), "Preserve me, O God" (16:1), "O Lord, rebuke me not" (6:1). There is much of the same in Roethke, and the pattern creates an immediacy, a rare sense of drama. "Delight me otherly, white spirit," he says in "I Cry Love! Love!" and "Lave me, ultimate waters" ("Praise to the End!"), or, in another mood, "Renew the light, lewd whisper " ("The Shape of Fire").

The pattern is used for both exhortation and supplication. When David wishes revenge on his enemies, the tone is tense and demanding: "Destroy, O Lord, and divide their tongues; for I have seen violence and strife in the city" (55:9); "Arise, O God, plead thine own cause: re-member how the foolish man reproacheth thee daily" (74:22). When he laments, the tone of the Psalmist is one of supplication: "Be merciful unto me, O God, be merciful unto me; for my soul trusteth in thee" (57:1), and, "O Lord, rebuke me not in thy wrath" (38:1). Roethke also uses exhortation and supplication, more and more often as the *Praise* sequence progresses and the poems gain intensity. For example, "Believe me, knot of a gristle, I bleed like a tree" ("Give Way, Ye Gates"), or "Mamma! Put on your dark hood:/It's a long way to somewhere else" ("Sensibility! O La!"). In the softer tones: "Sooth me, great groans of underneath,/I'm still waiting for a foot" ("O Lull Me, Lull Me"); "Voice, come out of the silence,/Say something,/Appear in the form of a spider" ("The Lost Son"). Or simply: "Father, forgive my hands" ("Praise to the End!").

To read this sequence aloud is to become acutely aware of how often Roethke uses these patterns, how strong the biblical echoes are. And we might well ask why a modern poet would choose such "archaic" forms in which to deliver his very contemporary song. An answer is immediately clear: the effect is incredibly powerful. Speech is formalized and inten-sified and all verbal excesses, all temptations to philosophize, are elimi-nated. The short, tight forms present the emotion with an immediacy that touches us far more quickly than any metaphor could. Indeed, there is a literalness in this language which is rare in modern poetry, and yet the mystery remains. When Roethke or David uses invocation, the ob-ject addressed, be it the Lord or a "white way to another grace" metamorphoses, quickens, as we are forced to focus on it so sharply. In marvelous contrast to the dramatic lines such rhetoric produces, the lyric passages in Roethke become all the more musical. Listen, for example, to the contrast in two stanzas from "I Cry Love! Love!":

> Mouse, mouse, come out of the ferns,
> And small mouths, stay your aimless cheeping:
> A lapful of apples sleeps in this grass.

That anguish of concreteness!—
The sun playing on loam,
And the first dust of spring listing over backlots,—
I proclaim once more a condition of joy.
Walk into the wind, willie!

. . . .

A fish jumps, shaking out flakes of moonlight.
A single wave starts lightly and easily shoreward,
Wrinkling between reeds in shallower water,
Lifting a few twigs and floating leaves,
Then washing up over small stones.

There is another rhetorical connection. Mitchell Dahood, in *The Anchor Bible*, mentions that "the dominating principle of . . . Biblical poetry is . . . that of balance or symmetry, the famous *parallelismus membrorum*." This balance shows most clearly in pairs of synonyms: rejoice-exault, foe-adversary, devoted ones-faithful ones.[4] But the translators of the Psalms usually provide a balance in rhythm or rhetorical structure also. Thus we hear David sing "I will praise thee, O Lord, among the people; and I will sing praises unto thee among nations" (108:3), and "All night I make my bed to swim; I water my couch with tears" (6:6).

Again, Roethke takes advantage of the Psalms pattern, especially as he moves from entreaty to celebration. The effect is incantatory. "You tree beginning to know,/You whisper of kidneys" ("Give Way, Ye Gates") leads to "In the high noon of thighs/In the springtime of stones" in the same poem. In "Praise to the End!" the youth urges: "Speak to me, frosty beard./Sing to me, sweet," and, having heard the singing, prays: "Wherefore O birds and small fish, surround me./Lave me, ultimate waters." The repetition sometimes intensifies, sometimes clarifies, as it does when the poet balances an abstraction in one line with something quite concrete in the next: "I could say hello to things;/I could talk to a snail" ("O Lull Me, Lull Me").

Such rhetorical similarities invite a more direct comparison of the two protagonists, but the relationship is subtle, oblique. The ancient heroic lad who faced Goliath with only a sling in his hand lends his voice to a modern child whose battles are all internal and whose giant is a ghost. This protagonist struggles slowly and painfully toward some understanding of his personal tragedy and his present condition. When Roethke reaches toward the David image, therefore, he seeks not a literal but an emotional reference for his sequence. The Psalms create for us David the singer, the poet-king who tells us of his great sorrows and his great joys, a lost son who seeks understanding and forgiveness from his Father. There is no lasting triumph for this singer; instead, the shifts of mood and tone and spiritual condition come through the powerful lyric poetry and we find ourselves alternately rejoicing or weeping as we read. And so we do for the lost son of this Roethke sequence, of which the poet says, ". . . at least you can see that the method is cyclic. I believe that to go forward as a spiritual man it is necessary first to go back. Any history of the psyche . . . is bound to be a succession of experiences, similar yet dissimilar. There is a perpetual slipping back, then a going forward; yet there is some 'progress.'"[5]

There are certain "facts" which become clear as the sequence progresses, however, that relate to those in the Psalms: events, themes, plot, and images. A central event is the death of the father, seen through the eyes of a very young child at the end of the first poem, "Where Knock is Open Wide." "He was all whitey bones/And skin like paper," the child says, sharing with us the traumatic event which colors all his perceptions. His instinctive emotional response to this event, "Kisses come back,/I said to Papa," establishes the intense feelings of loss, separation, and lack of love and communion which determine the child's response to all external sights and sounds. His rational response to the event, "God's somewhere else" and "Maybe God has a house./But not here," explains his sense of isolation and his continuing quest for a place or a time in which he can be enclosed by love.

The poems which follow in the sequence record that quest, described by John Wain as central to art, "an endeavor to break down the isolation of the human being . . . to bring us into a fruitful contact with *something.*" Wain goes on to say that Roethke is an "evangelical writer," that "the intensity of his lyric gift sprang directly from the hunger that raged at its center—a hunger for salvation."[6] Such hunger is also at the center of the Psalms, and the implied dramatic situation—of a passionate, lonely person with great emotional gifts and needs, awaiting and seeking reconciliation, union—could provide Roethke with just enough structure to shape his account of the restless psyche.

As Karl Malkoff notes, "the main themes of the entire sequence— birth and death, sexual guilt and confusion, separation from the father and God (the 'lost son' motif)—are explicitly considered in the first poem."[7] The themes are reiterated constantly, but always from a different point of reference and usually with some novel linguistic rendering. As the child grows up, he seeks solace from the mother, from associations with his past, from all elements of nature. His understanding comes after numerous descents to the "pit," a place familiar to David. To

Roethke, the pit symbolized the far reaches of a regressive journey, a place of mire, of primordial slime. These journeys are often accompanied by scenes of masturbation and consequent guilt, until the protagonist finally comes to realize a union with all things, which is sensual and ultimately sexual, for the regressive journeys have set off a fish-sperm association and, by extension, a fish-father-death-womb-water-life-light sequence. The young man's awareness of the cycle brings him, finally, to a sense of his own identity and to the understanding that "What the grave says,/The nest denies" ("Unfold! Unfold!"), that

> We met in a nest. Before I lived.
> The dark hair sighed.
> We never enter
> Alone.

> ["I Cry Love! Love!"]

The profound perception is reiterated in the final poem of the sequence, "O, Thou Opening, O":

> The dark has its own light.
> A son has many fathers.
> Stand by a slow stream:
> Hear the sigh of what is.

There is much more. The physical growth of the persona is accompanied by a parallel spiritual development; the union is mystical also. So too with the protagonist's aesthetic progress, for the child moves from a "small sing" in the first poem to a point where the grown persona cries in "Unfold! Unfold!":

> Sing, sing, you symbols! All simple creatures,
> All small shapes, willow-shy,
> In the obscure haze, sing!

As Roethke's sequence opens, the tie to David is immediate, albeit indirect. The title of the first poem, "Where Knock is Open Wide," is from Christopher Smart's *A Song to David.*[8] Smart asserts "Strong is the lion . . .," and in verse 77:

> But stronger still, in earth and air,
> And in the sea, the man of pray'r;
>   And far beneath the tide;
> And in the seat to faith assign'd,
> Where ask is have, where seek is find,
>   Where knock is open wide.

The unique diction renders Smart's version of Matthew 7:7, "Ask, and it shall be given you; seek, and ye shall find; knock, and it shall be opened unto you." Roethke's debt to Smart went beyond the use of that line for the title poem, for he also practices some of Smart's grammatical conversions and thus enlivens the rhetoric of the child protagonist. The title has implications which go beyond the original context, of course; it can have sexual connotations or even refer to the literal as well as the spiritual birth of a child. But the important thing, Smart's devotion to David, cannot be denied. His *Song* has 86 verses and he also did poetic "translations" of a number of the Psalms, many of which were set to music. Surely Roethke knew of this homage.

Interestingly, another poet whom Roethke cites was also especially devoted to David. Traherne was mentioned the first time Roethke spoke of "ancestors" for this sequence, and in a letter to John Crowe Ransom, Roethke mentions that it was Traherne's prose that most influenced him.[9] In the "Third Century" Traherne says,

> but as I read the Bible I was here and there Surprised with such Thoughts and found by Degrees that these Things had been written of before, not only in the Scriptures but in many of the fathers and that this was the Way of Communion with God in all Saints, as I saw Clearly in the Person of David. Me thoughts a New Light Darted in into all his Psalms, and finally spread abroad over the Whole Bible.[10]

After speaking of his new vision, Traherne wrote his own poem about David and then explicated some of the Psalms, giving contemporary exegetical associations. In *Thanksgivings*, Traherne echoes David strongly, seeing with David's poetic vision.

When Roethke was working on this sequence, with just a few of the poems done, he wrote to Kenneth Burke, "But God, I need a larger structure; something dramatic: an old story, —something. Most of the myths are a bore, to me. Wish I could talk to you about it."[11] His search quite obviously took him to the Bible, for his long poem, "The Lost Son" (first done for a collection with that title and later placed at the center of the *Praise to the End!* collection), contains a direct quote from Job 30:28, "Hath the rain a father?" And perhaps the words of Elihu to Job inspired the "plot" of the sequence: "His flesh shall be fresher than a child's: he shall return to the days of his youth" (Job 33:25), and "Lo, all these things worketh God oftentimes with man," "To bring back his soul from the pit, to be enlightened with the light of the living" (Job 33:29, 33:30).

The path from the pit to the places of light is long and difficult for adolescent or king, and Roethke fills his journey with an amazing number of images which are also found in the Psalms. Many of these images are traditional symbols, found often in our Western literature, but the Psalms provide an original emotional context for our poet. When Roethke echoes the pleading and anguish of David, he assimilates David's images and invests them with modern psychological symbolism. Thus the pit, for example, is not a place where evildoers are punished, as David saw it, but a dark, subconscious area in the psyche of the boy. It is a necessary stop on the journey of the spirit, and its exploration, however painful, can lead to union.

As we saw, it is easy to tie the theme of return to childhood to some later verses in Job, but the Psalms also open with images of generation and birth: "I will declare the decree: the Lord hath said unto me, Thou art my Son; this day have I begotten thee" (2:7). In the first poem of Roethke's sequence the child tells us: "Once upon a tree/I came across a time," and most critics agree that the time the child comes to is a prenatal time, a point at which he can ask "What's the time, papa-seed?" and when he can tell us "My father is a fish." The tree image is reiterated throughout the sequence, connected most often with sexual awakening or awareness. In an early poem he tells us, "When I stand, I'm almost a tree./Leaves, do you like me any?" ("Bring the Day!"), and later we hear "Believe me, knot of gristle, I bleed like a tree," and mention of "You tree beginning to know" ("Give Way, Ye Gates"). In "Sensibility! O La!"—in a time of joy—he notes, "I'm a twig to touch," and in "Unfold! Unfold!" he says "I stretched like a board, almost a tree." The idea of potency, caught by the image of a tree, is introduced early in the Psalms: "And he shall be like a tree planted by the rivers of water, that bringeth forth his fruit in his season; his leaf also shall not wither" (1:3). Later, with joy, David tells us "But I am like a green olive tree in the house of God" (52:8).

Roethke's choice of the voice of a child for these early poems is surely striking and appropriate, for David tells us, in Psalm 8:2, "Out of the mouth of babes and sucklings hast thou ordained strength because of thine enemies, that thou mightest still the enemy and the avenger." The enemy of Roethke's child is the ghost of the father, a ghost he must "still" and one that he finds in the wind or in the long grass. David's spiritual Father flies "on the wings of the wind" (18:10) and we know he spoke to Job from a whirlwind. Though Roethke's child comes to accept the wind later in the sequence, his first utterances are tense and compressed, showing the grammatical conversions Christopher Smart was so fond of. "How high is have?" he asks, "Have I come to always?" Or he sighs "Nowhere is out," or pleads "God, give me a near." This last clause has often been misprinted "God, give me an ear," an error which indicates just the kind of audible ambiguity Roethke intended. But it also echoes a number of David's cries: "Hear me when I call, O God" (4:1); "Give ear to my words, O Lord" (5:1); "Hear my prayer, O Lord, give ear to my supplication" (143:1); and finally, "Give ear to my voice, when I cry unto thee" (141:1).

At another moment the child begs, "Fish me out./Please." A strange image for a child to use, and difficult to explain, until we see that the Psalmist also used it: "He sent from above, he took me, he drew me out of many waters" (18:16), and again: "Deliver me out of the mire, and let me not sinketh: let me be delivered from them that hate me, and out of the deep waters" (69:14). David, in that same Psalm, moans "I am weary of my crying," a condition we noted before, in Psalm 6:6, where he tells us "I am weary with my groaning; all the night I make my bed to swim; I water my couch with my tears." In a beautiful contraction, intensified by the unusual rhetoric, the child tells us simply "My tears are tired."

In a regressive stage, Roethke's protagonist often mentions "a worm." In the first poem he cries, "A worm has a mouth./Who keeps me last?" and later: "It's still enough for the knock of a worm" ("Praise to the End!"). In "The Lost Son" is an early incantation, "Worm be with me./ This is my hard time." The image and the rhetoric belong to David also, in a song spoken from the same despairing mood: "But I am a worm, and no man; a reproach of men," and a few lines later: "Be not far from me; for trouble is near" (22:6 and 11). Similarly, and just as much a puzzle, is the boy's plea, "Bird, soft-sigh me hóme" ("The Lost Son"). The object of this address seems very general, until we note that David often cried to the Lord to hide him "in the shadow of thy wings," and connected the image with the soul in 11:1: "In the Lord put I my trust: how say ye to my soul, Flee as a bird to your mountain." For the modern poet, the image carries the weight of physical and spiritual connotations and is offered in terms as lovely. In "Give Way, Ye Gates": "Such music in a skin!/A bird sings in the bush of your bones." And in the poem just previous:

> O small bird awakening,
> Light as a hand among blossoms,
> Hardly any old angels are around any more.
>
> ["Bring the Day"]

Often repeated in Roethke's sequence is the image of bones, a reminder to readers of his very first book of published poems. There, in the first poem, "Open House," he presented himself as utterly open, "naked to the bone." This kind of nakedness meant total involvement for the persona, and the image grew in meaning in a later poem, "Cuttings, later," when the speaker felt in his veins and in his bones the "sucking and sobbing" of the plant beginning to root. In the most intimate moments of the *Praise* sequence, Roethke uses the bone imagery to express the intense emotions felt by the persona. At first the association is frightening: papa, dead, is "all whitey bones," and later he tells us "I dreamt I was all bones;/The dead slept in my sleeve." As he regresses in this poem, "Praise to the End!" he asks "Can the bones breathe? This grave has an ear." At the end of "The Lost Son," in a time of communion, he sees the light moving slowly "over the dry seed-crowns,/The beautiful surviving bones/Swinging in the wind," but just previous to this, in the heart of a "storm," he says "My veins are running nowhere. Do the bones cast out their fire?" At the very beginning of this poem, in fact, in a time of fear and longing for understanding, he tells us "I shook the softening chalk of my bones."

The Psalmist uses almost the same words in his expression of his fear and impotence: "I am poured out like water, and my bones are out of joint" (22:14). In fact, the bone imagery appears throughout the Psalms, just as it does in the Roethke sequence. In 31:10, David moans: "My strength faileth because of my iniquities, and my bones are consumed"; in 32:3, "When I kept silence, my bones waxed through my roaring all the day long"; and, in a joyful song, "He [the righteous] keepeth all his bones: not one of them is broken" (34:20). In the depths again: "Our bones are scattered at the grave's mouth" (141:7).

The most impressive connection of the sequence with the Psalms is probably the abundance of imagery associated with the pit or the mire. For Roethke, the journey backward was also a journey into the dark, the pit. He tells us: "Each poem . . . is complete in itself; yet each in a sense is a stage in a kind of struggle out of the slime, part of a slow spiritual process; an effort to be born, and later, to become something more."[12] When he wrote the "Lost Son" poem, before the others in this long sequence, he titled one of the sections "The Pit," indicating that "The Flight" of the previous section would take one to this dark interior. Any reading of the Psalms is bound to impress one with the same imagery, for the fear of the pit was omnipresent and we see that the wicked are always condemned to it (30:3, 30:9, 28:1, etc.). For David, the pit is dug by the offender, as we see in 7:15: "He made a pit, and digged it and is fallen into the ditch which he made." We feel his joy in his deliverance in 49:2: "He brought me up also out of the horrible pit, out of the miry clay, and set my feet upon a rock." When Roethke's protagonist comes to understanding, it is in reconciliation with the images of the pit, the "miry clay," as well as all else. He tells us in "Unfold! Unfold!": "I was far back, farther than anybody else," and describes how far that was:

> I was privy to oily fungus and the algae of standing waters;
> Honored, on my return, by the ancient fellowship of rotten stems.

Those images announce the move toward joy and light, a place both singers knew very well. In later poems Roethke often uses images of dancing to exclaim his joy; at one point he tells us "And everything comes to One,/As we dance on, dance on, dance on" ("Once More, The Round"). But the steps of that dance start here, in the final parts of this sequence, when his protagonist "danced in a simple wood." David also danced as he spoke to the Lord, "Thou has turned for me my mourning into dancing" (30:11). And the joy extends into new songs, too, as we see when David announces his faith in the Lord: "And now shall mine head be lifted up above mine enemies round about me: therefore will I offer in his tabernacle sacrifices of joy; I will sing, yea, I will sing praises unto the Lord" (22:7). In 40:3 we see that he has been brought up out of the pit, and immediately he says: "And he hath put a new song in my mouth." Again, in 144:9, the same impulse: "I will sing a new song unto thee, O God." For Roethke's protagonist the awakening brings a new awareness:

> I'm more than when I was born;
> I could say hello to things;
> I could talk to a snail;
> I see what sings!
> What sings!

> ["O Lull Me, Lull Me"]

In the final poem of the sequence he tells us "I've crept from a cry," "I sing the green, and things to come,/I'm king of another condition,/So alive I could die!" ("O, Thou Opening, O").

Such joy, such exaltation, is possible for all men, as David sees them in 103:15: "As for man, his days are as grass: as a flower of the field, so he flourisheth"; and it extends to all creation, too, for we see in Psalm 65 that God touches all things on earth and in the heavens, so that "the pastures are clothed with flocks; the valleys also are covered over with corn; they shout for joy, they also sing" (65:13). The realization comes also for the persona of Roethke's sequence, sometimes in the wild joy we have seen above, sometimes in the same image of the field which emanates life. The blessings were there, around him all the time, but the knowledge of such glory was hard to accept. In the first poem the child cried "Maybe God has a house./But not here." At the end of the sequence he sees

> A house for wisdom: a field for revelation.
> Speak to the stones, and the stars answer.
> At first the visible obscures:
> Go where the light is.

["Unfold! Unfold!"]

Theodore Roethke's work remains largely untouched by this investigation. The *Praise* sequence has many fathers, and is enormously rich in other themes and images, yet Roethke knew the wealth the Psalms held and was not afraid to sing with David's voice when he needed it. He acknowledged his debt to all his "ancestors" when he said: "In their harsh thickets/The dead thrash./They help." I believe he was thinking of David when he wrote

> See what the sweet harp says.
> Should a song break a sleep?

["O, Thou Opening, O"]

He answered affirmatively, awaking the harpist, so they could sing together.

Eleven

Saul and David in the Early Poetry of Yehuda Amichai

Noam Flinker

*I*n a series of poems first published in 1958,[1] a modern Israeli poet, Yehuda Amichai, revised the traditional stories of Saul and David to make these public, national heroes figures in the private world of an introspective speaker. His myths contrast markedly to the popular folk traditions about Saul and David that abound in the Israeli cultural landscape, extending from names of streets and hotels to the many folk songs and associated dances that sound the praises of these biblical heroes. Amichai focuses on their individual human qualities, while making only passing reference to the various traditions about Saul and David that the reader must keep in mind. The poems articulate a complex attitude toward the past by means of ironic tensions that neither embrace nor entirely reject the traditional details to which they allude.

"King Saul & I," "Young David," and "Mt. Zion" preserve the original historical continuity of selected biblical details from poem to poem, but the sequence presents a modernized view of them and thus elicits a contemporary identification with the ancient past. The David poem, at the center of the sequence, forms its focus. The longer Saul poem sets up a series of comparisons implicitly applicable to the Davidic focus. Young David's perceptions qualify those of "King Saul & I," just as they hover in the background of "Mt Zion." All the poems sound echoes in the author's mind. Together they are a poetic portrait of an inner landscape.

Amichai's sequence begins with a comparison between Saul and a contemporary first-person speaker ("King Saul & I"). The speaker uses Saul's career as a means of measuring and understanding himself. In the first stanza the speaker compares himself to Saul through three consecutive images, followed by a statement of their brotherly connection:

> They gave him a finger, but he took the whole hand
> They gave me the whole hand: I didn't even take the little finger.
>
> While my heart
> Was weightlifting its first feelings
> He rehearsed the tearing of oxen.
>
> My pulse-beats were like
> Drips from a tap
> His pulse-beats
> Pounded like hammers on a new building.
>
> He was my big brother
> I got his used clothes.[2]

Amichai's initial presentation of Saul contrasts with the biblical story where the future king's shy, retiring personality has him hiding "himself among the stuff" when Samuel wanted to make him king.[3] The modern poet stresses Saul's strength in the images which move from the physical power associated with "hand," to a gymnastic workout (or "rehearsal" in this translation), and finally to pulsebeats. The "tearing of oxen" appears as an example of apparently random violence. The biblical context for this particular detail is simply ignored in the poem.[4] In general, Saul's appearance in the first stanza projects a sense of power with ambition, aggression, and seething in qualified violence.

The contemporary first-person speaker contrasts himself pointedly with Saul. Although offered an entire hand, he refuses even a little finger. In the gym, he works out his primal feelings while his blood pressure remains low. But while these lines seem to suggest the total opposition between Saul and the speaker, the stanza concludes by making them brothers. The reader is left puzzled about the nature of those "used clothes." Implicit is a sense of connection with Saul's power and activity. If these qualities are his clothes, perhaps their being "used" conveys a lessening in the violence underlying his taking "the whole hand," or "tearing of oxen," or pounding "like hammers on a new building," but the basic nature of Saul's power and activity is not changed by use. The stanza thus ends with a contradictory sense of conflict and harmony between King Saul and "I."

Stanza two is entirely devoted to Saul. Here the seething violence of the first stanza is seen under greater control:

> His head, like a compass, will always bring him
> To the sure north of his future.
>
> His heart is set, like an alarm clock
> For the hour of his reign.
> When everyone's asleep, he will cry out
> Until all the quarries are hoarse.
> Nobody will stop him!
>
> Only the asses bare their yellow teeth
> At the end.

Saul's head is attuned to the future, much as the compass is in accord with the earth's magnetic field. There is something mechanical about Saul's attitude to the world, but with it comes the ability to deal with the realistic political situation in a firm, purposeful way. The next image, more mechanical still, compares Saul's heart to an alarm clock. There is not an immediate cosmic connection here between device and nature, such as that between compass and earth; clocks artificially measure time while compasses point direction by conforming to natural forces. Like an alarm clock, Saul has set his heart on being king, so that at the right time he can cry out to awaken the nation. Almost like God, who occasionally threatens to do something "at which both the ears of every one that heareth it shall tingle" (I Samuel 3:11), Saul's shouting, by echoing back and forth, makes the quarries hoarse. This sort of power and drive is not to be stopped. Nevertheless, the stanza concludes with a proleptic hint of Saul's tragic end. When the asses[5] "bare their yellow teeth" at the end of his path, Saul's control over fate and destiny will be gone. The lost asses, which once brought Saul to Samuel, become, in Amichai's poem, a reminder of the final destruction of a formerly exalted leader.

Stanza three returns to Saul's rise to power, after a few apparent digressions into the speaker's present:

> Dead prophets turned time-wheels
> When he went out searching for asses
> Which I, now, have found.
> But I don't know how to handle them.
> They kick me.
>
> I was raised with the straw,
> I fell with heavy seeds.
> But he breathed the winds of his histories.
> He was anointed with the royal oil
> As with the wrestler's grease.
> He battled with olive-trees
> Forcing them to kneel.
> Roots bulged on the earth's foreheads
> With the strain.
> The prophets escaped from the arena;
> Only God remained, counting:
> Seven . . . eight . . . nine . . . ten . . .
> The people, from his shoulders downwards, rejoiced.
> Not a man stood up.
> He had won.

The first-person references at the outset of the stanza are central to the poem, since they remind the reader of the relation between Saul's biblical past and the reality of contemporary existence. This relation is quite complicated and is presented here in terms of biblical images that unexpectedly reappear in a modern Israeli landscape. Like so many archaeological artifacts, the "asses," the "straw," and the "seeds" present an ambivalent attitude toward the past.

The lost asses are first mentioned in the Bible when Saul's father sends him to look for them (I Samuel 9:3). Later, Samuel predicts that two men will meet Saul and tell him: "The asses which thou wentest to seek are found" (10:2). In the previous stanza of the poem, the asses are a premonition of Saul's failure, and here he has "time-wheels" bring them to the contemporary speaker. The herd has had offspring. The inability of the speaker to handle them may at first appear as an indication of contemporary ineptitude in contrast to a past heroic age; yet, at the end of his path, Saul himself does not seem to be much more adept at handling the asses than the modern speaker, who gets kicked.

At this point Amichai adds another kind of biblical image in order to balance the comparison. "Straw" and "heavy seeds" are biblical metaphors, charged with traditional meaning and values. Separating wheat from chaff by winnowing on a hill takes on spiritual significance in Isaiah: "They shall flee far off, and shall be chased as the chaff of the mountains before the wind, and like a rolling thing before the whirlwind" (17:13). For the prophet, God's enemies are likened to the worthless chaff (the same Hebrew word that is translated "straw" in the poem) that is blown to the winds. The metaphor implies that the speaker's inability to deal with the kicking asses is not as derogatory as first appeared. Having found the asses, he is raised with the chaff but falls with the wheat, while Saul, "like the portion of them that spoil us, and the lot of them that rob us" (Isaiah 17:14), is blown away. On one level, Amichai reverses the biblical metaphor, with falling as negative and blowing[6] in the "winds of his histories" as positive, but on another level it is Saul who is found wanting in this traditional trope for distinguishing the good from the worthless. Thus, before describing Saul's rise to power, Amichai compares him with the modern speaker in rather ambivalent terms that present them almost as equals, with Saul's superiority less clear after the reversal of the wheat-chaff image.

The rest of the stanza treats Saul's anointment in images that recall the physical power and violence of stanza one. Anointment oil, probably an olive product, is associated with wrestler's grease ("oil" in Hebrew), which leads to a wrestling match with olives. Saul forces the olive trees to bow down, but then his opponent, Proteus-like, seems to change shape. The strain of the struggle, seen on the earth's forehead, is on the one hand a realistic impression of the soil of an olive grove, where the thick roots of the trees bulge within the soil much like blood vessels on a forehead. On a more metaphorical level, this struggle expands Saul's conflict into a Herculean wrestling match with the Antaeus-like olive grove, taking on some of the characteristics of a mythic personification of nature. With the flight of all the referees but God (the Hebrew *shoftim,* rendered "prophets" in the translation, literally means "judges" and is used for "referee" in contemporary sports events), the struggle is faintly reminiscent of Jacob's wrestling with the angel (Genesis 32). Although his victory is more complete than Jacob's, the rejoicing of the inferior crowds[7] and the absence of a real opponent places Saul in a less heroic light. He is victorious, but it remains unclear just whom he has defeated.

The fourth stanza places all this in a contemporary perspective. Saul's kingdom, justice, and ultimate historical verdict are juxtaposed against the day-to-day weariness of the speaker:

> I am tired,
> My bed is my kingdom.
>
> My sleep is just
> My dream is my verdict.
>
> I hung my clothes on a chair
> For tomorrow.
>
> He hung his kingdom
> In a frame of golden wrath
> On the sky's wall.
>
> My arms are short, like string too short
> To tie a parcel.
>
> His arms are like the chains in a harbour
> For cargo to be carried across time.
>
> He is a dead king.
> I am a tired man.

Here it is clear that Saul's energy and violence in the first stanza were not included in the "used clothes." Nevertheless, the tired speaker is not dead, like Saul. Saul's hanging "his kingdom/In a frame of golden wrath/On the sky's wall," as opposed to the Philistines, who "fastened his body to the wall of Beth-Shan" (I Samuel 31:10), is Amichai's version of the end first intimated by the bared yellow teeth of the asses. He thus avoids the interests of an earlier poet, Shaul Tchernichovsky, who interpreted Saul's last moments on Mt. Gilboa in heroic, nationalistic tones.[8] Saul's glory is manifest in Amichai's image, but it is juxtaposed against the speaker's prosaic hanging of clothes on a chair. Amichai's interest here is primarily in the speaker. Saul's final act is envisioned with ambiguous grandeur (whose wrath—Saul's? God's? David's?), but with a definite tone of finality. "He is a dead king" whose arms reach out across time to the tired speaker. The latter, despite his weariness and short arms, is in a position to wear his older brother's used clothes, and by using the harbor chains to lengthen the string, can participate in carrying the cargo of Saul's history into his own life.

"King Saul & I" thus articulates a view of biblical myth that makes a connection with contemporary consciousness possible. Despite his power, control of destiny, and initial victories, Saul was reduced to windblown chaff, at least in his final defeat, while the weary contemporary speaker, heavy like the wheat, is still capable of germination. The tired speaker, asleep and dreaming on his bed, sees himself as reliving, in miniature, Saul's regal career. The justice of the modern kingdom is achieved as a dream that acts as an imaginative leap beyond the realism of clothing and chains. Brotherly connection with Saul provides the speaker inspiration for imaginative activity that enlarges the significance of contemporary daily existence.

Once Amichai has reduced Saul's heroic stature to terms that make him relevant to his contemporary speaker, he moves on to "Young David," the giant killer, in a poem that probes the conquering hero's feelings upon returning to Saul's army with Goliath's head:

> David came back to the boys
> (Cheers still in his ears)
> And the noisy ones in armor
> Were terribly mature.
>
> They slapped him on the back, they laughed,
> Hoarse, and one cursed and a couple
> Spat. But David was lonely and felt,
> For the first time, that there were no more Davids.
>
> And suddenly he didn't know what to do with
> Goliath's head, he'd forgotten it, still
> Held by the curls.
>
> It was heavy. Who needed it, now?
> And like the birds of blood, flying far, he
> No longer heard the crowd roar.[9]

The octave describes David's return in colloquial language that imitates the talk of the young soldiers and then suddenly registers the hero's loneliness and sense of superiority. The sestet presents David as stunned before the roaring crowd, uncomfortably aware of the pointlessness of carrying his enemy's head. His loneliness at the conclusion of the octave is matched by the ambiguity of the final line of the sestet, where it is unclear in the Hebrew whether it is David or Goliath who, like the birds of prey, doesn't hear the crowd. In a sense, David is like his victim for an instant; and he is like Saul before the inferior crowd that rejoiced in their king's victory. The common people are merely able to shout, whereas

their heroic kings feel both their own superiority and the near absurdity
of the crowd's raucous noise.

There was a disparity in Saul's poem between the images of glory
attendant on his rise to power and the ironic retrospective on the end of
his story — "only the asses bare their yellow teeth/At the end" — which
the modern Israeli, knowing the whole story of Saul and the subsequent
history of his own Israel, cannot escape: "He is a dead king./I am a tired
man." David thus stands in contrast to both Saul and the speaker. In his
poem, we glance into his mind to see that he, unlike Saul, is aware of the
distance between the popular response to his dead and the real, almost
embarrassing significance; it's just a dead head in his hand. And unlike
the speaker, David was truly great. His irony was the irony of the strong
man who could see in his hands the little (if real) value of real, brave
deeds. The speaker's arms, we recall, "are short, like string too short/To
tie a parcel." The irony that David commands is the center of the
sequence.

The crowd's noise shifts to confusion with the beginning of "Mt.
Zion," the final poem of the sequence:

> As confusion tosses things up
> Suddenly, facing the closed wall,
> The psalms, the stairs, the cemetery stones
> And the barbed wire and the dark cypresses—they also
>
> Knew everything, but said nothing as
> They shot wailing rounds from
> Their prayer posts. And then the rams' horns
> Broke the silence past
>
> Repair. The wall stood, only the wall,
> And monks sang in Mary's Church,
> And the mosque tower pointed into
>
> The sky until it got cut off.
> But they covered their David with warm carpets
> Even though he wasn't there.

The confusion is everywhere. The Jewish worship with psalms,
weeping, and rams' horns is mixed with the chanting of the Christian
monks and the palpable silence of the Moslem mosque. The ungrounded
spiritualities weave in and out of the windings of wire and patterns of
bullets, which their conflict with one another somewhat resembles. The
cacophony of sound and purpose reaches a climax as the mosque tower is
"cut off" in the sky. This failure to reach heaven seems characteristic of
the organized efforts of all three religions at the site. The final sentence
strikes a blow at the national myth that made David's supposed tomb

into a Jewish and Israeli holy place, charged with representing the national ethos. His absence adds a degree of absurdity to the confusion.

Some things to make one hopeful do survive, however. There is an implicit longing for the time when the old city was open. And if David is gone and the three religions similarly ignore this in their worship, still there is among them a common groping toward some more universal myth. (All three shrines are actually on Mt. Zion.)[10] The poem offers no plan for composing such a myth, but its tone perhaps softens the denial of David's presence into an expression of longing and loss.[11] This might be the necessary preamble to an agreed upon opening of hearts and gates in the future, when David's clear understanding of the precise worth of things might be more universally enjoyed.

Amichai's sequence is primarily concerned with the contemporary relevance of biblical heroes such as Saul and David. His version of the biblical myth focuses attention on a few highly selected details in order to stress the ways in which Saul and David can help direct present thinking. In this way, in T. S. Eliot's terms, Amichai has "the past . . . altered by the present as much as the present is directed by the past."[12] The biblical materials are reshaped, with Saul as ambivalent hero against whose reduced public personality a private modern can view his own inner life. David's more extended popular reputation is reviewed through the musings of a quiet introvert who presents a very different image than the mythic king of Jewish tradition. Paradoxically, David's absence at the conclusion of the sequence helps to register a longing for Old Jerusalem, the city of David. Amichai's treatment of these biblical heroes reduces their traditional stature somewhat, to refashion a new, more acceptable view that can lend meaning and spiritual substance to the emptiness of daily existence. Saul, young David, and Mt. Zion must all be purged of certain traditions that blur their contemporary relevance. Then the alienated Israeli can attempt to see himself, both individually and collectively, in terms of the new tradition, which is itself a collage of ambivalently mixed details and feelings.

Notes

Introduction:
Transformations of the Myth of David

1. Murray Roston, *Biblical Drama in England* (Evanston, Ill.: Northwestern University Press, 1968), p. 254.

2. Elmer Blistein, Introduction to *David and Bersabe*, in *The Dramatic Works of George Peele* (New Haven: Yale University Press, 1970), p. 166.

3. Each age in its turn has taken part of the David story to itself, reinterpreting one or more incidents that it finds especially significant, or coming to the myth with the intellectual tools available only to that age. A study of the David myth in Western literature is, then, a survey of developing attitudes toward the Bible as literature, as well as a study of each age's elaboration upon one piece of the very complex David mosaic.

In tracing the various Davidic traditions, the following essays, containing bibliographies or making extensive mention of primary works on David, have proved helpful: J. M. McBryde, "A Study of Cowley's *Davideis*," *JEGP* 2(1899), esp. 469-76; R. F. Jones, "The Originality of *Absalom and Achitophel*," *MLN* 46(1931), 211-18; Inga-Stina Ewbank, "The House of David in Renaissance Drama: A Comparative Study," *Renaissance Drama* 8(1965), 3-40; Roston, *Biblical Drama in England*, *passim*; and Blistein, "Introduction," esp. 165-76.

4. In the article listed above and in *"The Love of King David and Fair Bethsabe:* A Note on George Peele's Biblical Drama," *English Studies* 39(1958), 57-62, Ewbank (Inga-Stina Ekeblad) analyzes both the dramatic and the Ovidian literature surrounding David's affair with Bathsheba. Simon A. Vosters has dedicated a lengthy chapter to David in Spanish Golden Age literature in *Lope de Vega y la Tradición occidental* (Madrid: Editorial Castalia, 1977).

5. Roston comments on the significance of Dryden's irreverence in terms of changing attitudes toward the Bible as literature (pp. 177-78). Interestingly enough, Chaucer's Pandarus, who gives his name in English to those who serve as a go-between in a love intrigue or cater to the sensual weaknesses of others, is probably a relation to a minor character in the David story: Jonadab, the "very shrewd man" who arranges Amnon's violation of Tamar (II Samuel 13). Cf. D. W. Robertson Jr., *A Preface to Chaucer* (Princeton: Princeton University Press, 1962), p. 479.

6. Moira Dearnley provides a neat summary of this controversy in chapter 7, *The Poetry of Christopher Smart* (London: Routledge and Kegan Paul, 1968). The battle between David's detractors and supporters is described in fuller detail by Arthur Sherbo in *Christopher Smart: Scholar of the Universe* (East Lansing: Michigan State University Press, 1967). Criticism of David's moral character was made as recently as 1933, by J. M.

P. Smith, in his inaugural address to a society of biblical scholars, which appeared as "The Character of David," *Journal of Biblical Literature* 52(1933), 1-11.

7. Barbard K. Lewalski, *Milton's Brief Epic: The Genre, Meaning, and Art of "Paradise Regained"* (Providence: Brown University Press, 1966), pp. 41, 80.

8. In describing Harapha, Milton echoes the biblical description of Goliath. Cf. John M. Steadman, *Milton's Epic Characters* (Chapel Hill: North Carolina University Press, 1968), pp. 185-93.

9. David has always been a popular subject in art. In *The House of David* (New York: Dutton, 1971), Jerry M. Landau reproduces dozens of art works, primarily medieval and Renaissance baroque, which interpret his story. Cf. also the entry under "David" in James Hall, *Dictionary of Subjects and Symbols in Art* (New York: Harper and Row, 1974), pp. 92-93; Louis Réau, *Iconographie de l'art chrétien* (Paris: Presses Universitaires de France, 1956); II, pt. I, 254-86; and for a study of continued representations of a single scene from the story, Elisabeth Kunoth-Leifels, *Uber die Darstellungen der "Bathseba im Bade"* (Essen, 1962).

10. In later ages David's slaying of Goliath becomes an especially appropriate and even apocalyptic vehicle for dramatizing a weak yet zealous minority's overthrow of a brutal and oppressive majority. Such diverse writers as nineteenth-century slave Phillis Wheatley, in "Goliath of Gath," and contemporary popular novelist Ann Fairbairn, in *Five Smooth Stones*, have used it, for example, in speaking of the American black's struggle for freedom and social equality.

11. H. C. McCusker points to structural parallels between Bale's play and William Tyndale's *Obedience of a Christian Man* that concern David in *John Bale: Dramatist and Antiquary* (New York: Books for Libraries Press, 1971), pp. 91-93. A near contemporary of Bale was Thomas Watson, whose use of the David story is examined by John Hazel Smith in *A Humanist's "Trew Imitation": Thomas Watson's ABSALOM* (Urbana: University of Illinois Press, 1964).

12. I am grateful to Noam Flinker for notes on Milton and Salmasius' use of Davidic references in their Latin Defenses in the 1650s. As he has pointed out to me, Merritt Y. Hughes' introduction and annotations of volume 3 of *Complete Prose Works of John Milton* (New Haven: Yale University Press, 1962) contain excellent summaries of the use made of David in the pamphlet duels between Royalists and Puritans.

13. George deF. Lord, "'Absalom and Achitophel' and Dryden's Political Cosmos," in *Writers and Their Background: John Dryden*, ed. Earl Miner (Athens: Ohio University Press, 1972), pp. 156, 177. In addition to Lord, one might consult the following on Dryden's use of the David myth: Leon Guilhamet, "Dryden's Debasement of Scripture in *Absalom and Achitophel*," *SEL* 9(1969), 395-413; Jones, "The Originality of *Absalom and Achitophel*"; George R. Levine, "Dryden's 'Inarticulate Posey': Music and the Davidic King in *Absalom and Achitophel*," *ECS* 1(1968), 291-312; and Stephen N. Zwicker, *Dryden's Political Poetry: The Typology of King and Nation* (Providence: Brown University Press, 1972), pp. 83-101. Joseph A. Mazzeo treats "Cromwell as Davidic King" in his *Renaissance and Seventeenth Century Studies* (New York: Columbia University Press, 1964), pp. 183-208.

14. Petrarch interprets his allegory in a letter to his brother (*De Familiari*, X.4), which is cited by Lewalski in *Milton's Brief Epic*, pp. 53-54.

15. Thomas Lodge, "Defence of Poetry, Music, and Stage Plays," in *Elizabethan Critical Essays*, ed. G. G. Smith (Oxford, 1904), 1:71. Sir Philip Sidney's *Apologie*, Thomas Becom's *Davids Harpe ful of moost delectable armony* (1542), and John Milton's *Reason of Church-Government* contain similar references.

16. Israel Baroway, "'The Lyre of David': A Further Study of Renaissance Interpretations of a Biblical Form," *ELH* 8(1941), 119-42. The passage quoted is on p. 122.

17. Much has been written on the influence of Wyatt and Smart on Browning. See, in particular, James McPeek, "The Shaping of *Saul*," *JEGP* 44(1945), 360-66; and Claude W. Sumerlin, "Christopher Smart's *A Song to David*: Its Influence on Robert Browning," *Costerus* 2(1972), 185-96.

18. Jeffrey Meyers says that Lawrence's "alternative search for satisfying relationships between men" is "modelled on the biblical friendship of David and Jonathan and not, as in works by practising and more reticent homosexuals, on the Greek ideal of male love" ("D. H. Lawrence and Homosexuality," in *D. H. Lawrence: Novelist, Poet, Prophet*, ed. Stephen Spender [New York: Harper and Row, 1973], pp. 135-46). The quote is on p. 135. For a discussion of the homosexual elements of the original story, see Tom Horner, *Jonathan Loved David: Homosexuality in Biblical Times* (Philadelphia: Westminster Press, 1978).

19. In a letter to the editors, Stephen M. Ross suggests that Baldwin's fascination with a father-son-brother triangle, as expressed in certain of his works before 1960, possibly derives from his interest in the David story.

20. Thomas Hardy did much the same for nineteenth-century England in *The Mayor of Casterbridge*. See Julian Moynahan, "*The Mayor of Casterbridge* and the Old Testament's First Book of Samuel: A Study of Some Literary Relationships," *PMLA* 71(1956), 118-30.

21. Frank Kermode, "A Modern Way with the Classic," *New Literary History* 5(1974), 418.

One:
Discriminations against David's Tragedy

1. The original division of the Hebrew texts, upon which the present division is based, was made to prevent the work from being too large for binding. The work is a unified whole. See Hans Wilhelm Hertzbert, *I and II Samuel: A Commentary*, trans. J. S. Bowden (London: SCM Press, 1974), the introduction.

For a complementary approach to the David story see Kenneth R. R. Gros Louis, "The Difficulty of Ruling Well: King David of Israel," *Semeia*, 8(1977), 15-33. Where this essay traces the doubleness of David's character as his tragic flaw, Gros Louis's remarkably comprehensive but compact essay traces "the complex relationship between moral individual order and political community order" (p. 15). He establishes a running analogy between David and Prince Hal of *Henry V* by Shakespeare: "As Prince Hal recognized, and painfully accepted when he banished Falstaff from his sight, a leader also has personal and private desires which, if unchecked, if not banished, can damage the public welfare he has been asked to maintain. . . . David can overcome and learn from the machinations of Saul, as Prince Hal moves beyond the guilt and paranoia of his father; he can put up with Joab, his blunt Hotspur; but he cannot, in the end, abandon entirely his heart's ease — he is unable to suppress his personal desire for Bathsheba, he is unable to carry out his public duty towards Absalom; he cannot, as does Prince Hal, banish Falstaff" (pp. 25,33).

2. Jean Daniélou in *Sacramentum Futuri* (Paris, 1950) and Henri de Lubac in *Exégèse Médiévale* (Aubier, 1959) make the point that Hebraic and Christian typological interpretations take their inspiration from texts such as this one: a primary text that is conscious of the typical quality of their characters and history. See also the discussion in Aage Bentzen, *King and Messiah*, ed. G. W. Anderson (Oxford: Basil Blackwell, 1970), pp. 110-11, n. 8.

3. The translation is that of S. Goldman in *Samuel: Hebrew Text and English Translation* (London: Soncino Press, 1959).

4. Hertzberg postulates on the evidence of this line that they did (p. 25).

5. At the height of David's power there appears the doctrine that the Lord had chosen David and his descendants to reign over Israel to the end of time (II Samuel 7) and had given him dominion over alien peoples (II Samuel 22, Psalm 18:44-51, and Psalm 2). The belief seems to be that David's present position will be inherited by an endless chain of succeeding links in his dynasty. After the collapse of David's empire, the hope remained that his house would rise again (Amos 9:11-12, Isaiah 11:10, Hosea 3:5; see also the discussion of how post-exilic editors reshaped the David story in light of this hope, n. 6). I Isaiah shifts the emphasis from the perpetuity of the dynasty to the qualities of the future king; the foundation of his throne will be justice (9:1-6, 16:4-5). II Isaiah reflects the doctrine that the future Messiah would suffer to bring justice about (52ff.). Bentzen traces the extra-biblical development of the image of the Messiah (see esp. pp. 73 ff.): "The fall of history did not confirm the faith . . . that Israel's happiness was secured through the presence of the anointed of Yahweh. The fall of both Israelite kingdoms in 721 and 587 necessarily made this discrepancy between faith and facts very keenly felt. Such is the background of the origin of Eschatology. Deutero-Isaiah worked in the faith and expectation of a 'new' world-age with a new myth." Christian exegetes build on this faith in their own way. See the discussion below.

6. One modern scholarly opinion is that the texts were successfully edited to convey this view. Wilhelm Hertzberg writes:

> The personal feelings and theological attitude of the final compiler are in closer sympathy with that part of the . . . tradition which regarded the development from Samuel to Saul as a mistaken one, even if it was permitted by Yahweh. One of the most attractive features of these texts is the way we can see how the friendly disposition towards the first king has not been eliminated, but has been overlaid by this different approach.
>
> David, on the other hand, is to the final compiler and the tradition which he uses, the man "with whom" Yahweh is, foreordained and specially chosen, the man whom II Samuel 7, which marks a highpoint in the whole narrative, sees arranged in messianic splendor [p. 20].

A bit later, he says of Samuel, Saul, and David that "each in his own way are [sic] forerunners and heralds of the real King," revealing his predisposition to see the prophetic point of view on the story, like generations of biblical exegetes before him, as decisive.

Hertzberg takes note of the episodes in the story where it seems that David's own initiative, or fate, or hazard, or miscalculation affects the outcome of events, only to point out the accompanying narrative assertions that God had given assent to whatever happened (I Samuel 2:1, 5:19, 23; II Samuel 8:6, 14). But he sees no narrative irony here. At the conclusion of his work he reiterates his conviction that chapter 7 in II Samuel (Nathan's messianic prophecy) "is the climax of this part and indeed of the book as a whole. The work of David is crowned by the promise which points towards the Messianic hope."

Another modern commentary of Samuel (R. A. Carlson, *David the Chosen King*, trans. Eric J. Sharpe and Stanley Rudman [Uppsala, 1964]) is more aware of the epic qualities of the David story. It can be read as the rise and fall of an earthly king whose very strengths of compassion and spontaneity win him a kingdom and finally trip him up. He rises and falls by principles of epic composition. But Carlson also sees the Deuteronomist editors (not a single compiler, as Hertzberg has it) subjugating this tragic pattern to the ancient literary-moral pattern of blessing-curse-blessing that syncopates the stories of Joshua and Judges. In this pattern, when the leaders and people follow God they receive a blessing, *be-ra-kah*—as David did from his anointing by Samuel to his ascending the throne of the consolidated kingdoms. When they fail to follow God, they receive a curse, *qe-la-bah*—as David did when he killed Uriah and lay with Bathsheba. To earn the blessing again, the people—David—must acknowledge the sin, suffer its consequences, and make atonement. In a concluding paragraph, Carlson wavers back and forth between stressing the tragic and providential rhythms of the story, until finally deciding the story is providential:

> The author of the succession story maintains a critical attitude towards the legitimate king, David, throughout. This is true, of course, most of all in the matter of Bathsheba and Uriah. But even David's treatment of Amnon, and later of Absalom, is portrayed in such a way that we can and are meant to see that here David has brought things from bad to worse, partly by excessive weakness, partly by his severity. Even his actions after the death of Absalom, his measures with Judah and Israel and his decisions about Amasa and Joab have serious and damaging consequences. There is a remarkable cogency in the course of events. K. Leimbach's title for chapters 11-20, "David's sin and its consequences" is right in so far as everything is, in fact, under the curse of the evil action which must go on to produce more and more evil actions. On the other hand we see the judicial righteousness which binds together guilt and punishment in a remarkable way. The sentence put in the mouth of Nathan, that the sword will never more depart from David's house, has a terrifying effect. *On the other hand, however, it is clear that the continuance of David's kingdom depends not on any ability of the king, but on the grace of the Lord who stands by his promise.* Therefore in these chapters David is humanly and in fact at his greatest when his external circumstances are at their worst, in his flight from Jerusalem. For the grace of God most frequently comes at the time of man's humiliation. Such considerations reveal that these narratives, too, are held together by the recognition that the Lord is directing events even in the smallest detail. [p. 378; emphasis added]

7. Leonhard Rost in *Die Uberlieferung von der Thronnachfolge Davids* (1926) develops a now widely accepted view that II Samuel 9-20 serves a utilitarian intent—to answer the question "who will occupy the throne of David" by ruling out those in line of succession who didn't. His slant obscures the possibility that part of the narrative intention could have been as well to expose to view the horrible consequences of David's tragic character.

On this point see David M. Gunn, "David and the Gift of the Kingdom," *Semeia*, 3(1976), 14-45. Gunn criticizes Rost for moving "our focus away from the primary object of interest, David, to minor characters [with] no literary presence whatsoever. This is a story about David and not any successor or potential successor."

8. Erich Auerbach inspires this method of analysis. Commenting on the characters' speech in the story of the sacrifice of Isaac he writes: "Their speech does not serve . . . to manifest, to externalize thought—on the contrary, it serves to indicate thoughts which remain unexpressed." Broadening the focus, he says: "The decisive points of the narrative alone are emphasized, what lies between is non-existence; time and space are undefined and call for interpretation; thought and feeling remain unexpressed . . . the whole . . . remains mysterious and 'fraught with background.'" He says of the David story: "How fraught with background, in comparison, are characters like Saul and

David! How entangled and stratified are such human relations as those between David and Absalom, between David and Joab!" Erich Auerbach, *Mimesis: The Representation of Reality in Western Literature*, trans. Willard Trask (Garden City, 1957), pp. 8-9.

9. See Wolfgang Roth, "You Are the Man! Structural Interaction in 2 Samuel 10-12," *Semeia*, 3(1976), for an intriguing study of the resonance of this line in David's and the reader's mind.

10. Gunn: "The tension between forgiveness (blessing) and retribution is never finally resolved" (p. 20). Gunn finds an ironic perspective in the narrative in his comprehensive study; in contrast, this analysis sees the narrator as less resolved. The narrative ambiguity balances hope in the future and reportage of the king's tragedy, without one perspective undercutting the other.

11. I follow R. J. Coggins, *Chronicles: A Commentary* (Cambridge University Press, 1976), pp. 3ff., on the manner and intent of the composition: "The material concerning David, though much of it is taken from earlier sources, is re-arranged in such a way as to stress David's concern for a proper place of worship rather than the more 'secular' side of his achievement."

12. *Chronicles: With Hebrew Text and English Translation*, commentary by Israel W. Slotki (London: Soncino Press, 1952).

13. The French edition of Josephus, edited by Théodore Reinach, contains a commentary by M. Julien Weill listing the sources Josephus used. The sections dealing with David draw exclusively on the Hebrew Bible, using none of the midrashic material drawn on for other sections.

14. Josephus, *Jewish Antiquities*, trans. J. Thackerary (Cambridge, Mass.: Harvard University Press [Loeb Library Edition], 1957), p. ix.

15. *Esther Rabba*, trans. Maurice Simon (London: Soncino Press, 1951), 10.

16. *Exodus Rabba*, trans. H. Freedman (London: Soncino Press, 1932), 1, 1.

17. *Midrash Samuel*, ed. Solomon Buber (Jerusalem, 1965 [reprint from 1893]), pp. 122-23; see also *Numbers Rabba*, XI, 3.

18. *The Talmud: Shabbath*, trans. H. Freedman (London: Soncino Press, 1938), vol. 1, 56a.

19. *The Talmud: Sanhedrin*, trans. H. Freedman (London: Soncino Press, 1935), vol. 2, 107a.

20. David was made free to play many roles in the folklore of midrashic times and after. He is often foolish, often kingly, often boyish and endearing, but never tragic. See the material on David collected in Louis Ginzberg, *The Legends of the Jews* (Philadelphia, 1946), 4:79-121, and in *Classical Jewish Folktales*, collected by Micha Joseph bin Gorian, ed. Emanuel bin Gorian, trans. I. M. Lask, intro. Dan Ben-Amos (Bloomington: Indiana University Press, 1976).

21. The translation closely follows *The New English Bible* (New York and London: Oxford University Press, 1971).

22. St. Augustine, *The City of God*, trans. E. M. Sanford, W. M. Green (Cambridge, Mass.: Harvard University Press [Loeb Classical Library], 1965). Augustine in this chapter says of David: "At the onset of his reign he was marvellously worthy of praise. Still, even he in his own person merely foreshadowed the future coming of Christ the Lord."

23. Augustine's title for chapter 8, as well as the general cast of Augustine's reading of the David story, illustrates what Erich Auerbach calls "figural interpretation." It "establishes a connection between two events or persons in such a way that the first signifies not only itself, but also the second, while the second involves or fulfills the first. The two poles of a figure are separated in time, but both, being real events or persons are within temporality" (*Mimesis*, pp. 64-65). In his discussion, Auerbach stresses that the connection can only be established if "both occurrences are vertically linked to Divine Providence, which alone is able to devise such a plan of history and supply the key to its understanding." The "horizontal" or "temporal" or causal relation need not link the figures compared.

He goes on to say however, that Augustine often, if not always, "endeavored to complement the figural-vertical interpretation by a representation of the intrahistorical chain of events . . . to give the highest measure of rational plausibility to an intrinsically irrational interpretation." But "there was no fully adequate substitute for the lost comprehension of rational, continuous earthly connections between things." In this light, the ambiguous perspective of the Kings narrative—focused both on providential patterns and "earthly connections—effects a momentary synthesis of vision which subsequent rabbinic dogma could not sustain, or patristic dogma revive.

24. St. Augustine, "Ennarationes in psalmos," *Opera Omnia: Patrologia Latine*, ed. J. P. Migne (Paris, 1891), 36:97 (hereafter PL).

25. St. Jerome, "Epistola XXII: ad Eustochium," *PL*, 22:2.

26. De Lubac, Premiere Partie, II, 459-66, gives a comprehensive analysis of the patristic literature on the adultery of David. He traces the sources of Augustine's ideas to Ambrose, Gregory, and others, and shows the profound influence of Augustine's formulations on later writers.

27. Rubert, abbot of Salzburg (d. 718), in his commentary on Kings sums up the tradition of close readings of the Bathsheba episode which precede his by saying that "the Fathers transform the damnable deed of David into a great and venerable mystery. In the Christian telling, David—whose story is literally embarrassing, and who could be taken by any reader as a strange devil, because he so stupidly and ridiculously sought to annihilate the essential dignity of his prophetic and kingly roles—is made out to mediate the pre-figuring wisdom of God." He then cites Eucherius and Isidore verbatim ("Reg. Lib II, caput 34," *PL*, 167:1135). Claude of Turin (623-703) also cites Eucherius verbatim in his commentary: "In Questiones XXX super Libros Regnum," *PL*, 104:703-4. Rebanus Maurus cites Isidore in his "Commentaria in Libros IV Regum," *PL*, 109:98, as does Walafrid the Squinter (*PL*, 113:21).

28. St. Eucherius, bishop of Lugdune, "Commentarii in Libros Regum, Lib. II," *PL*, 50:1090ff.

29. Eucherius' commentary illustrates what de Lubac calls "the most striking law of doctrinal exegesis . . . the great thesis of negative theology and one of the most ancient beliefs of humanity"—the law of "significations inversées" or "metaphores sans ressemblance." In these interpretations the obvious meaning of the text is taken to be exactly the opposite of the true or hidden meaning. Gregory the Great made the classic formulation early in the tradition: "Saepe res quaelibet per historiam virtus est, per significantionem culpa sicut aliquando culpa in facto, in scripto prophetiae virtus"; "Often something which seems literally to be virtuous, actually signifies a failing; similiarly what might seem a failing symbolizes a virtue" (*PL*, 75:634 B.C. [de Lubac, p. 462]). But de Lubac fails to note that this law often breaks down if the reading is close enough to catch an unmistakably literal meaning, as Eucherius and Isidore show.

30. St. Isidore of Seville, "Questiones in Vet. Testam, in Regum II," *PL*, 83:411, 2.

Two:

Frail Grass and Firm Tree

1. *The Book of Vices and Virtues*, ed. W. Nelson Francis, EETS 217 (London: Oxford University Press, 1942), pp. 225-26. On the value of the original, the *Somme le roi*, as a compendium of moral commonplaces see Rosemond Tuve, *Allegorical Imagery* (Princeton: Princeton University Press, 1966), pp. 57-60, 79-82. In the quotations in this paper I have retained original spellings, modernized such typographic and scribal practices as *u/v*, contractions and the thorn, and (except where otherwise noted) provided my own translations into English. Bible quotations are from the King James version, and in citing Psalms by number I follow the modern numeration, not that of the Vulgate. I recognize, with thanks, the support of a grant from the Folger Shakespeare Library and a sabbatical leave from Gordon College, which made the research for this essay possible.

2. *Legenda aurea*, trans. W. Caxton (Westminster, 1483), fol. 299^r.

3. The following sampling of references nicely spans the period dealt with in this paper: (1) Cassiodorus, in J.-P. Migne, *Patrologiae Cursus Completus . . . Series Latina* (221 vols.; Paris, 1844-64), 70:358; (2) Alcuin, 100:582; (3) Bruno of Würzburg, 142:477; (4) Honorius, 172:284; (5) Peter Lombard, 191:57; (6) Pseudo-Innocent III, 217:1070; (7) *Speculum Sacerdotale*, ed. E. H. Weatherly, EETS 200 (London:Oxford University Press, 1936), p. 22; (8) *Cursor Mundi*, ed. Richard Morris, EETS 57, 59, 62, 66, 68, 99, 101 (7 pts.; London, 1874-93), V, 1474-76; (9) *Legends of the Saints*, ed. W. M. Metcalfe, Scottish Text Society (3 vols.; Edinburgh, 1896), I, 205-7; (10) a Flemish prayer book c. 1450, Newberry Library MS. 56, fol. 189^r; (11) *Speculum Humanae Salvationis* (Paris, 1503), fol. 11^v —probably the longest list, which gives 26 examples in all; (12) John Fisher, *This treatise concernynge the fruytfull saynges of Davyd . . . in the seven penytencyall psalmes* (London, 1508), sig. A2^v; (13) Erasmus, *Enchiridion* 26, ed. R. Himelick (Bloomington: Indiana University Press, 1963), pp. 170-71; (14) William Lauder, *Ane Godlie Tractate or Mirrour* (1568), ed. F. J. Furnivall, EETS 41 (London, 1870), p. 14; (15) other sixteenth-century examples in Inga-Stina Ewbank, "The House of David in Renaissance Drama," *RenD* 8(1965), 9-10.

4. Claude of Turin, *Comm. in Libros Regum* (Migne, 50:1091); formerly attributed to St. Eucherius. On the authorship see Palémon Glorieux, *Pour Revaloriser Migne* (Lille: Facultés catholiques, 1952), p. 35. Other authors in Migne use this same formula verbatim.

5. *Homiliae dominicales aestivales*, 68, in Migne, 174:476.

6. E.g., a version of the holy rood legend in British Museum MS. Harl. 3185 (see A. S. Napier, ed., *History of the Holy Rood-Tree*, EETS 103 [London, 1894], p. 55); a twelfth-century Anglo-Norman paraphrase of 2 Samuel, whose author follows the biblical text quite closely on the Bathsheba affair until reaching this part of it, and then inserts another sentence repeating the trick on Uriah and adds a marginal note as well: "Cume Urie portad le brief de sa mort" (*Li Quatre Livre des Reis*, ed. E. R. Curtius, Gesellschaft für romanische Literatur 26 [Dresden, 1911], p. 78). In *Cursor Mundi*, line 7907 (ed. Morris, II, 456), we find a moral after this part of the story: Let this be a warning to "al letter-berers."

7. The best-known analogues are in the stories of Bellerophon and Hamlet.

Rudolf Zenker, *Boeve-Amlethus. Das altfranzösische Epos von Boeve de Hamtone und der Ursprung der Hamletsage*, Literarhistorische Forschungen 32 (Berlin: Felber, 1905), pp. 45-49, 283, 313-16, 402ff., cites several parallels. Laura A. Hibbard, *Mediaeval Romance in England* (New York: Oxford University Press, 1924), p. 122, considers 2 Samuel a possible source for the thirteenth-century *Beves of Hampton* on the basis of this motif. See also William H. Prescott, *History of the Conquest of Mexico*, I, vi (Modern Library ed., New York, n.d.), pp. 106-7; C. H. Tawney, "A Folklore Parallel," *The Indian Antiquary*, 10(1881), 190-91; Stith Thompson, *Motif Index of Folk Literature*, rev. ed. (6 vols.; Bloomington: Indiana University Press, 1955-58), IV, 359 (K978).

8. Friedrich Kluge, *Etymologisches Wörterbuch der deutschen Sprache* (17th ed.; Berlin: W. de Gruyter, 1957), p. 810: "geflügeltes Wort." Jacob and Wilhelm Grimm, *Deutsches Wörterbuch*, s. v. *Uriasbrief*, give a fuller account. The comparable allusion in classical times was to Bellerophon's letter: cf. Plautus, *Bacchides*, IV. vii. 12; Erasmus, *Adagia* II. vi. 82.

9. Pseudo-Innocent III, *Comm. in Septem Psalmos Poenitentiales*, in Migne, 217:1052.

10. *The ensamples of Vertue and vice, gathered out of holye scripture . . . Very necessarye for all christen men and women to looke upon*, trans. T. Paynell (London, 1561), sigs. X7ʳ, 2C2ᵛ, 2K6ᵛ, 2M2ᵛ, 2M6ᵛ, 2M8ʳ, 2X8ʳ, 2Y2ʳ. The last point, which sees in David's retirement from active campaigning at the head of his own armies a yielding to soft prosperity, is frequently stressed by commentators.

11. The *Postilla* of Nicolaus of Lyra appeared in many editions, both MS. and printed, often as a part of annotated Bibles running to several volumes. The quotation is from the beginning of his commentary on 2 Samuel 11. Negligence (i.e., of God) was also mentioned by St. Bruno (d. 1101) in his analysis of David's sin (Migne, 152:861).

12. *The Ship of Fools*, trans. Alexander Barclay, ed. T. H. Jamieson (2 vols.; Edinburgh, 1874), I, 86.

13. Gustav Weil, *The Bible, the Koran, and the Talmud; or, Biblical Legends of the Mussulmans*, trans. from the German (London, 1846), pp. 157-61. The reference toward the end to David's tears is supplied from Mary W. Montgomery, "David—In Mohammedan Literature," *Jewish Encyclopedia* (1925), 4:457. Cf. *Koran*, 38:16-24 (trans. J. M. Rodwell, 2d rev. and amended ed. [London, 1876], pp. 119-20), which gives the story of the trick judgment, does not mention that the pleaders were angels, and emphasizes David's readiness to do penance, whereby Allah was pleased.

14. Johann Albert Fabricius, *Codex Pseudepigraphus Veteris Testamenti* (Hamburg and Leipzig, 1713), pp. 1,000-1,001; for the last quotation, Louis Ginzberg, "David—In Rabbinical Literature," *Jewish Encyclopedia* (1925), 4:455-56.

15. See C. A. Huttar, "Old Testament Sainthood," *N&Q*, 11 (1964), 86-88.

16. Ginzberg, pp. 455-56. See also "David," *Encyclopaedia Judaica* (16 vols.; New York: Macmillan, 1971-72), pp. 1328, 1331.

17. Augustine, *Christian Doctrine*, 23.21; trans. J. F. Shaw, in Philip Schaff, ed., *A Select Library of the Nicene and Post-Nicene Fathers of the Christian Church*, 1st ser. (14 vols.; 1886-90; reprinted Grand Rapids: Eerdmans, 1956), II, 565. The last two quotations are from Honorius (Migne, 172:283), who has followed Augustine closely. His version, in turn, also appears almost verbatim in Gerhoh of Reichersberg in Austria (Migne, 193:1602). Cf. also Chrysostom (d. 407), *Homilies on Romans*, 16, trans. J. B. Morris and W. H. Simcox, in Schaff, XI, 466.

18. Hanape, *Ensamplès of Vertue and vice*, sig. 2S1ʳ. Cf. Gerhoh of Reichersberg

(d. 1169), *Opera Inedita*, ed. D. and O. Van Den Eynde and A. Rijmersdael (2 vols. in 3; Rome: Apud Pontificium Athenaeum Antonianum, 1955-56), II, 361, 502.

19. Filippo Picinelli, *Mundus Symbolicus . . . Nunc . . . in Latinum Traductus* (Cologne, 1687), I, 202. Picinelli attributes the point to Augustine.

20. Migne, 70:359.

21. "Penitential Psalms," lines 41-48, in *Collected Poems of Sir Thomas Wyatt*, ed. Kenneth Muir and Patricia Thomson (Liverpool: Liverpool University Press, 1969), p. 100. Both Wyatt and his source for this stanza, Pietro Aretino, *I Sette Salmi de la Penitentia di David* (Venice, 1536), sig. B1^{r-v}, used traditional details.

22. The idea of nakedness occasionally recurs; perhaps it has some symbolic value. In *Middle English Sermons*, ed. W. O. Ross, EETS 209 (London: Oxford University Press, 1940), p. 110, we read, "Thou that arte in dedely synne, will thou see how that thou arte downe and also naked?" Cf. Ps. 32:1, "Blessed is he . . . whose sin is covered," and Gen. 3:7ff.

23. Lines 49-56. Cf. the similar attention to iconography in lines 305-8.

24. A. O. Belfour, ed. and trans., *Twelfth Century Homilies in MS. Bodley 343*, EETS 137 (London: K. Paul, Trench, Trübner, 1909), p. 47.

25. *Epist.* 77 (Migne, 22:692); trans. W. H. Fremantle, in Philip Schaff and Henry Wace, eds., *A Select Library of Nicene and Post-Nicene Fathers*, 2d ser. (14 vols.; 1890-1900; reprinted Grand Rapids: Eerdmans, 1952-56), VI, 159.

26. E.g., Cassiodorus (Migne, 70:358, 359); Alcuin (Migne, 100:582); *Glossa ordinaria*, Ps. 51 (Migne, 113:918), citing Cassiodorus. Augustin Calmet, as quoted in G. L. Haydock, ed., *The Holy Bible* [Douay Version] . . . *with Useful Notes* (2 vols.; Manchester, 1811), I, 440, cites an early Greek homily that presented "the chief lords of the court" as being in attendance.

27. British Museum MS. Royal 2 B. VII; in George F. Warner, ed., *Queen Mary's Psalter* (London: British Museum, 1912), pl. 101; translation, p. 87. Other examples in fourteenth-century painting may be seen in M. R. James, ed., *The Bohun Manuscripts* (Oxford: Roxburghe Club, 1936), pl. 67(a), and D. D. Egbert, ed., *The Tickhill Psalter and Related Manuscripts* (New York Public Library and the Department of Art and Archaeology, Princeton University, 1940), pl. LVII.

28. 1 Chron. 21:12, 16, 27, 30; 2 Sam. 12:10 (cf. verse 9, where "the sword" has just appeared twice in a different sense).

29. Arsenal MS. 5211, fol. 154^v; reproduced in Hugo Buchthal, *Miniature Painting in the Latin Kingdom of Jerusalem* (Oxford: Clarendon Press, 1957), pl. 70.

30. Ekkehard IV, "Tituli für den Dom zu Mainz," lines 51-52, in Julius von Schlosser, *Quellenbuch zur Kunstgeschichte des abendländischen Mittelalters* (Wien, 1896), p. 170.

31. Ed. Muir and Thomson, lines 38, 331-33.

32. Still other variants specify 80 days or 6 months (S. Baring-Gould, *Legends of the Patriarchs and Prophets* [New York: Hurst, 1889], pp. 395, 388).

33. *The Life of Solitude*, II.v.4; trans. Jacob Zeitlin (Urbana: University of Illinois Press, 1924), p. 257. For David's condemnation of the city, Petrarch's authority is Ps. 55:10-11.

34. *Trionfi*, I.iii.42; in *Rime, Trionfi e Poesie Latine*, ed. F. Neri (Milan and Naples: Ricciardi, 1951), p. 496.

35. E. H. Wilkins, *Petrarch's Later Years* (Cambridge, Mass.: Harvard University Press, 1959), p. 176. It was in this cave that Petrarch wrote a Latin poem on the saint.

36. In this instance I use the text of the Great Bible version (1539), as it was one of Wyatt's sources (Muir and Thomson, eds., p. 357).

37. See E. O. James, *From Cave to Cathedral* (New York: Praeger, 1965), pp. 37-50; R. M. Harmer, "Embalming, Burial, and Cremation," *New Encyclopaedia Britannica* (1975), 6:738; Maud Bodkin, *Archetypal Patterns in Poetry* (1934; reprinted New York: Vintage, 1958), pp. 98, 100, 121-23.

38. British Museum MS. Add. 49999, fol. 67^v. Cf. George F. Warner, *Descriptive Catalogue of Illuminated Manuscripts in the Library of C. W. Dyson Perrins* (2 vols.; Oxford: at the University Press, 1920), I, 23; Sydney C. Cockerell, *The Work of W. de Brailes*, Roxburghe Club (Cambridge: at the University Press, 1930), p. 24. A few other MSS. and a wood painting show a similar scene, but without the verbal explanations. In another study I hope to trace the background for this iconography, including its relationship to traditional illuminations for Psalms 69 and 130.

39. Fol. 70^r. Caxton's authorship of the Old Testament section is well established. I have not yet identified the written source in which his informant, Sir John Capons, "had redde" this legend.

40. Davies Gilbert, *The Parochial History of Cornwall* (4 vols.; London, 1838), II, 262. As a further instance of the impact of asceticism, note the presence of a flagellant's scourge alongside David's harp in a fifteenth-century painting of the kneeling penitent; Newberry Library MS. 42, fol. 92^r. Cf. also Brailes *Horae*, fols. 72, 79 (Warner, *Descriptive Catalogue*, I, 23-24).

41. *South English Legendary*, in Richard Morris, ed., *Legends of the Holy Rood*, EETS 46 (London, 1871), p. 30; cf. "Canticum de Creatione," ed. C. Horstmann, *Anglia*, 1(1878), 327. Many vernacular versions of the rood legend sprang up, and they vary considerably. They are surveyed in Esther C. Quinn, *The Quest of Seth for the Oil of Life* (Chicago: University of Chicago Press, 1962). The incorporation in the legend of the story of David and Bathsheba apparently occurred in the thirteenth-century versions: see Wilhelm Meyer, "Die Geschichte des Kreuzholzes vor Christus," *Abhandl. des Philos.-Philol. Classe der k.-b. Akad. der Wissenschaften*, 16, 2(1882), 143-44.

42. R. Morton Nance and A. S. D. Smith, *Davyd hag Urry*, Extracts from the Cornish Texts 6 (St. Ives: Federation of Old Cornwall Societies, 1958), p. 11. In this bilingual edition, the literal translation is by Nance. F. E. Halliday, *The Legend of the Rood* (London: Duckworth, 1955), pp. 77ff., converts this translation into more polished English verse. A less reliable translation may be found in Edwin Norris, *The Ancient Cornish Drama* (2 vols.; Oxford, 1859). On the longevity of this play see Norris, II, 455; Halliday, p. 14; and F. E. Halliday, *A History of Cornwall* (London: Duckworth, 1959), p. 207.

The biblical account says only that the rich man had "exceeding many flocks and herds," but some narrators preferred to specify—50 sheep in the Brailes *Horae*, 99 in the Muslim legend, and here 100.

43. Norris trans., I, 177. Cf. "Canticum de Creatione" (ed. Horstmann, p. 328), in which work on the temple proceeds for 24 years until an angel calls a halt because "thou has don so muchel synne."

44. In the *Ordinalia's* "principal source" (Halliday, *Legend*, p. 49), the *Cursor Mundi*, the more general reason had been retained: "And mani men slan wit thin hand" (II, 478 [above, note 3]).

45. Other factors that possibly contributed to this association are (1) the importance of the temple in the rood legend, since the wood of this same tree was taken for its construction (cf. other versions of the legend, e.g., *The Story of the Holy Rood* in Morris, *Legends*, p. 78); (2) the fact that Solomon, God's appointed templebuilder, was a later offspring of the marriage with Bathsheba, who played a key role in ensuring his succession (1 Kings 1:11-31); (3) the fact that, in the much earlier episode in which David's offer to build a temple was rejected, Nathan was the prophet who bore God's message (2 Samuel 7:4ff.); (4) the placement of David's *preparations* for Solomon's work of construction (1 Chronicles 22:1-16) immediately after the episode of the census and the consequent epidemic, whose attachment to the Bathsheba episode in medieval times we have already noted.

46. In the rood-legend section of the *Cursor Mundi*, a Northumbrian work roughly contemporaneous with Brailes, it is an angel, sitting on a bough of the holy tree, which takes over Nathan's role in 2 Samuel 7 of forbidding David to build a temple (II, 478).

47. Even one of the rood writers, faced with the plain evidence of Psalms whose titles connected them with other events in David's life, listed three exceptions to the statement that "he composed the whole Psalter under the holy tree" (Napier, p. 55). Still, the association of the entire psalter with this episode was sufficiently current to receive casual reference in popular verse: see F. J. Furnivall, ed., *Political, Religious, and Love Poems*, EETS 15 (London, 1866), p. 126.

48. Cassiodorus, writing after 540 (Migne, 70:371, 60), says he is following "the usage of the churches" in referring to them as "septem psalmi poenitentium" (not yet "poenitentiales"), but it is not clear whether he means that they are to be recited by those who are penitent or that they were written in the personae of penitents (cf. col. 24). Jerome (d. 420) calls three of them Psalms "of penitence" or spoken by penitents (*Opera*, ed. Erasmus [Basel, 1516], VIII, fols. 4^r, 27^v, 35^v), but uses no such language of the other four; I take it he is describing, not classifying. Augustine (d. 430) is reported to have asked, on his deathbed, for "the psalms of David concerning penitence, which are very few," to be written on the wall where he could see them (Possidius, *Vita s. Aug.*, in Migne, 32:63), but even if the story is true, it does not indicate how many nor which Psalms. In his *Enarrationes in Psalmos*, an early work (c. 392-94), Augustine does not speak of the Seven Penitentials. Hilary (d. 367), who expounded all the numerical peculiarities of the psalter (Migne, 9:231-47), apparently was not aware of the Seven Penitentials. H. Lesêtre, *Le Livre de Psaumes* (La Sainte Bible . . . avec Commentaires 6 [Paris, 1883]), p. lxn, says the grouping goes back still earlier, to the time of Origen; but he offers no documentation, and E. J. Boyce, "The Psalter," in *Prayer-Book Commentary* (London: SPCK, 1894), p. 160, observes that this grouping was "not known to the Eastern Church."

49. Cassiodorus ties in the Seven Psalms with one or two other septenaries (Migne, 70:60, 1014) and Pseudo-Innocent in his *Commentarium* lists some 28 other scriptural sevens (Migne, 217:969-71). Cf. also Alcuin (Migne, 100:571-72), Honorius (Migne, 172:282), and, as an instance of the continuing fascination exerted by the septenaries, Johannes Mösch, *Tractatulus . . . de horis canonicis* (Basel, 1483), sig. A5^v-6^r. See Tuve, *Allegorical Imagery*, pp. 112-13.

50. E.g., H. Eobanus Hessus (d. 1540), *Psalterium Davidis Carmine Redditum* (London, 1575). Cf. Johann Bugenhagen, *Psalter wol verteutscht auss der heyligen sprach* (Basel, 1526), fol. 1^r-8^v; Geneva Bible (1560), headnotes to Pss. 102, 130, 143. Some caution had entered the picture much earlier: Nicolaus of Lyra considered Psalm 130 exilic.

51. The phraseology is that of H. A. Mason, *Humanism and Poetry in the Early Tudor Period* (London: Routledge and Kegan Paul, 1959), pp. 211, 213.

52. Accounts of their development may be found in Victor Leroquais, *Supplément aux Livres d'Heures Manuscrits de la Bibliothèque Nationale* (Mâcon: Protat frères, 1943), p. xxi, and S. J. P. Van Dijk and J. H. Walker, *The Origins of the Modern Roman Liturgy* (Westminster, Md.: Newman, 1960), pp. 20, 121, 138, 218, 270ff. See also Mason, *Humanism and Poetry*, pp. 207-8.

53. See, as a few examples, Whitley Stokes, ed., *Middle-Breton Hours* (Calcutta, 1876), p. 33; Carl Horstmann, ed., *Yorkshire Writers* (2 vols.; London, 1895-96), II, 315; *Portiforium* (Pollard and Redgrave STC 15833; Paris, 1535), sig. H1^v-3^r, and as a rule *all* the Sarum Breviaries. Cf. William Maskell, *Monumenta Ritualia Ecclesiae Anglicanae* (3 vols.; London, 1846-47), II, 79-89*nn*, Morton W. Bloomfield, *The Seven Deadly Sins* (East Lansing: Michigan State College Press, 1952), p. 178; Tuve, *Allegorical Imagery*, p. 92.

54. E.g., Egbert of York (d. 766), *Penitential*, in A. W. Haddan and W. Stubbs, eds., *Councils and Ecclesiastical Documents Relating to Great Britain and Ireland* (3 vols.; Oxford, 1869-73), III, 425; Regino (d. 915), *De eccles. disciplin. 2.* 251 (Migne, 132:333); *Speculum Sacerdotale* (post-Lateran III; ed. Weatherly, EETS 200), pp. 75-89.

55. Elliott V. Dobbie, ed., *The Anglo-Saxon Minor Poems*, Anglo-Saxon Poetic Records 6 (New York: Columbia University Press, 1942), pp. lxxx, 93-94.

56. Fisher (above, note 3), sig. 2G2^v-4^v. The explicit statement that David's purpose was to set a pattern for us occurs again in John Hall, *The Court of Virtue (1565)*, ed. Russell A. Fraser (New Brunswick, N.J.: Rutgers University Press, 1961), p. 79 (lines 10-11).

57. Joannes Herold, ed., *Orthodoxographa Theologiae* (Basel, 1555), pp. 1330-52. Ailly's work was also reprinted under the name of his more famous pupil, Jean Gerson, but Ailly's claim to its authorship is preferred.

58. Cf. P. Pourrat, *Christian Spirituality*, trans. W. H. Mitchell and S. P. Jacques (3 vols.; London: Burns, Oates, and Washbourne, 1922-27), II, 268.

59. One indication of this is the extent to which Wyatt is influenced by currents of Protestant theology: see Mason, *Humanism and Poetry*, pp. 206-7, 214-21, and Muir and Thomson, eds., pp. 356-90 *passim*.

60. *Fortior ex lapsu*, emblem in Johannes Michael van der Ketten, *Apelles Symbolicus* (2 vols.; Amsterdam and Danzig, 1699), I, 421.

Three:
Two Views of the Evangelical David

1. See my *The King's Progress to Jerusalem: Some Interpretations of David during the Reformation Period and their Patristic and Medieval Background* (Malibu, Calif: Undena Publications, 1976 [*Humana Civilitas*, 2]). Hundreds of Psalm commentaries were written during these periods. Some idea of the vastness of the literature may be gained by scanning F. Stegmüller's *Repertorium Biblicum Medii Aevi* (7 vols.; Madrid: 1950-1961) and B. Smalley's *The Study of the Bible in the Middle Ages* (Notre Dame, Ind.: University of Notre Dame Press, 1964).

2. That is, a dehistoricized figure whose faith was not concrete or personal but merely representative of a *homo mysticus*, undifferentiated from other *homines mystici*, who served only to validate the retention of the Old Testament as part of Christian canonical literature. Cf. J. S. Preus, *From Shadow to Promise: Old Testament Interpretation from Augustine to the Young Luther* (Cambridge, Mass.: Harvard University Press, 1969), pp. 121-22.

3. Augustine, *Sermo II (PL* 38, col. 30). Quoted in E. Mâle, *The Gothic Image*, trans. Dora Nussey (New York: Harper Torchbook, 1958), pp. 135-36: "Brothers, I warn you in the name of God to believe before all things when you hear the Scriptures read that the events really took place. . . . Do not destroy the historic foundation of Scripture, for without it you will build in the air."

4. Augustine, *De doctrina christina*, III, 10.14 *(PL* 34, col. 71): "Whatever appears in the divine Word that does not pertain to virtuous behavior or to the truth of faith, you must take to be figurative." Cf. also Augustine, *De civitate dei*, XVI, 26: "The Old Testament is nothing but the New covered with a veil, and the New Testament is nothing but the Old unveiled."

5. This is the generic name for Augustine's expositions of the Psalms, many of which were delivered as sermons. They can be found in the *Corpus Christianorum: Series Latina*, vols. 38-40, and in J.-P. Migne, ed., *Patrologiae latinae cursus completus omnium ss. patrum, doctrum, scriptorumque ecclesiasticorum*, vols. 36-7.

6. *PL* 37, coll. 1855-57.

7. *Loc. cit.*

8. Nicolaus de Lyra, *Postilla moralis super psalterium*, in *Postilla moralis super totam bibliam* (Cologne: Johannes Kölhof de Lübeck, 1478), fol. t7 recto & verso. Lyra's *postillae* were written between 1322 and 1339. On the use made by Lyra of Rashi and other rabbinical sources, see H. Hailperin, *Rashi and the Christian Scholars* (Pittsburgh: University of Pittsburgh Press, 1963); on the fortune of the printed editions of his works, see my "A Listing of the Printed Editions of Nicolaus de Lyra," *Traditio 26(1970), 399-426.*

9. Lefèvre and Beza both knew Augustine's and Lyra's commentaries. As is clear below, Lefèvre criticized Lyra's hermeneutic, while Beza and other Protestants were positively influenced by it.

10. On Lefèvre d'Etaples (Fauber Stapulensis), see A. Renaudet, *Préréforme et humanisme à Paris pendant les premières guerres d'Italie, 1494-1517* (Paris: Librairie d'Argence, 1916/1953), *passim*; E. F. Rice Jr., *The Prefatory Epistles of Jacques Lefèvre d'Etaples and Related Texts* (New York: Columbia University Press, 1972), *passim*. On Theodore Beza, see P.-F. Geisendorf, *Théodore de Bèze* (Geneva: Jullien, 1967). Gosselin, *King's Progress*, chaps. 3 and 6, discusses Lefèvre's and Beza's concepts of David.

11. He particularly admired the Pseudo Dionysius, Raymond Lull, Cusanus and Pico della Mirandola. On his intellectual interests, see E. F. Rice Jr., "The Humanist Idea of Christian Antiquity: Lefèvre d'Etaples and His Circle," *Studies in the Renaissance*, 9(1962), 126-60; idem, "Lefèvre d'Etaples and the Medieval Christian Mystics," in *Florilegium Historiale*, ed. J. G. Rowe and W. H. Stockdale (Toronto: University of Toronto Press, 1971); idem, "The Meaning of 'Evangelical,'" in *The Pursuit of Holiness in Late Medieval and Renaissance Religion*, ed. C. Trinkhaus and H. A. Oberman (Leiden: E. J. Brill, 1974); H. Heller, "The Evangelicism of Lefèvre d'Etaples: 1525," *Studies in the Renaissance*, 19(1972), 42-77; and *idem*, "Nicholas of Cusa and Early French Evangelism," *Archiv fdiur Reformationsgeschichte*, 63(1972), 447-64.

12. *Quincuplex Psalterium* (hereafter cited as *Quin. Psalt.*) (Paris: Henri Estienne, 1509). This text is an edition of a medieval triple psalter (a *Psalterium iuxta Hebraeos,*

Gallicanum et Romanum). The three versions are set in parallel columns. To these Lefèvre added a *Psalterium vetus* and a *Psalterium conciliatum* (the former being the version and the churches used before Jerome's revisions; the latter being the Vulgate version corrected from Jerome's *Psalterium iuxta Hebraeos*).

For this quotation, see Rice, *Epistles*, p. 193, and H. A. Oberman, *Forerunners of the Reformation*, trans. P. L. Nyhus (New York: Holt, Rinehart and Winston, 1966), p. 297.

13. Lefèvre, *Quin, Psalt.* (Rice, *Epistles*, p. 194; Oberman, *Forerunners*, p. 298).

14. Lefèvre, *Quin. Psalt.* (Rice, *Epistles*, pp. 193-94; Oberman, *Forerunners*, p. 298). Also *ibid.* (Rice, *Epistles*, p. 194; Oberman, *Forerunners*, pp. 298-99).

15. Lefèvre, *Quin. Psalt.*, Ps. 7, fol. 13r.

16. *Loc. cit.*

17. Lefèvre's idea that the *sensus propheticus* is the true literal sense, and Lyra's opinion that the *sensus historicus* is, both stem from Thomas Aquinas' discussion of the meanings of Scripture. Cf. Gosselin, *King's Progress*, pp. 5-6, and Preus, *Shadow*, pp. 51-4 ("According to [Aquinas'] definition, the *sensus litteralis* is that which the divine author intended"). See also Thomas Aquinas, *Summa theologiae* 1.1.10.

18. Lefèvre, *Quin. Psalt.*, Ps. 33, fol. 55r.

19. Ibid., Ps. 62, fol. 95r.

20. Ibid., Ps. 24, fol. 42r and v.

21. *Psaultier de David* (hereafter cited as *Psaultier*) (Paris: Simon de Colines, 1525). Critical editions of its preface and the "exhortation en la fin" can be found in Rice, *Epistles*, nos. 140 and 142.

22. See A. Levi, S. J., "Humanist Reform in Sixteenth-Century France," *Heythrop Journal*, 6(1965), 447-64, esp. pp. 454-55.

23. Lefèvre, *Psaultier*, "exhortation en la fin" (Rice, *Epistles*, p. 488).

24. Lefèvre, *Psaultier* (Pss. 1-3), fol. Siii recto (Pss. 22 and 24), fol. Siiii recto (Ps. 54), fol. Svi recto.

25. This fact is evidenced one time in the *Psaultier*, in his comments on Psalm 50 (*Psaultier*, fol. Svi recto).

26. For a detailed study of Luther's, Melanchton's, Calvin's, and Beza's treatments of David, see Gosselin, *King's Progress*, pp. 67-118.

27. By "Protestant David" we mean the David found in the commentaries of Luther, Melanchthon, Calvin, Beza, and Martin Bucer. We suspect that the general agreement among these commentators concerning David would be duplicated in the commentaries of other exegetes from the so-called "Right Wing of the Reformation." We exclude, however, from our rubric of the "Protestant David" any interpretation of David by the so-called "Left Wing Reformers," i.e., the Anabaptists and Spiritualists.

28. Theodore Beza, *Les Pseaumes de David et les Cantiques de la Bible, avec les argumens et la Paraphrase de Théodore de Beèze* (s.l. [Geneva]: J. Berjon, 1581), Ps. 13, p. 42.

29. Beza, *Pseaumes de David*, Ps. 19, pp. 55-56.

30. Ibid., Ps. 16, pp. 47-48.

31. Ibid., Ps. 70, p. 332.

32. Philip Melanchthon, *Commentarii in psalmos*, in *Corpus Reformatorum*, vol. 13 (New York: Johnson Reprint Corp., 1963), col. 1059. (Our italics.)

33. Beza, *Pseaumes de David*, Ps. 101, pp. 496-98.

34. Ibid., pp. 497-98; cf. also ibid., Ps. 72, p. 342, and Ps. 16, pp. 47-48.

35. Ibid., Ps. 26, pp. 95-96.

36. For a discussion of the *Droit* and Beza's political theory, see Théodore de

Bèze, *Du droit des magistrats sur leurs suiets.* . . . , ed. R. M. Kingdom (Geneva: Droz, 1970), and E. A. Gosselin, "*David in Tempore Belli:* Beza's David in the Service of the Huguenots," *The Sixteenth Century Journal*, 7(1976), 31-54.

37. Melanchthon, who had defended just resistance against tyranny, was able to find only forbearance in David's conduct, and was thus unable to use David as an advocate of militant resistance; the same holds true for Calvin. See Gosselin, *King's Progress*, pp. 93-97.

38. Beza, *Pseaumes de David*, Ps. 109, pp. 559-60. It would have been very easy for a Huguenot to see the Guises, Catherine de' Medici, and Henri III in the Psalm and in its commentary. Beza already had drawn an explicit comparison between the persecution of David and that of Huguenots. See ibid., Ps. 52, p. 240.

39. Foreseeing the hostility of the Catholic League to Henri IV, Beza creates the myth that David was "elected" king by the "tribes of Israel." Beza creates a historical parallel between the "tribes of Israel" and the Huguenot *gens de bien et de vertu*. Thus, since Henri will have the support of the Huguenots, he will have been "elected" by what Beza calls "the healthiest part" of the kingdom. Cf. Beza, *Pseaumes de David*, Ps. 133, p. 681. Cf. also Kingdon, ed., *Droit*, p. 53, for Beza's use of "la plus saine partie" as "the healthiest part" of the kingdom. On the importance of the myth of election in French monarchical thought, see R. E. Giesey, "The Jouristic Basis of Dynastic Right to the French Throne," *Transactions of the American Philosophical Society*, n.s. 51 (1961), and Gosselin, "*David in Tempore Belli*," pp. 36, 49-50.

Four:

"Wait upon the Lord"

1. The Nordic Amleth, who goes far back into Scandinavian folklore, feigns madness, although Hamlet's coming upon Claudius at his prayers and sparing him seems to be an innovation in the old story (see Geoffrey Bullough, *Narrative and Dramatic Sources of Shakespeare* [New York: Columbia University Press, 1957-74], VII, 6, 38). Behind Shakespeare's work stands a lost Hamlet play, probably by Thomas Kyd, who did much to form the genre of revenge tragedy and whose *Spanish Tragedy*, with its possible David allusion, is discussed below. Any conscious adaptation of the story of David would probably have been done by Kyd. Shakespeare, however, knew and employed I Samuel in other plays. Richmond Noble, *Shakespeare's Biblical Knowledge* (London: Society for Promoting Christian Knowledge, 1935), p. 152, tabulates 18 verbal parallels and quotations from I Samuel, scattered throughout the corpus. Four of the allusions are to the chapters in which David spares Saul and two are to Saul's visit to the witch of Endor. Noble lists no verbal connections to *Hamlet*.

2. Northrop Frye, *Anatomy of Criticism* (Princeton: Princeton University Press, 1957), p. 56.

3. Murray Roston, *Biblical Drama in England* (London: Faber & Faber, 1968), p. 117, observes that Renaissance writers tended to shy away from working directly with biblical material, since the word of God was not to be manipulated, changed, or trivialized for fear of blasphemy and prosecution. The Mystery plays on biblical subjects were, of course, long established, though opposed by the Puritans and their predecessors. Roston also comments that the story of David was one of the most popular themes in the biblical drama of the early Renaissance (p. 55), though he does not cite any plays on the subject of David's flight. (George Peele's *David and Bathsabe* will be discussed below). Elmer Blistein's introduction to Peele's play in *The Dramatic Works of George Peele* (New Haven: Yale University Press, 1970) gives more detailed background, observing that the David story figured more prominently on the Continent than in England.

4. Francis Schaeffer, "David: Lawful and Unlawful Vindication," in *No Little People* (Downers Grove, Ill.: InterVarsity Press, 1975), pp. 125-40. My reading of the story of David draws heavily upon Schaeffer's exegesis.

5. See Madeleine Doran, *Endeavors of Art: A Study of Form in Elizabethan Drama* (Madison: University of Wisconsin Press, 1964), pp. 256-57 and *passim.*

6. William Empson, *"The Spanish Tragedy," Nimbus,* 3 (1956), reprinted in Ralph J. Kaufmann, ed., *Elizabethan Drama* (New York: Oxford University Press, 1961), p. 60.

7. Eleanor Prosser, *Hamlet and Revenge* (Stanford: Stanford University Press, 1967), pp. 36-73.

8. See ibid., pp. 54-56.

9. Ibid., p. 55. See also note 20 below.

10. The story of David, as it is presented in the books of Samuel, is a powerful and provocative narrative in its own right. Robert Pfeiffer, ranking it with the other national epics, such as those by Homer, calls it "a masterpiece, unsurpassed in historicity, psychological insight, literary style, and dramatic power" (*Introduction to the Old Testament* [New York: Harper, 1941]), pp. 357, 359; see also William G. Pollard's introduction to *The Hebrew Iliad*, trans. Robert H. Pfeiffer (New York: Harper, 1957), and W. R. Arnold, *Ephod and Ark* (Cambridge, Mass.: Harvard Theological Studies [no. III], 1917), p. 118*n*. The Book of Common Prayer provided for the public reading of practically the entire Bible in the course of a year. Every April, Elizabethans would have the books of Samuel read to them in church, during the morning and evening prayers (attendance was compulsory). Thus every year on his birthday William Shakespeare would hear, read to him, the death of Saul and the coronation of David. (See Blistein's appendix to his edition of *David and Bethsabe* for a table of readings drawn from the Book of Common Prayer.) On April 24 the reading for matins was II Samuel 1 and the reading for evensong was II Samuel 2. See also S. Schoenbaum, *William Shakespeare: A Compact Documentary Life* (New York: Oxford University Press, 1977), pp. 55-59, for an account of Elizabethan churchgoing and Bible reading. Although any comparisons of *Hamlet* to Peele's play or to the scriptural narrative are to be taken only generically, it would be unusual if the Hebrew epic did not touch the imagination of Shakespeare or his contemporaries, or if it did not suggest resonances of meaning for an audience that saw similar motifs in secular literature.

11. For David as poet see Sidney's *Apology for Poetry*, passim. Sylvan Barnet, *A Dictionary of Literary Terms* (Boston: Little, Brown, 1960), p. 64, comments on David in relation to the pastoral.

12. Except when otherwise indicated, scriptural citations are modernized from the facsimile Geneva Bible (1560) (Madison: University of Wisconsin Press, 1969), the translation known by Shakespeare and his contemporaries. Revenge was an important moral issue in the Renaissance, as is reflected in the biblical translations of the time, just as modern translations reflect contemporary concerns. The Renaissance translations of Romans 12:19 read "Vengeance is mine"; the New English Bible reads "Justice is mine." Because of this difference in emphasis, as well as the desire to avoid any sense of anachronism and to leave open the possibility of historical influence, I am using the Geneva Bible and, occasionally, the King James Version.

13. François de Belleforest, "Histoires Tragiques," trans. Joseph Satin, in *Shakespeare and His Sources* (Boston: Houghton Mifflin, 1966), p. 399.

14. Compare also Edgar's adopting the role of Tom O'Bedlam in *King Lear* (II.iii). Quotations from Shakespeare are from Peter Alexander, ed., *The Complete Works* (London: Collins, 1951).

15. Ernest Talbert, *Elizabethan Drama and Shakespeare's Early Plays* (Chapel Hill: University of North Carolina Press, 1963), pp. 62-63.

16. Prosser, *Hamlet and Revente*, p. 8.

17. Cf. *As You Like It* (I.i.105-9) and *Two Gentlemen of Verona* (IV.i).

18. See Prosser's discussion of this scene in *Hamlet and Revenge*, pp. 183-91. For David's scruples about harming "the Lord's anointed" see the handling of the theme of regicide in Beaumont and Fletcher, *The Maid's Tragedy*.

19. For the theory of composition, a sorting out of the material, and other helpful information, see the introduction and notes to the books of Samuel in the *Oxford Annotated Bible* (New York: Oxford University Press, 1973).

20. Hamlet's desire not only to kill but to damn his enemy eternally has justifiably horrified audiences and readers of the play; it too has a David connection. Eleanor Prosser (*Hamlet and Revenge*, pp. 268-69), in her study of "the convention of immortal vengeance," observes that the earliest parallel to the situation in *Hamlet*, and indeed the only one she mentions that is prior to the date of *Hamlet* (c. 1601), is in Peele's *David and Bethsabe* (c. 1593). Absalon swears that Ammon, his half-brother, who incestuously raped their sister, "shall bear his violence to hell" (1.348). Absolon thereupon arranges a feast, and while his brother is drinking, kills him, carefully forestalling his revenge until "Ammon's heart/Is merry and secure" (11.864-65), so that he will "die accurst" (1.756).

Peele was extrapolating from II Samuel 13:28: "Now had Absalom commanded his servants, saying, 'Mark now when Amnon's heart is merry with wine, and when I say unto you, smite Amnon, kill him, fear not, for have not I commanded you? Be bold therefore, and play the men.'" The thought seems to be that Amnon must be caught unawares purely from a practical standpoint, with the splendid irony of Absolom, who does not do the deed himself, martially exhorting his men to have courage in the rather cowardly act of stabbing a man who is unsuspecting and drunk. The theological implications of dying unprepared, possibly in a state of mortal sin, were developed of course much later. Peele, though, brought his own religious assumptions to the reading of Scripture and found in Absolom's waiting for revenge until his enemy is drunk a further desire to damn his soul.

21. Prosser, *Hamlet and Revenge*, p. 183.

22. See Doran, *Endeavors of Art*, pp. 305-6.

23. The witch-of-Endor episode, and whether the ghost was that of Samuel or a manifestation of Satan, as the gloss in the Geneva Bible avers, was a familiar example on both sides of the Elizabethan controversy surrounding witches and ghosts. See "Endor Witch" in Russell Hope Robbins, *The Encyclopedia of Witchcraft and Demonology* (New York: Crown, 1959), pp. 159-60. For a discussion of Elizabethan ghostlore and its crucial importance in interpreting *Hamlet* —whether Hamlet's ghost is "a spirit of health or a goblin damn'd" (I.iii.40)—see Prosser, *Hamlet and Revenge*, pp. 97-142.

24. E.g., A. C. Bradley, *Shakespearean Tragedy* (New York: Macmillan, 1949), pp. 134-36, for the most distinguished version of this reading of the play.

25. Lily B. Campbell, "Theories of Revenge in Elizabethan England," *Modern Philology*, 28(1931), 281-96; Fredson Bowers, *Elizabethan Revenge Tragedy, 1587-1642* (Gloucester, Mass.: Peter Smith, 1959).

26. Prosser, *Hamlet and Revenge*, p. 4.

27. Campbell, "Theories of Revenge," pp. 281-82.

28. Schaeffer, "Lawful and Unlawful Vindication," pp. 133-34. Again, this reading of the David story in its theme of revenge is indebted to Schaeffer's exegesis.

29. The exclamation "How are the mighty fallen!" captures well the structure, along with the pity and fear, of *De casibus tragedy*, the fall of princes, of which the story of Saul is an archetypal example.

30. Schaeffer finds David's overindulgence with Absalom, his refusal to punish Absalom's killing of Amnon, eventuating in the final rebellion. C. I. Scofield, on the other hand, thinks David was not radical enough in his forgiveness. Commenting on David's refusing to see his son for two years after his return, Scofield thinks that "had David at this time taken Absalom into intimacy, the rebellion might have been averted" (*The Scofield Reference Bible* [New York: Oxford University Press, 1909], p. 370).

31. Typologically, David represents Christ, whose unconditional love is in tension with the absolute justice also inherent in the Godhead. David's lament for Absalom, "Would God I had died for thee!" is a typological foreshadowing of the atonement, in which God *does* die for his children, lovingly taking upon himself the punishment justly deserved by human sin, and thereby reconciling justice and love.

32. Cf. Milton's desire for a Christian, or biblical, heroism based on "the better fortitude/Of patience and heroic martyrdom" (*Paradise Lost*, IX, 31-32), rather than the traditional, but pagan, heroic ideal based on violence and war.

33. Campbell, "Theories of Revenge," p. 282.

34. Ibid., *passim*.

35. Ibid., p. 282. See also Doran, *Endeavors of Art*. pp. 120-21.

36. Campbell, "Theories of Revenge," p. 290. See also J. M. R. Margeson, *The Origins of English Tragedy* (Oxford: Oxford University Press, 1967), p. 112 and *passim*.

37. Campbell, "Theories of Revenge," p. 293.

38. Again, see Prosser's *Hamlet and Revenge* for a detailed study of Hamlet's struggle with the moral issue of revenge throughout the play.

39. For an extreme example of the Renaissance view that God himself works justice on the evildoer and that the virtuous revenger must restrain himself to let God work, see Cyril Tourneur's *The Atheist's Tragedy*. In this play the ghost of the murdered father appears to *prevent* his son from taking revenge, arguing that "patience is the honest man's revenge" (V.ii.278). The son, with great conflict, rejects revenge and seems helpless at the hands of the atheistic villain who finally has the young man at the execution block. The villain raises the ax—and providentially knocks his own brains out. For the concept of leaving vengeance to God in Shakespeare, see (e.g.) *Richard III* (I.vi.200-205, 221-25) and *Richard II* (I.ii.6-8, 39-41), cited by Campbell (pp. 290-91). For a more comprehensive survey see Prosser's chapter, "Shakespeare and Revenge" (pp. 74-94). Bowers cites Belleforest, a major source for *Hamlet*, as ascribing the reason for Hamlet's delay to "la tardiue vengeance de Dieu" (p. 87).

40. Cf. Psalm 37, "A Psalm of David," which speaks of evil, justice, and the necessity to "wait upon the Lord," a concept analogous to Hamlet's famous hesitation:

> Fret not thyself because of evildoers, neither be thou envious against the workers of iniquity.
> For they shall soon be cut down like the grass, and wither as the green herb.
>
> . . . .
>
> Commit thy way unto the Lord; trust also in him; and he shall bring it to pass.
> And he shall bring forth thy righteousness as the light, and thy judgment as the noonday.
> Rest in the Lord, and wait patiently for him: fret not thyself because of him who prospereth in

his way, because of the man who bringeth wicked devices to pass.

Cease from anger, and forsake wrath: fret not thyself in any wise to do evil.

For evildoers shall be cut off: but those that wait upon the Lord, they shall inherit the earth.

For yet a little while, and the wicked shall not be: yea, thou shalt diligently consider his place, and it shall not be.

But the meek shall inherit the earth; and shall delight themselves in the abundance of peace.

[Psalms 37:1-2, 5-11]

David's aphorism, repeated by Jesus in the Sermon on the Mount, seems surprising in its context of God's wrath, but in the story of David and in the tragedy of Hamlet, meekness becomes a method through which God's justice is revealed.

Five:

David as Epic Hero

1. *The Works of Michael Drayton*, ed. William J. Hebel (Oxford: B. H. Blackwell, 1961), III, 687-94. All line references are to this edition.

2. Kathleen Tillotson in *The Works of Michael Drayton*, ed. William J. Hebel (Oxford: B. H. Blackwell, 1961), V, 228.

3. Lily B. Campbell, *Divine Poetry and Drama in Sixteenth Century England* (Cambridge: Cambridge University Press, 1961), p. 105.

4. Compare the power of Orpheus' lyre over trees, beasts, and birds in Ovid's *Metamorphoses*, ed. H. Gregory (Toronto: Viking Press, 1960), X, 128-51, 205-11.

5. *Paradise Lost*, in *Milton: Complete Poetical Works*, ed. Harris F. Fletcher (Cambridge: Riverside Press, 1941), I, 762-75.

6. Joan Grundy, *Spenserian Poets* (London: Arnold, 1969), p. 214.

7. Hebel, ed., *Works of Drayton*, V, 228.

8. Apart from his occasional development of biblical subjects, Drayton anticipates one or two of Milton's leading ideas. Like the Milton of *Areopagitica*, he seems to have considered that poetry is "of power beside the office of a pulpit to inbreed and cherish in a great people the seeds of virtue and public civility" (Grundy, p. 214). With regard to the heroic, Drayton contended in *England's Heroicall Epistles* (1597) that human "greatness of Mind" was as useful a qualification as the divine fathering of (say) Hercules or Achilles. Drayton himself drew directly on Homeric strategies as Milton would do, somewhat after his example.

Six:

Cowley's Davideis *and the* Exaltation of Friendship

1. J. M. McBryde Jr. lists over 60 works in "A Study of Cowley's *Davideis*," *JEGP*, 2(1899), 469-76; R. F. Jones adds to that list in "The Originality of *Absalom and Achitophel*," *MLN*, 46(1931), 211-18; and several additional titles appeared after the publication of Dryden's poem.

2. Pietro Martire Vermigli, *The Common Places of the Most Famous and Renowmed* [sic] *Diuine Doctor Peter Martyr*, trans. Anthonie Marten (London: At the cost of Henrie Denham, *et al.*, 1583), pt. III, pp. 258-59. Peter Martyr died in 1562, and his *Common Places* was first published, in Latin, in 1576.

3. William Smith Clark II, ed., *The Dramatic Works of Roger Boyle* (2 vols.; Cambridge, Mass.: Harvard University Press, 1937), 2:702-64. The play was first published, anonymously, in 1703. Clark convincingly argues Orrery's authorship (I, 55-58) and assigns its composition to a period between 1677 and 1679.

4. Quarles' offering is "Davids *Epitaph on* Jonathan," a 16-line poem in tetrameter couplets, written in 1620 or later and published in *Divine Francies* (1633). In 1656, Cowley wrote: "if any man design to compose a *Sacred Poem*, by only turning a story of the *Scripture*, like Mr. *Quarles's* . . . into *Rhyme;* He is so far from elevating of *Poesie*, that he only *abases Divinity*" (Preface, p. 14; see note 9 below). In 1712, Thomas Ellwood published his own *Davideis: The Life of David, King of Israel: A Sacred Poem in Five Books.* He had written the first three books—that part of the poem covering the friendship of David and Jonathan—in 1688. According to Ellwood's prefatory "To the Reader," he had not read Cowley's *Davideis* until he had completed his own, but he includes Cowley's epic among those poems whose influence he avoided because they "consist mostly in their *Extravagant*, and almost *boundless Fancies; Amazing*, and even *Dazeling Flights; Luxurious Inventions; Wild Hyperble's Lofty Language;* with an *Introduction* of *Angels, Spirits, Daemons*, and their respective *Deities*, &c."

5. *The Letters of Dorothy Osborne to William Temple*, ed. G. C. Moore Smith (Oxford: Clarendon Press, 1928), pp. 169-70. The letter in question (no. 67) was undoubtedly written in 1654, and Smith conjecturally assigns it to June 15.

6. E.g., Cowley's scientific and philosophical attitudes in *Davideis* are examined in Robert Hinman, *Abraham Cowley's World of Order* (Cambridge, Mass.: Harvard University Press, 1960); the political content of the poem receives considerable attention in Arthur H. Nethercot, *Abraham Cowley: The Muse's Hannibal* (Oxford: Oxford University Press, 1931 [reprinted with corrections; New York: Russell and Russell, 1967]).

7. In this century, the lengthiest treatments of the David and Jonathan friendship in the poem (both brief) have appeared in Hinman, pp. 265-66, and James C. Taafe, *Abraham Cowley* (New York: Twayne, 1972), pp. 88-89. Unfortunately, throughout his chapter on *Davideis*, Taafe confuses Dorothy Osborne with Katherine Philips, "the matchless Orinda."

8. See J. B. Fletcher, "Précieuses at the Court of Charles I," *Journal of Comparative Literature*, I(1903), 120-53, and Philip Webster Souers, *The Matchless Orinda* (Cambridge, Mass.: Harvard University Press, 1931, and New York: Johnson Reprint Corp., 1968), pp. 258-60.

9. All quotations from Cowley's preface to the 1656 edition of his *Poems* and from *Davideis* (including Cowley's notes to the poem and the prose arguments which introduce each book, labeled "The Contents") follow the text of Abraham Cowley, *Poems*, ed. A. R. Waller (Cambridge: Cambridge University Press, 1905). Locations are cited parenthetically in the text; and for *Davideis* itself, line numbers are supplied.

10. The classical sources for these ideas are Plato's *Lysis*, Aristotle's *Nicomachean Ethics*, Cicero's *De amicitia*, and Seneca's *Ad Lucilium*, IX. See L. Dugas, *l'Amitie antique* 2nd ed.; Paris: Alcan, 1914). Laurens J. Mills, in his pioneering study *One Soul in Bodies Twain: Friendship in Tudor Literature and Stuart Drama* (Bloomington, Ind.: Principia Press, 1937), notes that "the most potent single literary production in reviving the theme [of friendship in the sixteenth century] was Cicero's *De amicitia*" (p. 10).

11. *Eth. Nic.*, 1169[a], 20-22, trans. W. D. Ross, in Richard McKeon, ed., *The Basic Works of Aristotle* (New York: Random House, 1941), pp. 1087-88.

12. Although the concept originates in classical literature, the English phrasing may have been used first by Nicolas Grimald, whose poem "Of frendship," found in all editions of Tottel's *Miscellany*, contains these lines: "Behold thy frend, and of thy self the pattern see:/One soull, a wonder shall it seem, in bodies twain to bee" (11. 15-16). Grimald made the most popular English translation of Cicero's *De officiis* in the Renaissance. See Mills, *One Soul*, p. 113.

13. The best discussion of this subject is Nesca A. Robb, *Neoplatonism of the Italian Renaissance* (London: Allen & Unwin, 1935; reprinted New York: Octagon Books, 1968). See also the introduction to Sears Reynolds Jayne, trans. and ed., *Marsilio Ficino's Commentary on Plato's "Symposium"* (University of Missouri Studies, vol. 19, no. 1) (Columbia: University of Missouri, 1944). One of the most available documents outlining Neoplatonic love theory in the Renaissance was Castiglione's *Il libro del cortegiano* (1528), which has Cardinal Bembo as a prominent character. Sir Thomas Hoby's famous translation, first published in 1561, enjoyed wide readership in England.

14. R. T. Wallis, *Neoplatonism* (New York: Scribner's, 1972), p. 86.

15. G. Blakemore Evans., ed., *The Plays and Poems of William Cartwright* (Madison: University of Wisconsin Press, 1951), p. 26. See also Kathleen Lynch, "Conventions of Platonic Drama in the Heroic Plays of Orrery and Dryden," *PMLA*, 44(1929), 456-71; L. J. Mills, "The Friendship Theme in Orrery's Plays," *PMLA*, 53(1938), 795-806; and Clark's introductions to Orrery's plays.

16. Part II, no. 1, question 28, articles 1-4. *The Summa Theologica of St. Thomas Aquinas*, trans. Fathers of the English Dominican Province (London: Thomas Baker, 1914), pp. 326-34.

17. "To Mr. *Cowley* on his *Davideis*," first published in full in Ted-Larry Pebworth, "The Earl of Orrery and Cowley's *Davideis*: Recovered Works and New Connections," *MP*, 76(1978), pp. 136–48, from which the subsequent quotations are taken.

18. "Cowley as a Man of Letters," *Transactions of the Wisconsin Academy of Sciences, Arts and Letters*, 27(1932), 128.

19. Although Cowley's first biographer, Thomas Sprat, states that *Davideis* was written while Cowley was still at Cambridge, Nethercot has argued that the poem underwent lengthy revision prior to its publication (pp. 49, 153-54, etc.), and Frank Kermode has asserted that "there are grounds for believing that the whole poem was written after 1650" ("The Date of Cowley's *Davideis*," *RES*, 25[1949], 158). Neither argument is totally convincing.

Seven:

David, the Military Exemplum

1. Biblical quotations are taken from the King James version, except where the quotation is taken directly from the sermon under discussion and is presented exactly as it appears in that sermon.

2. For a history of the London Artillery, see George Alfred Raikes, *The History of the Honourable Artillery Company* (London: Bentley and Son, 1878), 2 vols.

3. John Davenport, *A Royall Edict for Military Exercises:* Published in a Sermon preached to the Captaines and Gentlemen that Exercise Armes in the Artillery Garden at their Generall Meeting June 23, 1629 (London: Elizabeth Alde for Ralph Mab and Nicholas Bourne, 1629), p. 10. The Reverend John Davenport later emigrated to the colonies and was a leader in the founding of New Haven Colony.

4. *The Necessity of a Well Experienced Souldiery, Or, A Christian Common Wealth ought to be well Instructed & Experienced in the Military Art.* Delivered in a Sermon upon an Artillery Election June the 10th: 1675. By J. R. (Cambridge, Mass.: Samuel Grene, 1679), p. 4. It has been generally accepted that J. R. stands for John Richardson of Newbury, Massachusetts. Although the Ancient and Honorable Artillery Company reprinted this sermon in 1839, understanding it to have been delivered before their Artillery Company, this is not altogether certain; the sermon may well have been delivered to another Artillery Company either in Cambridge or Charlestown.

5. For a history of the Artillery Company, see Oliver Ayer Roberts, *History of the Military Company of Massachusetts now called the Ancient and Honorable Artillery Company of Massachusetts 1637-1888* (Boston: A. Mudge and Son, 1895-1901), 4 vols.

6. Oliver Peabody, *An Essay to revive and encourage Military Exercises, Skill and Valour among the Sons of God's People in New England*, A Sermon Preached before the Honourable Artillery-Company In Boston, June 5th, 1732 (Boston: T. Fleet for J. Eliot and J. Phillips, 1732), pp. 26-27, 29.

7. Thomas Symmes, *Good Soldiers Described and Animated* A Sermon Preached before the Honourable Artillery Company in Boston, June 6th. 1720 (Boston: S. Kneeland for S. Gerrish and D. Henchman, 1720).

8. Thomas Symmes, *Lovewell Lamented, Or A Sermon Occasion'd by the fall of the Brave Capt. John Lovewell in the Late Heroic Action at Piggwacket.* Pronounc'd at Gradford, May 16, 1725 (Boston: B. Green for S. Gerrish, 1725), p. 6.

9. Mather Byles, *The Glories of the Lord of Hosts, and the Fortitude of the Religious Hero.* A Sermon preached to the Ancient and Honourable Artillery Company June 2, 1740. (Boston: Thomas Fleet & Joseph Edwards, 1740), pp. 8-9.

The David-Goliath combat also inspired Mather Byles to poetry. A selection from his limping couplets on this subject, "Goliah's Defeat," is given below; the poem is included in Mather Byles, *Poems on Several Occasions* (Boston: S. Kneeland and T. Green, 1744), pp. 18-22.

> Fearless, the Hero heard the thundering Peals
> Drive thro' the Rocks, and rattling round the Hills.
> Disdain flash'd dreadful from his martial Eyes,
> And thus aloud his dauntless tongue replies.
> "Cease, empty Vaunter, cease thy impious Breath,
> This stone shall fly commission'd with thy Death:
> Your's is the Sword and Spear you vainly boast,
> The Vict'ry's mine, for mine's the LORD OF HOST!"
> He said; then whirl'd his Sling, the Pebble slung,
> It flew impetuous, and triumphant sung;
> On his broad Front it strook the Wariour full,
> And Death drove furious thro' his crashing Scull.
> Down fell the mighty Bulk; Hills, Fields and all,
> Shook when he fell, and echo'd to the Fall.
> In Dust and Blood awhile his Members roll,
> Then Night eternal rush'd upon his Soul.
> A Length enormous in the Plains he show'd
>   Like a vast Island in a Sea of Blood!

10. Samuel Mather, *War is lawful, and Arms are to be proved.* A Sermon preached to the Ancient and Honourable Artillery Company on June 4, 1739 (Boston: T. Fleet for Daniel Henchman, 1739), p. 7.

11. James Cogswell, *God the Pious Soldier's Strength and Instructor.* A Sermon delivered in Brooklyn in Pomfret to the Military Company under the Command of Capt. Israel Putnam 13th day of April 1757 (Boston: John Draper, 1757), pp. 15-16.

12. Abraham Keteltas, *The Religious Soldier; Or, the Military Character of King David Displayed and Enforced* in A Sermon Preached March 8, 1759 to the Regular Officers and Soldiers in Elizabeth-town (New York: H. Gaine, 1759), pp. 3-13.

13. Ibid, pp. 14-15. See also Samuel Davies, *Religion and Patriotism The Constituents of a Good Soldier* A Sermon Preached to Capt. Overton's Independent Co. of Volunteers in Hanover County, Virginia Aug. 17, 1755 (Philadelphia: James Chattin, 1755).

Eight:

"Blest Light"

1. *Parleyings With Certain People of Importance in Their Day* (London: Smith, Elder & Co., 1887), p. 86.

2. W. H. Bond, ed., *Jubilate Agno* (London: Rupert Hart-Davis, 1954), pp. 115-19. Subsequent references to sections and line numbers of this work will be included parenthetically in the text.

3. Norman Callan, ed., *The Collected Poems of Christopher Smart* (London: Routledge & Kegan Paul, 1949), p. 352. Subsequent references to this edition will be included parenthetically in the text.

4. Arthur Sherbo, *Christopher Smart: Scholar of the University* (East Lansing: Michigan State University Press, 1967), p. 171. See also Moira Dearnley, *The Poetry of Christopher Smart* (London: Routledge & Kegan Paul, 1968), pp. 170-76. Dearnley argues, reductively, that Smart's prime motive in the composition of *A Song to David* is to defend his hero against the attacks of Pierre Bayle and others. If the *Song* were the only evidence of Smart's interest in David, this argument would be more plausible.

5. *Lectures on the Sacred Poetry of the Hebrews,* trans. G. Gregory (Boston, 1815), p. 31.

6. Thorough study of Smart's views on language remains to be done. The best account, so far, is in Robert Brittain's "Introduction" to *Poems by Christopher Smart* (Princeton: Princeton University Press, 1950).

7. *The Fate of Reading* (New Haven: Yale University Press, 1975), pp. 81-82.

8. Moira Dearnley, for example, finds the *Psalms* long-winded and unreadable: "Not even the most partisan of Smart's admirers could find the slightest literary merit in his *Translation of the Psalms.* The interminable periphrasis, as each verse of the Coverdale version is laboriously expanded into a stanza of English verse, makes the *Translation of the Psalms* almost impossible to read with the least spark of interest" (*The Poetry of Christopher Smart*, p. 240). The difficulty with this criticism is that periphrasis, in its technical sense, is relatively rare in Smart's *Psalms* and, as I hope I have demonstrated, if only on a small scale and with few examples, the expansions frequently add poetic and dramatic interest to the otherwise pithy and brief originals. To ask such paraphrase to share the characteristics of Coverdale's earlier version is simply irrelevant.

Nine:

Faulkner's Absalom, Absalom! *and the David Story*

1. I am using the King James Bible throughout this essay, because that is the Bible Faulkner was familiar with.

2. Modern Library ed. (1951), p. 353. *Absalom, Absalom!* was originally published in 1936. All page references hereafter cited in text.

3. *Faulkner in the University: Class Conferences at the University of Virginia, 1957-1958*, ed. Frederick L. Gwynn and Joseph L. Blotner (New York: Vintage Books, 1965), p. 167.

4. See, for example, Lawrence Thompson: "How do the analogies operate here? Did Thomas Sutpen make any such lament [as David's]? He did not. It is thus at the very point where the mythic analogy breaks down, or becomes inverted, that the most important values of all those analogizings illuminate the crucial point in the Sutpen story. The ultimate tragedy here is that Sutpen's dream was indeed only Sutpen" (*William Faulkner: An Introduction and Interpretation* [New York: Barnes and Noble, 1963], p. 65).

5. The novel contains a recurring pattern of doors being barred against someone. Rosa listens behind doors, and is stopped by Clytie from bursting into Judith's room; Wash Jones is barred from the Sutpen house by Clytie; Quentin is chased away from Sutpen's Hundred.

6. Since Sutpen is getting old when he takes up with Milly, she also reminds us of the virgin brought to old King David's bed to warm him (I Kings 1:2).

7. Appropriate to the novel's crucial racial nexus (though perhaps a stretching of specific comparisons) is the possible analogy between the black race and the covenant of God. Faulkner elsewhere has characters argue that slavery imposed a commandment upon whites to protect blacks—a Calvinist version of the "white man's burden" argument (hence the name Joanna Burden in *Light in August;* see also part iv of "The Bear"). When Sutpen hauls his slaves in wagons to Mississippi, he brings the moral equivalent of the "Ark of the Covenant of God" that David triumphantly leads back into Jerusalem (II Samuel 6:12). Sutpen proceeds to "build an house" not for the Ark of God but for his dynasty—though, in a nice ironic touch, the slaves (Clytie, Jim Bond) ultimately occupy Sutpen's Hundred. David dances naked before the ark (to his wife Michal's disapproval); the naked Sutpen wrestles and bloodies his slaves (to his wife Ellen's disapproval), a fitting perversion of David's spontaneous worship of the Lord.

8. Critics draw from I Samuel for facts about David's past, but only Ralph Behrens calls attention to the parallels between Jonathan-David and Henry-Bon. Behrens, unfortunately, feels forced to apologize for Faulkner's "somewhat incongruously from the analogical point of view . . . shifting the biblical story." Behrens, like Thompson, assumes that the only function of the analogies between the biblical David story and *Absalom, Absalom!* is to demonstrate Sutpen's moral inferiority. Ralph Behrens, "The Thematic Center of *Absalom, Absalom!*" *PMLA*, 89 (January, 1974), 24-33.

9. The clear analogy between Tamar and Judith Sutpen reinforces Irwin's use of the Oedipal triangle. No sister plays such a role in the Jonathan-David relationship, though David has married the king's daughter Michal. In the pattern father-son-brother, the sister plays a symbolic role, representing the authority of the father (the authority, ultimately, to prohibit incest). Thus Amnon's rape of Tamar, Absalom's later taking of David's concubines, Bon's intent to marry Judith are all direct assaults on the father's authority.

10. Saul, David, and Jonathan speak of each other as "father," "son," and "brother"; see I Samuel 24:11, 26:17, and II Samuel 1:26 respectively. Faulkner repeats the scene in which Jonathan gives David his robe (I Samuel 18:4), though he reverses the giver and receiver: Bon gives Henry his cloak (p. 356). A more important parallel is the offer David makes to Jonathan, that if he has done any wrong Jonathan should kill himself ("if there be in me iniquity, slay me thyself" [I Samuel 20:8]). Bon hands Henry the gun so Henry can shoot him: *"His hand vanishes beneath the blanket and reappears, holding his pistol by the barrel, the butt extended toward Henry.*
—Then do it now, he says (p. 357).

11. See, however, Irwin's fine discussion (*Doubling and Incest*, pp. 104-5) of power and authority.

12. We could fill in the roles in the following manner: role I, Father-King: Saul, David, Sutpen, (Henry); role II, Son: (Jonathan), David, Amnon, Charles Bon, Henry[1], Absalom[1]; role III, Brother: (David), Jonathan, Absalom, Henry. (Parentheses indicate a secondary role played by a character, a role less important to the story and to the character than other roles. Prime [1] indicates a second role assumed by a character, a role at least as equal in importance as his first role. Thus Absalom *becomes* a Son when he foments civil war.

13. For discussions of other literary "sources" for *Absalom, Absalom!* see Michael Millgate, *The Achievement of William Faulkner* (New York: Random House, 1966), pp. 150-64, and Stephen M. Ross, "Conrad's Influence on Faulkner's *Absalom, Absalom!*," *Studies in American Fiction*, 2(Autumn 1974), 199-210.

14. Eric Auerbach, *Mimesis: The Representation for Reality in Western Literature* (New York: Anchor Books, 1957), pp. 9-10.

15. Interview with Loic Bouvard (1952), reprinted in *Modern Fiction Studies*, trans. Henry Dan Piper, 5(Winter 1959-1960), 362.

16. The events of Sutpen's career do not occur in the same order as the events in David's, nor are events *told* in the same order; the order of implication, however, is the same.

17. Saul's desperation is reflected in his visit to a witch (I Samuel 28).

18. See Irwin, *Doubling and Incest*, p. 150.

19. Faulkner also wrote a chronology and a genealogy for *Absalom, Absalom!* —still another "version" of the Sutpen story, just as Chronicles in the Old Testament provides another summation of the David story.

20. *Selected Letters of William Faulkner*, ed. Joseph Blotner (New York: Random House, 1977), p. 79.

21. See Irwin, *Doubling and Incest*, pp. 113-15.

Ten:
The Words of Their Roaring

1. From "The Waking," *The Collected Poems of Theodore Roethke* (Garden City: Doubleday, 1966), p. 108. All quotations are from this edition, although I prefer the order of the sequence as Roethke himself arranged it for *Words for the Wind*, with "The Lost Son" central in the sequence, beginning part 2. Quotations from Psalms are from the King James version of the Bible.

2. See Roethke's "Open Letter," in *On the Poet and His Craft: Selected Prose of Theodore Roethke*, ed. Ralph J. Mills, Jr. (Seattle: University of Washington Press, 1965), pp. 37-41. In this essay Roethke also describes the complexity of this poetry:

Much of the action is implied or, particularly in the case of erotic experience, rendered obliquely. The revelation of the identity of the speaker may itself be a part of the drama; or, in some instances, in a dream sequence, his identity may merge with someone else's or be deliberately blurred. . . . Disassociation often precedes a new state of clarity. . . . [A]nd, finally in this kind of poem, the poet should not "comment," or use any judgment words; instead he should render the experience, however condensed or elliptical that experience may be.

3. I am aware that the authorship of Psalms is in dispute by modern biblical scholars, and that only seventy-three are traditionally attributed to David. See, for example, the introduction to the section on Psalms in *The Dartmouth Bible*, ed. Chamberlin and Feldman (Boston: Houghton Mifflin, 1961), p. 467. For the sounding of his echoes, however, Roethke relies on a literary reality, not a historical one. It is that same literary reality that I invoke in my characterization of David in this paper.

4. *Anchor Bible: Psalms I*, trans. Mitchell Dahood (Garden City: Doubleday, 1966), p. xxxiii.

5. "Open Letter," *Selected Prose*, pp. 37-41.

6. John Wain, "The Monocle of My Sea-Faced Uncle," *Theodore Roethke: Essays on the Poetry*, ed. Arnold Stein (Seattle: University of Washington Press, 1965), p. 57.

7. Karl Malkoff, *Theodore Roethke: An Introduction to the Poetry* (New York: Columbia University Press, 1966), pp. 76-77.

8. See Roethke's note mentioning his indebtedness to Smart in *Selected Letters of Theodore Roethke*, ed. Ralph J. Mills Jr. (Seattle: University of Washington Press, 1968), p. 252.

9. *Letters*, p. 131.

10. *Traherne: Centuries, Poems and Thanksgivings*, ed. H. M. Margoliouth (London: Oxford, 1958), II, 148.

11. *Letters*, p. 147.

12. "Open Letter," *Selected Prose*, p. 38.

Eleven:

Saul and David in the Early Poetry of Yehuda Amichai

1. The poems discussed in this paper were originally published in *B'Merchak Shtei Tikvot: Shirim* [Two Hopes Away: Poems] (Tel Aviv: Hakibbutz Hameuchad Publishing House, 1958), pp. 65-70. When reprinted in *Shirm* [Poems]: *1948-1962* (Tel Aviv: Schocken, 1962), pp. 101-5, the order was slightly changed. The original arrangement began with "Young David," then "King Saul & I," then another poem (deleted in *Shirim*), and finally "Mt. Zion." In the most recent (1977) edition of *Shirim*, Amichai has restored all the poems deleted in 1962, and has returned to the original order of *B'Merchak Shtei Tikvot*. Nevertheless, it is my position in this discussion that the rearrangement of the poems in 1962 presented them in a sequence that has poetic significance which has been somewhat lessened in the 1977 edition.

2. All citations from "King Saul & I" are to Yehuda Amichai, *Selected Poems*, tr. Assia Gutmann and Harold Schimmel with the collaboration of Ted Hughes (Harmondsworth, Eng.: Penguin, 1971), 15-17. The poem "King Saul & I" written by Yehuda Amichai and translated by Assia Gutmann in *Selected Poems of Yehuda Amichai* (1968) is reprinted by permission of the publisher, Cape Goliard.

3. I Samuel 10.22 All citations from the Bible are from the King James Version.

4. In I Samuel, Saul held his peace when, after his public presentation, "the children of Belial said, How shall this man save us? And they despised him, and brought him no presents" (10:27). Only when the Ammonites threatened Jabesh-Gilead did Saul resort to threats and violence in order to see that his call to arms was not ignored: "And he took a yoke of oxen, and hewed them in pieces, and sent them throughout all the coasts of Israel by the hands of messengers, saying, Whosoever cometh not forth after Saul and after Samuel, so shall it be done unto his oxen. And the fear of the LORD fell on the people, and they came out with one consent" (11:7).

5. The word "ass" here renders the Hebrew *athon* (lit. she-ass), which, like most early English uses of the word before 1500 (cf. *OED*, 1.c), has no depreciatory associations. Had Amichai been interested in pejorative connotation, he could have used the more common Hebrew word *chamor*.

6. The line Gutmann translates "But he breathed the winds of his histories" could have been rendered "But he blew in the wind of his chronicles." The verb *nashav* is ordinarily used for wind and not people, so that both alternative interpretations are possibilities in a context that is quite deliberately ambiguous. Since wind is definitely related to separating wheat from chaff, poetic logic associates Saul with the wind-blown chaff, even though the nature of his activity in the winds of time (history) is not very clear.

7. When Saul first appears in I Samuel he is "a choice young man, and a goodly: and there was not among the children of Israel a goodlier person than he: from his shoulders and upward he was higher than any of the people" (9:2). Amichai reverses the point of view, with the people rejoicing "from his shoulders downward." This, of course, contributes to the theme of the inferiority of the crowds, as opposed to the hero's isolation.

8. Tchernichovsky wrote a number of poems about Saul. In "The King" (*Kitvei* [Writings of] *Shaul Tchernichovsky* [Tel Aviv: Dvir Co., 1966], I, 313-17), he made the secretly anointed Saul relevant to his own romantic world of universal brotherhood, expanding upon the story in I Samuel (10:10). Saul becomes inspired by the prophetic spirit and breaks into a series of dances that remove the barriers between king and people, Jew and Gentile, man and beast, living things and the rest of creation. In "On the Hills of Gilboa" (I, 341-42), Tchernichovsky interpreted the tragic end of Saul's career in a ballad that makes the suicide into a call for national resurgence: "Is Israel a lamb? Shall we be slaughtered like ewes? . . . Arise, take the places of the fallen and failing!" Gershon Shaked discusses the shifts in modern Hebrew poetic treatments of Saul in "Chamisha Shirim Al Hamelech Sha'ul: Al Shireihem Shel Tchernichovsky, Alterman, Pan, Gilboa V'Amichai" [Five Poems on King Saul: Tchernichovsky, Alterman, Pan, Gilboa, and Amichai], *Masa*, 8, nos. 20 and 21 (May 16 and 23, 1958).

9. The translations of "Young David" and "Mt. Zion" are by Burton Raffel and Noam Flinker.

10. Cf. Zev Vilnay, *The Guide to Israel* (Jerusalem: Da'at Press, 1968), pp. 93-99.

11. In a related yet more traditional view of Mt. Zion, Shimshon Blaukopf, the agnostic artist in S. Y. Agnon's novel *Temol Shilshom* [Only Yesterday] says:

> I don't know if I believe in God, but I do know that he believes in me and has shown me what every eye doesn't see. . . . As you know, I don't knock my feet about holy places. I leave that to those who run from one such place to another. For me it's enough that I'm in Jerusalem. But there is one place in Jerusalem where I go once a year on Shavuoth [Pentecost], and that's King David's tomb, because King David is dearer to me than all the Jews in the world. He was a powerful king always troubled by wars with Goliath the Philistine and all the other malefactors, and, with all due distinction, even the Jews surely gave him enough trouble; nonetheless, he would take the time to play the harp and compose psalms for all the miserable and the depressed—How can you help loving such a king?! Thus every year at Shavuoth I go to his tomb in the morning. And when I go to David, I eat nothing, not even a drop of cocoa, so that I won' lord it over the poor and needy who stand there praying all night. And I wear my fine jacket with red embroidered stripes that I wore at my wedding, and likewise my other best clothes, as befits a man who is going to a king. (*Kol Sipurav Shel Shmuel Yosef Agnon*, 2nd ed. [1953; reprinted Tel Aviv: Schocken, 1964], V, 215-16. This novel was first published in 1945. The translation is my own.)

Blaukopf's love for Mt. Zion and King David is characteristically idiosyncratic, since he prefers Mt. Zion to other holy places at a time when Jews had access to the old city (i.e., before 1948). In any case, the tradition Blaukopf maintains (along with thousands of less sophisticated persons every year at Shavuoth) is relevant as background for Amichai's poem.

12. "Tradition and the Individual Talent," *Selected Essays* (1951; reprinted London: Faber & Faber, 1961), p. 15. For a more extended discussion of Amichai's use of literary tradition, see my essay in *Denver Quarterly*, 12, no. 2 (Summer 1977).

Contributors

Marie L. Ahearn is professor of English, Southeastern Massachusetts University. Research for her essay was assisted by participation in a 1976 National Endowment for the Humanities Summer Institute at Brown University on "The Puritan Imagination."

Anthony Allingham is an instructor in English at Southern Alberta Institute of Technology, Calgary, Canada. His main area of research is the Bible in Renaissance literature.

Thomas F. Dillingham teaches English and Japanese literature at Stephens College and is completing a study of transformations of poetic form in the late eighteenth century.

Noam Flinker, a lecturer at the University of Haifa in Israel, has written articles on John Donne, Thomas Hobbes, Matthew Arnold, and Robert Frost, in addition to collaborating with Burton Raffel on translations of Yehuda Amichai's verse and drama.

Raymond-Jean Frontain (co-editor) is completing his Ph.D. at Purdue University. He directs the Spirituality and the Arts Institute at Victorynoll, Huntington, Indiana.

Edward A. Gosselin is associate professor of Renaissance and Reformation history at California State University, Long Beach. Among his publications are *The King's Progress to Jerusalem: Some Interpretations of David during the Reformation* and an edited translation of Giordano Bruno's *La Cena de le Ceneri.*

Charles A. Huttar is professor of English at Hope College and a past president of the Conference on Christianity and Literature. He is the editor of *Imagination and the Spirit* and author of articles on biblical aspects of Renaissance and contemporary literature.

M. L. Lewandowska is a poet and associate professor of English at San Jose State University.

Ted-Larry Pebworth is professor of humanities at the University of Michigan (Dearborn), chairman of the biennial Seventeenth Century Conference there, and author of many articles on seventeenth-century literature, as well as a book-length study of Owen Fellthem. He is at work on a history of the seventeenth-century prose essay.

Stephen M. Ross has published various material on Faulkner and black literature, is on the editorial board of *Modern Fiction Studies,* and teaches at the United States Naval Academy.

Gene Edward Veith, Jr., teaches religion and literature at the University of Kansas, where he is working on his Ph.D. in Renaissance drama.

Jan Wojcik (co-editor) is associate professor of English at Purdue University. In addition to articles on medieval and comparative literature, he is the author of *Muted Consent: A Casebook in Modern Medical Ethics.*